BUSH LEAGUE
DIPLOMACY

BUSH LEAGUE
DIPLOMACY

HOW THE **NEOCONSERVATIVES** ARE PUTTING
THE WORLD AT RISK

CRAIG R. EISENDRATH
AND MELVIN A. GOODMAN

 Prometheus Books

59 John Glenn Drive
Amherst, New York 14228-2197

Published 2004 by Prometheus Books

Inquiries should be addressed to
Prometheus Books
59 John Glenn Drive
Amherst, New York 14228–2197
VOICE: 716–691–0133, ext. 207
FAX: 716–564–2711
WWW.PROMETHEUSBOOKS.COM

08 07 06 05 04   5 4 3 2 1

Library of Congress Cataloging-in-Publication Data

Eisendrath, Craig R.
    Bush league diplomacy : how the Neoconservatives are putting the world at risk / Craig R. Eisendrath and Melvin A. Goodman.
        p. cm.
    ISBN 1–59102–176–6 (hardcover)
    1. United States—Foreign relations—2001- 2. Bush, George W. (George Walker), 1946—Views on international relations. 3. Conservatism—United States. 4. War on Terrorism, 2001- 5. United States—Military policy. 6. Unilateral acts (International law) 7. Militarism—United States. 8. National security—United States. 9. Security, International. I. Goodman, Melvin A. (Melvin Allan), 1938- II. Title.

E902.E37 2004
327.73'009'0511—dc22

                                                                                    2004001535

Printed in Canada on acid-free paper

To Alexandra Kate Stubin and James Ekedahl Tauber . . . may these beautiful

grandchildren grow up in a safer and saner world.

M. A. G.

CONTENTS

PART TWO: FOUNDATIONS OF FAILURE

PART THREE: FROM THE WRONG TO THE RIGHT PATH

ACKNOWLEDGMENTS

The authors wish to thank Daniel E. Goodman for his invaluable work as research assistant and Robert McGiffert for his editorial clairvoyance. Our wives, Roberta Spivek and Carolyn Ekedahl, provided the most valuable assistance of all. They read every chapter and brought to it their keen editorial minds for organization, logic, and clear prose—despite their own professional demands.

PART ONE
PATH OF FAILURE

CHAPTER ONE
FALL FROM GRACE

AMERICA ABANDONS COLLECTIVE SECURITY

*We all have to recognize that no matter how great our strength,
we must deny ourselves the license to do always as we please.
No one nation . . . can or should expect any special privilege
which harms any other nation. Unless we are all willing to pay
that price, no organization for world peace can accomplish its
purpose. And what a reasonable price that is!*

— President Harry S. Truman, 1945

In the aftermath of the war against Iraq in 1991, there was widespread
reaffirmation of both the role of the United Nations and the rule of law.
The United States went to war with a carefully crafted coalition of thirty-
four nations that included many Islamic states, even Syria. There was an
international consensus and sympathy in support of the war, known as
Desert Storm, to end the Iraqi invasion and occupation of Kuwait. The
coalition involved not only troops but treasure. Countries such as Japan,
which found it too controversial to send military forces to the Persian Gulf,
sent enormous funds to the United States in support of the war effort. In
fact, the international community absorbed the bulk of the war's costs.

In 2001 the United States went to war against Afghanistan in self-defense after the traumatic terrorist attacks in New York City and Washington, DC. Again, it received international support and even greater international sympathy. Masses and marches all over the world expressed profound sadness for what had taken place in the United States and conveyed support for virtually any U.S. response. The French newspaper *Le Monde* demonstrated unprecedented empathy for America with the banner headline "We Are All Americans."

In 2003 the United States again went to war; on this occasion, however, there was virtually no international sympathy for the United States and little international support for its actions. Within the United Kingdom, the only serious supporter of the war, there were huge demonstrations against Operation Iraqi Freedom, and Prime Minister Tony Blair was attacked in the British parliament for his willingness to be the cat's paw of the United States. The political positions of both Blair and President George W. Bush suffered when it was demonstrated that both Washington and London had lied at the highest levels to gain congressional and parliamentary support for the decision to go to war.

The popularity and credibility indexes of both Blair and Bush continued to decline in the wake of the war because of their miserable handling of the postwar Iraqi situation. Whereas President Franklin D. Roosevelt had begun planning for the post–World War II situation three years before the end of the war, there was little or no planning in Washington and London for the postwar period in Iraq. The Bush administration's disdain for multilateralism and its crude exploitation of the 9/11 attacks to justify the war against Iraq pointed to a cynical, unsophisticated, and dangerous policy process.

It became apparent in the immediate postwar period that the U.S. decision to use force against Iraq had been both rash and senseless, ignoring the fundamental premise that force should be the last, and not the first, option. There was no near-term threat to the United States or to U.S. interests. Yet the United States made no attempt to use diplomacy or to build a coalition. Rather, it approached the problem assuming that, as the world's dominant military power, it had no need to gain the cooperation of the world community that was organized to meet such international challenges. In his State of the Union speech in January 2004, President Bush said that the United States would not seek a "permission slip" to defend American interests.

This unprecedented U.S. use of force as the first option reflects the approach championed by neoconservative groups for the past decade. Theirs is a doctrine of unilateral and preemptive use of force and disdain for diplomacy, collective security, and multilateral organizations.

With the invasion of Iraq in 2003, the vision of the world held by the United States since the end of World War II was shattered. That war, which saw twelve million Americans under arms and the entire economy mobilized, was the most destructive war in world history. To avoid another such cataclysm, this country embarked on a new policy that embraced collective security and international diplomacy. We pursued that policy with considerable success for over fifty years; it began to erode in the 1990s and was shattered by the Bush administration in the first three years of the twenty-first century. Today, the United States is strikingly isolated in the international community, with universal criticism of the militarization of U.S. foreign and national security policies.

Over one hundred million people died in World War II as the war was fought not only against armies but against whole peoples and eventually involved almost every country in the world. None of the so-called rules of war was honored as millions of innocent civilians in Europe and Asia were annihilated, whole cities were left in ruins, and national economies were wrecked. Over eleven million people perished in Nazi concentration camps. At war's end, the atomic bombs dropped on Hiroshima and Nagasaki, more powerful than any previous weapon in history, posed the threat of the potential destruction of our species. Dropping the atomic bombs may have shortened the war, but the annihilation of hundreds of thousands of innocent civilians presented an appalling and apocalyptic vision of what the future might hold. Many in the United States and Europe embraced the concept of a new collective order.

In December 1945 the delegates of fifty nations attended the conference in San Francisco that produced the UN Charter establishing both a General Assembly of all member states, each nation with a single vote, and a Security Council of eleven members. The charter stated that the primary purpose of these institutions was to avoid the "scourge of war." The document was a ringing endorsement of the universal desire to establish a different system of international relations in order to prevent the unnecessary devastation and loss of the twentieth century's two world wars. It was an effort by world leaders who, in the aftermath of so much suffering, recognized a common humanity.

The framers of the UN Charter were tentative in outlining a system of effective collective security, but they had begun a journey designed to solve common geopolitical problems and alleviate international suffering. The Economic and Social Council, an International Court of Justice, a Trusteeship Council, and a Secretariat were part of the sophisticated architecture of an attempt to deal with global governance. Article 51 of the charter significantly noted that "nothing in the present Charter shall impair the inherent right of individual or collective self-defense." Article 41 called for a Military Staff Committee as a framework for establishing UN forces to deal with problems of peacekeeping and peacemaking. The five permanent members of the Security Council (the United States, Britain, the Soviet Union, France, and China) were given veto power over any UN action to protect the national interests of the winners of the war and to avoid the political problems that had defeated the efforts of President Woodrow Wilson to establish the League of Nations.

By the end of 1947, with the Cold War a reality and the wartime alliance with the Soviet Union shattered, cooperation through the Security Council was no longer possible on issues involving major East-West conflicts. In 1950, when North Korea invaded South Korea, the United States managed to cobble together an international force of nineteen nations and obtained a UN endorsement only because the Soviet Union had walked out of the Security Council in a dispute over the claim to China's seat on the council. More than fifty years after the end of the Korean War, there was no peace treaty between North and South and no sign of a solution to political and military tensions on the peninsula. Nevertheless, the Korean War was an important reminder that diplomacy was of critical importance to international security, that collective security was essential, and that the threat of confrontation required new efforts to prevent the scourge of war.

In many ways the UN Charter and the new international organizations created a framework for collective diplomacy and for cooperation across a broad front of interests—economic, social, cultural, and political. The framework envisaged the kind of international peacekeeping operations that could keep warring sides apart, such as the United Nations Emergency Force in the Middle East after the 1956 Suez War, which marked the UN's first peacekeeping operation. American statesman Ralph Bunche, working with UN secretary general Dag Hammarskjold, designed a force that allowed the withdrawal of British, French, and Israeli troops from Egyptian soil. Hammarskjold and Bunche also developed a UN peacekeeping mission for the Congo in 1960, with the assistance of a large U.S. airlift. The UN force in Cyprus after the Greek-Turkish crisis of 1973 and the international missions that eventually settled destructive civil wars in El Salvador, Guatemala, and Cambodia also reflected President Franklin D. Roosevelt's concept of a system that allowed the major powers to effect solutions to regional wars and crises without risking direct confrontation.

The UN Charter provided a framework for agreements, working arrangements, and international law in such fields as civil aviation, international telecommunications, postal traffic, tariffs and trade, world health, and international refugees. In every area in which nations could cooperate, the United Nations offered a forum for nations to talk to each other and, particularly, for new states to establish full diplomatic relations with other countries. For the United States it offered an opportunity to provide not domination but leadership, and to persuade others to support effective collective security.

The UN's global consciousness was epitomized by the Nuremberg trials through which the United States and its allies put the Nazi leaders on the stand, not only for their part in conducting the war but particularly for their "crimes against humanity." In making these leaders responsible for the outrages of the concentration camps, the Nuremberg trials made clear that the rulers of nation-states were responsible to the world community for both their conduct toward other nations and their treatment of their own citizens. The world community became the court of last resort for people who had found no justice in their own nations. The trials were a model for trials held in The Hague to deal with war crimes in Bosnia and Croatia in the 1990s.

But it was only a beginning. A widening of the concept of international civil rights emerged in 1948 with the UN Declaration of Human Rights. Like the United Nations itself, the declaration was the product of U.S. leadership. It declared that "all human beings are born free and equal, in dignity and with rights." It then spelled out these rights, particularly the right to "life, liberty, and security of person." The declaration included a ban on slavery and inhuman punishment and provided for equality before the law, fair legal procedures, privacy and free expression, and the free movement of peoples. It also made a matter of right equal participation in government, social security, a free choice of employment, and an adequate standard of living and education. These were the international standards to which this country and the other members of the United Nations subscribed.

In its earliest days, the United Nations recognized that it must find a way to deal with the problems of the atomic bomb and atomic energy. Only two weeks after its first meeting in 1946, the UN commissioned a study of the control of atomic energy. Six months later American elder statesman Bernard Baruch proposed an "international atomic development authority to which the United States would turn over its atomic bomb secrets, provided that there was an international control and inspection of bomb production not subject to big-power veto and that further manufacture of bombs would cease and existing stocks be destroyed."[1] The Baruch Plan was rejected by the Soviet Union as the Cold War was gaining momentum. The Soviet takeover of Eastern Europe and the division of Europe between the Soviet-dominated Warsaw Pact and the U.S.-dominated North Atlantic Treaty Organization delayed serious discussion of disarmament. It was not until the Cuban missile crisis of 1962 that the two major nuclear powers, the United States and the Soviet Union, who had gone to the brink of nuclear war, developed a disarmament agenda with a new sense of purpose and direction.

In the forty years that followed Hiroshima and Nagasaki, two approaches to dealing with nuclear armaments worked together to help create security: international arms control and nuclear deterrence. In 1949 the Soviet Union exploded its first atomic bomb, and in the next few years it caught up with the United States in producing hydrogen bombs and perfecting intercontinental ballistic missiles (ICBMs). These were the ultimate weapons, not only because of their destructiveness but because there was no way they could be stopped.

Soon each side had tens of thousands of nuclear missiles; in a few years each could be armed with multiple warheads, capable of inflicting destruction by orders of magnitude greater than the atomic bombs that leveled Hiroshima and Nagasaki. Studies by organizations such as the U.S. Air Force–financed Rand Corporation in the 1960s put casualties at over a hundred million in a first exchange between the two superpowers and concluded that subsequent nuclear exchanges would virtually eliminate the populations on both sides and pollute the planet to levels that threatened all life. The living would envy the dead, as Soviet leader Nikita Khrushchev warned in the 1950s. Even the horrors of World War II began to pale in comparison with such a nuclear holocaust.

The arms race demonstrated that deterrence was at best only a temporary solution. Even if each side offered the credible threat that it could destroy the other, there was still the possibility that nuclear war might break out, particularly if strategic weapons spread to other countries. The other alternative was arms control, a direct lesson of the Cuban missile crisis that forced President John F. Kennedy and Soviet leader Khrushchev to the negotiating table. In 1963 the two sides concluded both the Partial Test Ban Treaty, which prohibited the testing of nuclear weapons on the surface of the earth, in the atmosphere, and in outer space, and a Hot Line agreement to allow the two sides to establish communications immediately in a crisis in order to avoid the use of force, particularly the use of lethal systems that were on strategic alert.

The 1968 Nonproliferation Pact was another vital agreement. Nonnuclear states declared they would not acquire nuclear weapons, and the nuclear powers pledged they would not share their nuclear technology with nonnuclear states. The nuclear powers also agreed to significantly reduce their nuclear arsenals, a goal that every administration pursued until the Bush administration became the steward of American national security in 2001 and abandoned arms control and disarmament.

Arms control worked. Fifty years after Hiroshima, there were only a handful of nuclear powers—the United States, the United Kingdom, France, Russia, China, India, Pakistan, and Israel. No nuclear weapons were used during this period, and many countries that might have gone nuclear stayed in the nonnuclear camp because they were not threatened by nuclear neighbors. Without such a system, the world would have witnessed greater proliferation of nuclear weapons and conceivably even a nuclear exchange.

The United States not only promoted arms control and disarmament but tried to create economic conditions in other countries that would lead to political stability. After World War I the victorious allies had imposed a harsh peace on a defeated Germany. With the Versailles Treaty of 1919, Germany was not only saddled with high reparation payments, but it was deprived of key pieces of its own territory. As a result, Germany suffered a drastic inflation that ruined its middle class. The growth of Hitler's National Socialists was directly related to economic instability. Prior to the crash of 1929, during a period of economic stability, the Nazi Party lost votes in the parliament, but it quickly regained them once the world depression hit. In 1933 the Nazis took over the government of Germany.

Seeing the close relationship between economic and political instability, the United States created the Marshall Plan in 1947, which eventually distributed $79 billion (in 2003 dollars) to key Western European nations threatened with economic and social instability. The funds helped create a solid bulwark against communism by assisting the Western European countries. Secretary of State George C. Marshall, in his commencement speech at Harvard in June 1947, argued that the European heritage of legal, economic, and parliamentary systems; productive agriculture; innovative industry; vibrant culture; and solid education would stabilize Western Europe and serve as a model for Eastern Europe. When Britain could no longer afford to maintain its security commitment to Greece and Turkey and to build the solid economic base that would allow them to resist communist pressure, the United States introduced the Truman Doctrine, which replaced the role of the British in the eastern Mediterranean. The United States also began to see that economic aid in other parts of the world would shore up its allies and create economic conditions that would foster democracy.

All these developments—the United Nations, the growth of international law, the concept of arms control, and the extension of economic aid—complemented a growing set of alliances that the United States formed to create collective security in order to resist the spread of communism. With the subversion of Eastern Europe after World War II, particularly the overthrow of the government in Czechoslovakia, the Soviet drive to build a buffer zone in the region became palpable. The United States moved to use yet another aspect of collective security—strong multilateral alliances—to defend itself and key vulnerable nations in Europe. The North Atlantic Treaty Organization (NATO), established in 1949, included not only Canada and the countries of Western Europe but eventually Greece, Turkey, and West Germany. Considering an armed attack against any member as an attack against all, the NATO nations provided for collective self-defense in conformity with Article 51 of the Charter of the United Nations. It also provided an essential U.S.–Western European political forum and encouraged economic and social cooperation.

The primacy of diplomacy distinguishes this period, marked by a brilliant generation of security architects that included Gen. George C. Marshall and Secretary of State Dean Acheson. Policy initiatives, such as the containment doctrine of George F. Kennan, came primarily from the State Department, with interagency coordination arranged by the National Security Council.[2] The National Security Act of 1947 created the National Security Council, the Department of Defense, the U.S. Air Force, and the Central Intelligence Agency. The CIA was the nation's first intelligence organization placed outside the policy process to provide independent intelligence judgments to policymakers.

Until the Bush administration, diplomacy was not just another option but the primary means by which the United States worked with other states to create collective security. Until recent years, military force was used only when diplomacy failed. An important exception was the gradual slide into the Vietnam War in the 1960s, which also was marked by the misuse of intelligence information and the failure to gain international support and create an international coalition. Although the United States was not directly involved, there is no better example of the futility of war than in the Middle East, where the wars of 1948, 1956, 1967, 1973, and 1982 demonstrated the failure of diplomacy. More aggressive international diplomacy might have prevented the Arab attacks on Israel in 1948 and 1973; the British-French-Israeli coalition warfare in 1956; the Israeli attack against Egypt and Syria in 1967; and the disastrous Israeli invasion of Lebanon in 1982.

The use of diplomacy seeks to prevent bilateral and regional antagonisms from descending into violence and to create the means for building mutual advantage. Diplomats are trained to lance tense situations and create peaceful solutions. Military action, which should always be the last option, often creates unintended consequences that worsen geopolitical situations and leave behind desolation and bitterness, as in Afghanistan and Iraq. From 1945 to 2000, U.S. policymakers relied primarily on diplomatic instruments and collective security and when they did not, as in Vietnam in the 1960s, they created economic and social weakness at home.

A supportive feature of all policy making and diplomacy is prompt and relevant intelligence, which often permits the best decision making in times of crisis. The current international environment is not as dangerous as the nuclear balance of terror during the worst days of the Cold War, but it is marked by increasing instability. In the period before World War II, the United States had the least developed intelligence system of any major power. Henry Stimson, secretary of state in the Hoover administration, was so opposed to modern intelligence that he refused to consider a system to classify documents or send messages in code. He opposed breaking the codes of other countries and remarked in 1931, "Gentlemen do not read each others' mail." Ten years later a massive intelligence failure contributed to the U.S. lack of preparedness for the Japanese attack on Pearl Harbor. Both Pearl Harbor and, forty years later, 9/11 demonstrated a failure to provide trenchant intelligence analysis for policymakers.

Emerging from the wartime Office of Strategic Services, the Central Intelligence Agency was established by the National Security Act of 1947 to provide intelligence to the president in the increasingly bleak Cold War atmosphere. The CIA provided excellent intelligence during the Vietnam War, but it was largely ignored by the policy community or distorted by the interagency intelligence community. The intelligence failure of 9/11 led to the deaths of more than three thousand Americans and profound changes in our way of life that will seemingly never end. The deliberate misuse of intelligence in the run-up to war in Iraq in 2003 rivals the falsification of intelligence during the Vietnam War in the 1960s and the politicization of intelligence on the Soviet Union in the 1980s as the greatest intelligence scandals in the history of the Republic. Today, the director of central intelligence (DCI) has virtually no influence over thirteen different intelligence agencies, including the Federal Bureau of Investigation and extremely sophisticated technical agencies such as the National Security Agency (NSA), the National Reconnaissance Office (NRO), and the National Geospatial-Intelligence Agency (NGA). These are essential parts of U.S. intelligence collection and analysis but are subordinated to the policy dominance of the Pentagon. President Truman's intent to create an intelligence community that was not beholden to the policy community, and thus could provide objective intelligence analysis, has been subverted, and the United States is more insecure as a result.

To make matters worse, the USA PATRIOT (Uniting and Strengthening America by Providing Appropriate Tools Required to Intercept and Obstruct Terrorism) Act of 2002 raises the specter of potential use of the intelligence community to weaken the civil liberties of all Americans. The CIA is prohibited from domestic spying against American citizens, but these prohibitions were observed in the breach in the 1960s when President Lyndon B. Johnson used the Vietnam War as a pretext for CIA monitoring of student movements and antiwar protests. These violations led Congress to conduct major bipartisan hearings in the House, chaired by Rep. Otis Pike (R-NY), and in the Senate, chaired by Sen. Frank Church (D-ID), to establish select bipartisan intelligence oversight committees to end domestic abuses and make sure that there would never again be domestic transgression by the CIA or any other agency in the intelligence community.

Unfortunately, during much of the Bush administration the chairmen of the Senate intelligence committee, Sen. Pat Roberts (R-KS), and the House intelligence committee, Rep. Porter Goss (R-FL), were self-proclaimed "advocates" for the CIA and the intelligence community and used their political power to prevent oversight and investigation of intelligence failure. The Senate and House intelligence committees blocked an immediate investigation of the intelligence failure that led to the 9/11 attacks and demonstrated little interest in getting a grasp on the serious misuse of intelligence that preceded the war against Iraq. Unlike the commissions that investigated Pearl Harbor, neither committee has offered a serious reform proposal for revamping the policy process and preventing another failure such as 9/11.

Throughout the period of the Cold War, the government worked best when it acknowledged the constitutional balance between Congress and the executive branch and stressed the importance of bipartisanship in the conduct of foreign policy. Not only did Congress keep control of the purse, but it regularly demanded and received accurate information from the executive branch of its activities, which provided the basis for essential budgetary decisions. The delicate balance between the executive's power to initiate foreign policy moves and Congress's power to approve and sustain them through supportive legislation was upheld. Currently, the nation's single most expensive weapons system, the so-called national missile defense, is being developed and deployed without proper congressional oversight and review.

Despite heavy Cold War demands, Congress maintained under both parties the basic features of government that had been developed in the 1930s. These included an extension of basic privileges for all citizens in such areas as social security, health, and education. There was a bipartisan consensus that citizens should pay for these benefits in proportion to their income, an assumption that formed the basis of the graduated income tax, estate taxes, and the taxation of corporate dividends and profits. Unlike Europe, however, where reform policies had been introduced by such conservatives as Otto von Bismarck and Benjamin Disraeli, in the United States they often came tainted with the brush of liberal or leftist politics— at least from the perspective of political conservatives.

In the post–World War II period, the United States experienced not only the full maintenance of our constitutional democracy but also a growing standard of living in which virtually all elements of society benefited. The other side of collective security was a prosperous, socially responsible democracy, here and in Western Europe. The vision that guided this period was that increasingly all the countries of the world could in their own ways achieve prosperity in a supportive, multilateral system.

If we put the period of 1945 to 2000 into perspective, it reveals a number of salient features. The United States:

- Pioneered a system of world diplomacy, including the United Nations, that looked to increasing cooperation among nations along a broad front of peacekeeping as well as political, social, and economic programs.
- Fostered a peaceful, viable Western Europe, which was helpful not only in our fight against communism but also in providing a rich, democratic life for its citizens. In so doing, we avoided much of the acrimony that led to two world wars earlier in the century. We also furnished economic aid to other countries to increase their stability.
- Cooperated with other nations to develop a rich tapestry of international law that sought to protect human rights. Through numerous treaties and agreements, we worked cooperatively with other nations in dozens of other areas, including transportation, immigration, and health, to regulate relations between states.
- Entered its first multilateral alliance in more than 150 years, with the creation of NATO, which contained the Soviet Union and contributed to the fall of the Berlin Wall in 1989 and the dissolution of the Soviet Union in 1991.
- Worked with other nations to curb the development of nuclear

weapons, limit the number of nuclear powers, and create an international arms control regime.

- Lowered its military budgets after 1987, aided by the decline of the Soviet Union and various arms control agreements.
- Developed an effective intelligence system that, while still geared to the Cold War, had the potential to provide the U.S. government with the objective intelligence it needed to create effective policy.
- Maintained civil liberties at home and continued vital social services initially established under the New Deal. The constitutional balance between the executive and congressional branches was sustained, and the economy, with containable dips and rises, supported a continuing growth in living standards for the great majority of the population.
- Gave supremacy to diplomacy and reaped enormous benefits in the collective security system both at home and abroad.

The direction taken by the United States after World War II, despite some lapses, worked to create a safer world and a democratic and prosperous democracy at home. These are developments in which we should take pride and which we should have the determination and will to continue.

When we turn to the period following the national election of 2000, we see that our government has put many of these achievements in jeopardy. The post-2000 period is characterized by the abandonment of diplomacy as our principal means of conducting foreign policy and by an increased reliance on military force. In every area we have defined, the United States finds itself in full retreat from the accomplishments of the preceding half century.

THE UNITED NATIONS

Following the 1994 congressional elections, a triumph for conservative Republicans and particularly the neoconservatives, the guiding philosophy of American foreign policy began to shift toward unilateralism. This is the idea that the United States, as the world's surviving superpower, can do what it wants without the need for cooperation with other states. Unilateralists maintain that the United States has the power to enforce its will and that U.S. policies benefiting the United States will automatically be beneficial to other nations.

The first victim of this policy was our relationship with the United Nations, a target of the neoconservatives since the Reagan administration. Reagan's disdain for the UN culminated with the sarcasm of his deputy ambassador to the United Nations, Charles Lichenstein, who exploded at delegates in 1983 for complaining about the treatment of diplomats in the United States. Lichenstein lectured the complainers that if they did not like the treatment, they should "seriously consider removing themselves and this organization from the soil of the United States." "We will put no impediment in your way," he went on, "and we will be at dockside bidding you a fond farewell as you set off into the sunset."[3]

Conservative Republicans in the 1990s, led by Sen. Jesse Helms, withheld regular UN dues and peacekeeping assessments and adamantly refused to even consider the establishment of a readily deployable UN force for peacekeeping operations. Without such a force, the United Nations remained unable to meet many of the challenges to which, as the world organization, it should have been able to respond. These included crises in the Balkans, Africa, and the Middle East. The failure of President Clinton to provide logistical support for sending French troops to Rwanda in 1994 contributed to one of the worst holocausts in history.

Following the attacks on September 11, 2001, the Bush administration, sensing the need for cooperation to fight terrorism, paid most of America's back dues to the United Nations and gave lip service to selective international cooperation, but its basic tone did not change. In Iraq, particularly, it chose to go ahead with an invasion without the United Nations or a supporting Security Council resolution, to cut off UN inspections, and to give the world organization only a nominal role in the provision of aid, economic and social reconstruction, and the formation of a new Iraqi government.

The United States has also failed to provide adequate support to the world organization in other areas. In the Congo current estimates put casualties as high as four million in a violent struggle over the past decade, which could have been avoided with a strong UN presence. Former Liberian president Charles Taylor exported his violent ways to all his neighbors, but in 2003 the Bush administration waited months before introducing a pathetically modest peacekeeping presence to assist a West

African force, headed by Nigeria. When the United States parked this modest presence off the Liberian coast until President Taylor had left the country, the Nigerian president remarked that he found the U.S. action comparable to sending a fire department to the scene of a conflagration but refusing to get involved until the fire was extinguished.

ECONOMIC AID

Despite the chronic need for economic aid in Afghanistan, the United States pulled back from virtually every economic commitment it had made prior to military action against the Taliban regime in Kabul. As a result, Afghanistan continues to suffer widespread hunger, disease, and economic despair. In 2002 Afghanistan again became the world's leading supplier of heroin. The U.S.-imposed government has not established control beyond the suburbs of Kabul, and Taliban and al Qaeda forces have returned to southeastern Afghanistan. Everywhere else in the country, warlords reign.

In Iraq a similar pattern of economic neglect in favor of military dominance is being shaped. The cost of maintaining the U.S. military force in 2003 is roughly fifty times what is being spent on nonmilitary support. Here again, the lesson of the Marshall Plan—that economic reconstruction must follow military victory if peace and stability are to be restored—is being lost. To throw out Saddam Hussein but fail to reconstruct the economy of Iraq is to invite another dictator in the future. The United States did no planning for the postwar situation until two months before the invasion, gave the Pentagon complete control over the transition period, and made no attempt to seek assistance from international or nongovernment organizations. The United States even initially allowed Ba'athist Party members to resume their old positions, causing bitter resentment.

The failure of the United States to extend international economic aid is particularly deplorable. This country ranks sixteenth among the sixteen most developed nations in money it spends on international economic aid as a percentage of its own gross national product. It extends only one-tenth of 1 percent of its GNP to international assistance. Thus, the richest country in the world ranks among the stingiest in helping the planet's poor. Conditions that breed war are being neglected throughout the developing world.

While insisting on free trade, the United States has maintained high tariffs and subsidies for its agricultural products, making it difficult for developing countries to feed their populations. Through its strong influence on international lending institutions, such as the International Monetary Fund and the World Bank, the United States has imposed policies that have decreased living standards in the developing world in favor of protecting the financial community.

INTERNATIONAL LAW

Rather than dealing with suspected terrorists captured during the Afghanistan war through the mechanism of international law, the U.S. government opted for its own military tribunals and the suspension of accepted judicial procedures. It abandoned judicial guarantees for people arrested in the United States, often with no evidence of involvement with terrorism. It ignored existing legal structures, such as the United Nations' International Court of Justice, which could have provided a legal procedure based on international law. It rejected established judicial civil procedures that guarantee the rights of the accused, including the right to know the charges, to be represented by an attorney, to have a speedy trial, and to have access to evidence and witnesses for defense.

In another dramatic repudiation of international law, the country that helped conduct the Nuremberg trials, pioneered the UN's Universal Declaration of Human Rights, and advanced the idea that the world community could define crimes against humanity refused to join the International Criminal Court (ICC). This tribunal, created in 2003, was supported by every other major country in the world. The U.S. objection was that American citizens might be tried for international crimes, even though the ICC Charter clearly stipulates that the court will not try individuals whose countries will do this job themselves. Not only has the United States refused to participate in the ICC, it has done virtually everything it can to undermine the court's authority by negotiating thirty-seven agreements with individual states that prevent the extradition of U.S. citizens in order to be tried by the court. It has refused to grant desparately needed economic aid to countries in Asia and Africa unless they agree to these conditions. The United States also has pulled away from signing international conventions on the rights of children and women and on climate control. Finally, the United States has virtually ended international arms control.

USE OF FORCE VERSUS ARMS CONTROL

In a series of policy declarations, the Bush administration proclaimed that the United States will consider the preemptive use of nuclear weapons against nonnuclear states and that it will consider military action against any state that might challenge the United States. In so doing, it has repudiated the standard of the UN Charter that force can be used only in self-defense. In general, it has rejected or withdrawn from international agreements that restrict U.S. military development, including the the Comprehensive Nuclear Test Ban, the 1972 Anti-Ballistic Missile Treaty, and pacts on biological weapons, small arms, and land mines. The United States is also planning to develop outer space as a new theater of direct military activity in opposition to UN resolutions, and the administration is seeking to create small nuclear devices that will require a resumption of underground nuclear testing. Spurred on by these developments, a number of states appear to be moving more aggressively toward their own nuclear capacity, particularly North Korea and Iran.[4] The tearing up of the fabric of arms control created over a fifty-year period puts our security and that of the world in jeopardy.

DIPLOMACY

Diplomacy has been shamefully abused since the 2000 election, particularly in the buildup to the Iraq war. For their refusal to support the United States going into Iraq without a Security Council resolution, many of our closest NATO allies, most prominently the French and the Germans, were roundly insulted, particularly by officials in the Department of Defense. The French were prohibited from taking part in NATO air exercises in the United States, which compromises the future cooperation of Western forces. France, Germany, and Russia were prohibited from contracting for the postwar development of Iraq, at the same time that the United States wanted these nations to provide financial assistance to Iraq. The international community has been particularly vexed that, after decades in which the United States was the leader in fostering close cooperation with the Atlantic Alliance, spokesmen for the Bush administration, particularly the secretary of defense, reveled in crude statements, delivered pointed snubs, and engaged in conduct that was simply out of line in civil diplomatic exchange.

THE INTELLIGENCE SYSTEM

The intelligence community, particularly the CIA, has been compromised by the politicization of intelligence to support the use of force in Iraq and its co-optation by the Pentagon to support military operations rather than provide objective information. The result has been blunders that included the U.S. bombing of a pharmaceutical plant in Khartoum, Sudan, in 1998 and the Chinese embassy in Belgrade in 1999. The September 11 attacks demonstrated a massive intelligence failure, comparable to Pearl Harbor, but there has been no effective investigation, let alone reform, of the intelligence system and no attempt to correct the institutional deficiencies that led to the failure. Unsurprisingly, no one has been held accountable, which has been a major source of anguish to the survivors of the 9/11 victims.

The Iraqi scandal, particularly the unverified claims that Iraq had a sufficient stock of weapons of mass destruction to constitute an imminent threat and that it was working closely with al Qaeda terrorists, has compromised the credibility of not only the intelligence community but the president as well.

MILITARY SPENDING AND THE MILITARIZATION OF FOREIGN POLICY

Reversing a trend from prior to the fall of the Soviet Union, the United States has increased its military budget to more than $400 billion, and projections suggest a defense budget of $500 billion before the end of the decade. Led by Secretary of Defense Donald Rumsfeld, the Department of Defense has moved aggressively to eclipse the State Department as the major locus of our foreign policy and to take over significant sections of the intelligence system. The diplomacy of the Department of State has increasingly been ignored as power has shifted to the Defense Department. Senior Defense Department officials, particularly Deputy Secretary of Defense Paul Wolfowitz, make diplomatic forays traditionally performed by State Department counterparts. Funding of the Department of State has become so meager that it has had to close consulates around the world and assign personnel of the well-funded intelligence agencies to its diplomatic and consular posts, compromising it in the eyes of other nations. While defense spending represents 17 percent of American spending, we allocate less than 1 percent of the federal budget to the needs of the State Department.

DEMOCRACY AT HOME

This period has seen massive infringement on civil rights and privacy through the PATRIOT Act and the suspension of judicial fairness in our dealings with both citizens and noncitizens. The balance between Congress and the executive branch has been tipped in favor of the executive branch in violation of the U.S. Constitution. There has been massive withholding of information from Congress on items involving U.S. security and weapons development, with the executive branch refusing to give Congress a role in the withdrawal from the ABM Treaty. Social fairness has also suffered in this period as the gap between the rich and the rest of our society has been aggressively widened by massive tax cuts for the wealthy and a marked cutback in social services. There have been more jobs lost in the Bush administration than in any administration since Herbert Hoover's during the depression. Some critics have characterized this period as a move back to the more restrictive role of government in the era of President William McKinley at the turn of the twentieth century.

These policies have left the economy in a precarious position. An overwhelming number of Nobel laureates in economics believe that tax cuts will not revitalize the economy, as the Bush administration maintains, and that the continuing budget deficits, projected to be over $400 billion a year, coupled with unfavorable trade balances, pose the severe danger of recession or deflation in the next few years. The $5.6 trillion surplus that was predicted for the decade ending in 2011 is a $2.3 trillion cumulative deficit under the best-case predictions of the Congressional Budget Office announced at the end of August 2003.[5]

Not too long ago, the nation was celebrating the collapse of the Berlin Wall and the dissolution of the Soviet Union, believing that the Cold War had ended and a new era of peace and prosperity had begun. With the fall of the Soviet Union over a decade ago, the United States had a unique opportunity, as the surviving superpower, to lead the world toward a period of greater cooperation through the use of diplomacy, international organization, and international law. This great opportunity is being squandered as the world drifts toward military anarchy and even our own democracy is being compromised at home.

With the invasion of Iraq, we witnessed the end of the so-called post–Cold War era and the escalation of a worldwide and continuous war on terrorism that has increased our insecurity. Today, more than 150,000 American forces, including more than 80,000 reservists and National Guard members, are occupying Iraq and Afghanistan, which have become havens for terrorists, and, in the case of Iraq, for the first time. Nor has the U.S. presence in either country led to domestic stability. Moreover, the United States, having branded Iran and North Korea as part of an "axis of evil" in 2002, has created a domestic and international concern that the Bush administration will soon resort to the use of preemptive force once again. Key Islamic nations, observing U.S. pressure tactics against Syria and Iran, believe that they will soon be added to the shortlist of nations that will require a military solution and that the United States will try to enforce regime change in Tehran and Damascus.

Instead of living in a whole new era, we may be witnessing an ugly epilogue to the Cold War that will find the United States acting alone instead of working with its traditional allies. Following World War II, the United States was revered and respected for its role in defeating the Nazi menace and standing up to the possibility of Communist conspiracy. Now many of our traditional friends in Europe and Asia view us with hostility as they question the moral basis of our foreign policy. This book is designed to explain how the United States as a nation arrived in this terrible cul-de-sac and how the nation should debate and adopt policies to reverse the Bush administration's dangerous course.

NOTES

1. Robert H. Ferrell, *American Diplomacy: A History* (New York: W. W. Norton, 1969), p. 680.

2. The National Security Council was an organization created during the Truman administration, which includes the president, vice president, secretary of state, secretary of defense, director of the CIA, the heads of the Joint Chiefs of Staff, and the president's national security advisor and deputy advisor. In the case, particularly, of Henry Kissinger, who was for some time head of the NSC under President Nixon, central diplomatic direction came for some years directly through that agency.

3. Stanley Meisler, *United Nations: The First Fifty Years* (New York: Atlantic Monthly Press, 1995), p. 186.

4. Republican congressman Curt Weldon reported that the North Koreans had directly justified their nuclear program by the U.S. action against Iraq. Chris Mondies, "N. Korea Ties Nuclear Push to U.S. Action," *Philadelphia Inquirer*, June 3, 2003, p. A2.

5. David Firestone, "Dizzying Dive to Red Ink Poses Stark Choices for Washington," *New York Times*, September 14, 2003, p. A1.

CHAPTER TWO
TERRORISM AND PEACEKEEPING

THE AFGHANISTAN PRECEDENT

THE 9/11 ATTACKS

On September 11, 2001, two hijacked jetliners slammed into the World Trade Center in New York City and one into the Pentagon in Washington, DC. A fourth airliner, reportedly destined for the U.S. Capitol building, was forced to crash into a field in Pennsylvania. The next day President Bush labeled the attacks "acts of war" and invited our allies to join the "war on terrorism." NATO immediately declared that the attacks were directed at all nineteen member states and that it would cooperate closely with the United States in its war against terrorism and in support of rebuilding Afghanistan. The fact that the fundamentalist Taliban regime in Afghanistan had harbored Osama bin Laden, the mastermind of the attack, made it certain that the United States would target both the Taliban and bin Laden's al Qaeda organization.

The September 11 tragedy, one of the most devastating attacks on American soil in history, was traumatic for the American people, reminding us that the world in which we live had become increasingly dangerous. The attacks also provided an opportunity for the Bush administration to radically change the direction of American national security policy. A continuous, worldwide war against terrorism would soon begin, and the seeds of a preemptive war against Iraq had been planted.

The decision to use force against Afghanistan received widespread international support as an act of self-defense. Unlike the invasion of Iraq eighteen months later, which was challenged and criticized by nearly all of the key members of the United Nations, international opinion sanctioned the invasion of Afghanistan to remove the Taliban government and to run al Qaeda into the ground. A UN Security Council resolution demanded that the member states take sweeping action against terrorism. There was almost complete sympathy and support from the international community as pro-U.S. demonstrations occurred all over the world.

It is noteworthy that in both Afghanistan and Iraq the United States has created perilous postwar situations for which this country was not prepared and for which it failed to develop effective civil administrations. The power vacuum in both countries constituted ideal conditions for increasing anarchy and terrorism. In neither case had the Bush administration done the difficult strategic planning that might have facilitated a smoother transition to stable governance. More Americans were killed and wounded in the first four months after the war in Iraq than during the six-week conflict that ended on May 1, 2003, when President Bush proclaimed the "mission accomplished" on the aircraft carrier USS *Abraham Lincoln*; the loss of blood and treasure has continued unabated into 2004. The U.S. Central Command no longer releases information on wounded Americans unless asked, which makes the combat injuries of the postwar situation one of the untold stories of the war.[1]

THE U.S. RESPONSE

When the terrorist attacks took place on 9/11, President Bush was in Florida, promoting his education agenda; Secretary of State Powell was in Lima, Peru, having breakfast with the new Peruvian president; and CIA director George Tenet was having breakfast at the St. Regis Hotel, only three blocks from the White House, with his former boss at the Senate Select Intelligence Committee, former Oklahoma senator David L.

Boren. Among the key members of the eventual "war cabinet," only Vice President Cheney, who was in the West Wing of the White House, and Secretary of Defense Rumsfeld, who was in the Pentagon, were working at their desks. Twenty-four hours later, all were present as Bush convened the first National Security Council meeting to begin planning the war against Afghanistan and al Qaeda.

The United States immediately moved into a war posture, calling up reservists and securing Pakistani support for attacks on neighboring Afghanistan and the Taliban regime that was harboring al Qaeda leader bin Laden. On September 18 the Taliban leaders responded by calling on Muslims around the world to wage holy war on the United States if it attacked Afghanistan. The following day the Pentagon ordered combat aircraft to the Persian Gulf. Among our NATO allies, only the British were particularly anxious to take part in the conflict and prepared a thousand men to join their American comrades in possible ground operations in Afghanistan. On October 7, American bombs and missiles began to rain down on Afghanistan; all nine of al Qaeda's training camps, nine Afghan airfields, and twenty-four military barracks were totally destroyed or out of commission within days.

At home, with the country frightened and behind the president, the war strategy was not challenged. A huge increase in military appropriations was secured through Congress, although many of the increases for weapons systems had little to do with terrorism. Declaring that the war had no time limit and might take generations, the president described the campaign against terrorism as the first step in an unlimited war against terrorist organizations and their sanctuaries. In what became known as the Bush Doctrine, the president emphasized, "We will make no distinction between those who planned these acts and those who harbor them."[2] This decision was reportedly made without any consultation with Cheney, Powell, and Rumsfeld, and it sent the first signals to the European members of NATO that the Afghan war would be merely the first in a series of U.S. military actions.

There was only weak Afghan resistance to the American invasion. Afghanistan had been in a virtual state of war since the Soviet invasion in December 1979, and even before that a civil war had been waged for nearly a decade with devastating results. There was no effective government in Afghanistan and no real governing authority. The authority of the Taliban was largely limited to the areas around Kabul and Kandahar. The country was impoverished, and the Taliban used tools of fear and terror to institute fundamentalist Islamic authority. Nevertheless, the United States would not have been so successful in such a short period of time without the United Front, also known as the Northern Alliance, a group of Tajiks, Uzbeks, and Hazaras who had represented the only serious armed opposition to the Taliban regime and who bore the brunt of the fighting in the war. The Central Intelligence Agency had developed and maintained close relations with many of the leaders of the Northern Alliance, dating from the anti-Soviet resistance of the 1980s. The CIA's planning shaped the logistical, military, and political role of the anti-Taliban resistance group. Cooperation with the Northern Alliance created a problem in U.S. relations with Pakistan, however, because Islamabad had developed close ties with the Taliban and al Qaeda and feared the alliance's close ties with both Russia and Iran.

The ground campaign of the Northern Alliance north of Kabul and the U.S. air campaign across the country led to the routing of the Taliban militia after only a month of fighting. The CIA and U.S. Special Forces enlisted spotters from the alliance in order to direct fire from the air without endangering substantial numbers of U.S. troops on the ground. The first U.S. ground operation in Afghanistan took place on October 19, when only one hundred U.S. Army rangers and other special forces carried out a hit-and-run operation in and around the Taliban stronghold of Kandahar. This mission was designed to decapitate the terrorist network, but bin Laden and the al Qaeda leadership proved elusive. By mid-November the Taliban's retreat had become a rout, with Herat in the west, Jalalabad in the east, and Kandahar in the south in the hands of hostile local leaders.

The unexpectedly quick Taliban collapse permitted representatives of the various Afghan political factions to meet in Bonn, Germany, under the auspices of the UN Special Representative of the Secretary General for Afghanistan, to plan for Afghanistan's future. After tortuous negotiations among Afghan military commanders, representatives of Afghanistan's different ethnic groups, Afghan expatriates, and representatives of the exiled monarch, the Bonn Agreement was signed on December 5, 2001. The delegates agreed on the creation of a new constitution, an interim government (the Afghan Transitional Administration), and elections in 2004. They also agreed on security arrangements, reconstruction of the country, and the protection of human rights. With such widespread participation, the arrangement seemed to offer hope of a bright future for Afghanistan.

The problems were huge, however. There were still significant pockets of resistance in Afghanistan. Taliban and al Qaeda fighters were holding out at various points around the country, with positions in Kunduz, Herat, and even Kabul posing the greatest threat. The country itself was virtually destroyed after three decades of civil war; all its political institutions, including the parliament, courts, civil service, and education, health, and transportation systems, were in tatters. Nearly half of Afghanistan's twenty-seven million people lived in poverty; 50 percent were unemployed, and 70 percent were illiterate.

At Bonn, the United States and its allies committed themselves to underwriting Afghanistan's recovery, and in Tokyo in January 2002, the international community promised to provide over $4.5 billion of assistance over the next five years. This was a rather minimal sum, far short of that requested by Afghanistan's interim president, Hamid Karzai, who wanted $15 billion. Neither the United States nor the rest of the international community followed through with even their modest commitments, however.

Some of the heaviest fighting of the war for U.S. forces began in March 2002; the assault called Operation Anaconda occurred in eastern Afghanistan, where U.S. troops and some European detachments tried to destroy the remnants of al Qaeda that were holding out in Paktia province, south of Gardez. Whereas the U.S. air campaign and the ground fighting of the Northern Alliance successfully removed the Taliban regime from Kabul in short order, the U.S. ground campaign against al Qaeda was far more difficult. Despite heavy fighting, Taliban and al Qaeda agents slipped through the dragnet and found refuge in Pakistan or elsewhere.

RECONSTRUCTING AFGHANISTAN

By June 2002 the *loya jirga*, the Grand Council of Afghanistan, had created the framework for the new government. Unfortunately, the control of the Karzai government did not extend far outside Kabul, and regional warlords continued to control much of the country. President Karzai needed a national army and a responsible police force if he was to reverse the pattern of chaos and corruption that had dominated the country for thirty years, but the warlords remained dominant.

In addition, many legitimate Afghan factions believed they were not adequately represented in Kabul. This attitude was particularly strong among the majority Pashtun group, a situation that parallels the discontented Shiite majority in Iraq. The Pashtun were alienated by the use of American airpower and rockets that killed hundreds of civilians as well as by U.S. disregard for local customs and laws.

In the de facto alliance with the Afghan warlords in the fight against the Taliban, the United States left the country mostly under their rule, making governance almost impossible. While encouraging the growth of the central government, the United States also continued to support local militias and warlords battling against Muslim extremists, thus weakening the central government. Sarah Sewall, a former deputy assistant secretary of defense, summed up the problem: "By insisting that the United Nations do the 'dirty work' of nation-building without ensuring a secure foundation upon which to build, President George W. Bush is effectively setting up the UN to fail in Afghanistan. . . . The U.S. refusal to support disarming and defusing the warlord culture renders even the most effective nation-building efforts a Band-Aid at best."[3]

The U.S. policy left the country in virtual anarchy—the roads unsafe, human rights abuses rampant, and poverty spreading. The one hundred thousand men in private armies fought and stole from one another and destroyed economic assets. Peacekeepers were stationed in Kabul, while the rest of the country sank into chaos. Proposals to extend the range of the peacekeeping force, including those by President Karzai and the United Nations, were blocked by the United States and other key nations, including France, Canada, Australia, Germany, and the Netherlands.

In August 2003 the North Atlantic Treaty Organization took control of Afghanistan's multinational peacekeeping force, its first mission beyond Europe's frontiers in its fifty-five-year history. NATO had provided more than 90 percent of the troops for the five-thousand-member International and Security Assistance Force in Afghanistan, and its decision to take command promised greater continuity and stability to the operation. Since its formation in February 2003, a different country had led the force each month. NATO took over command from the joint leadership of Germany and the Netherlands, and the first NATO commander was German Lt. Gen. Lotz F. E. Gliemeroth.

Afghan and UN officials strongly endorsed the NATO role and urged that the NATO-led force take up positions outside of Kabul. U.S. ambassador to NATO Nicholas Burns was less enthusiastic, stating that expansion of the force "will need to be considered seriously once NATO has settled into its role in Kabul."[4] The United States has troops in the NATO force, separate from the nearly 11,500 U.S. troops in Afghanistan. The larger U.S. presence is dedicated to hunting for Taliban and al Qaeda remnants, but the narrowness of that search has led to great criticism and dissatisfaction with the U.S. commitment. Additionally, the United States, Britain, and New Zealand have formed provincial reconstruction teams of sixty to seventy soldiers to operate in areas outside of Kabul.[5]

The task of improving security was divided among five donor nations: the United States (military reform), Germany (police reform), Japan (disarmament and demobilization), United Kingdom (counternarcotics), and Italy (judicial training). Progress on all fronts has been slow. Not enough funds were allocated, resulting in inadequate forces, poor morale, and a high rate of desertion. Plans to build a national army, numbering seventy thousand, quickly stalled, with only about four thousand members trained by 2003 and only nine thousand projected by 2004. The new Afghan military, moreover, was splintered by factionalism, and the police force was largely untrained. The international peacekeeping force itself was small in relation to the population. Where Kosovo had one peacekeeper for every 48 people, and East Timor one for every 86, Afghanistan had one for every 5,360 people.[6]

The result, not surprisingly, has been a lack of security, which in turn slows reconstruction. Security issues have made it almost impossible for U.S.-backed education officials to work in twenty-four of the nation's thirty-four provinces, and other central administration functions were seriously inhibited.[7] Despite Defense Secretary Rumsfeld's statement that the bulk of the country was secure, there were numerous signs that this was not so. In the south, the Taliban and other spoiler forces became increasingly menacing.[8] Renewed fighting broke out between warring groups in the north, specifically the Tajik and Uzbek factions. As in Iraq, the continued U.S. presence drew fire from the population, particularly as Afghans were detained and held by U.S. troops, often without charges.

U.S. economic aid, supplemented by other countries, has been woefully inadequate for the tough job of reconstructing a country beset by three decades of conflict and impoverishment, and there is virtually no private investment. In early 2003 Congress stepped in to fund nearly $300 million in humanitarian and reconstruction funds even though the Bush administration had inexplicably failed to request such funding. The Afghan economy was not strong enough to provide needed local funding. Tax collection was insufficient to pay police and other vital government agencies. Limited funds went to emergency relief, and infrastructure items such as dams, roads, and telephone and power systems went begging. Despite modest gains in education and health, particularly in Kabul, schools, roads, health programs, and other vital services throughout the rest of the country remained woefully inadequate. The total amount pledged or donated by the international community, including the United States, was insufficient, and only a small percent of donated money reached the Afghan government. This further diminished the authority of the Karzai government, a problem for Iraq's transition authority as well.

The population, discontented with the slow progress of economic reconstruction, has grown increasingly skeptical about the commitment of the United States and its allies. The amount of financial support is between a third and a half of the funds that the Afghans and the World Bank believe are needed for reconstruction. The duration of the pledges (no more than five years) is far less than what will be required to meet the chronic, long-term needs of the country.

The political signs are mixed. A loya jirga in December 2003 and January 2004 produced a new constitution that endorsed a strong president—Hamid Karzai—who is favored to join elections later this year.[9] On the other hand, judicial reform, which included the difficult goal of equality for women, is also proceeding very slowly. The justice system remains dominated by religious conservatives who have more in common with the Taliban than with the Karzai government. Human rights groups believe that too much power has been given to religious fundamentalists.

Despite these gains, in many ways Afghanistan has returned to its pro-Taliban conditions.[10] The Afghan government and the United Nations have avoided the issue of accountability for past human rights abuses; human rights are often ignored, as delegates from warlord groups were allowed to participate although they had engaged in human rights abuses. Afghanistan has also returned to its position as the world's leading producer of heroin, with much of the money from heroin going to the warlord foes of the central government.[11] By 2002 Afghanistan already was producing more than eighteen times the amount of heroin produced during the last year of Taliban rule, and future years promised to be even more bountiful. In 2004 a third of the Afghan economy will be drug related, and most of the heroin shooting into European veins will be Afghan in origin.

Afghanistan requires a commitment of noninterference by its neighbors, an objective that was addressed by the December 2002 Kabul Declaration on Good-Neighborly Relations. The declaration, which pledged noninterference in Afghanistan, was signed by Pakistan, Uzbekistan, Turkmenistan, China, and Iran. Pakistan and Iran, however, have been providing support to regional leaders; Pakistan, moreover, has been harboring some Taliban leaders. Such nonsigners of the declaration as Russia have supported longtime clients in northern Afghanistan, and the United States has also provided military supplies to certain warlords in an effort to win their support. A viable Afghanistan requires an end of arms shipments to regional leaders, acceptance of Afghan borders, and the promotion of normal relations. Pakistan must stop the penetration of the Taliban across the Durand Line separating Pakistan and Afghanistan.

Deploying a credible security force outside of Kabul to take on the daunting task of disarming the warlords would require the infusion of large sums of money and the participation of many nations. Until there is some level of stability, regional development teams will struggle to improve conditions. Meanwhile, anarchy reigns. Only days after NATO took command of the International and Security Assistance Force, Afghanistan recorded its most violent twenty-four-hour period since the war ended. Fifty guerrilla fighters, government soldiers, and innocent civilians, including six children, were killed. Fifteen of the deaths took place in Helmand in southern Afghanistan, where a bomb exploded on a bus. Twenty government soldiers and insurgent fighters were killed in eastern Afghanistan in the province of Khost, only a few miles from the border with Pakistan. Afghan officials have accused Pakistan of allowing Taliban insurgents to operate in Afghanistan. Clashes between rival warlords led to another twenty deaths, and in Kabul a bomb killed two university students.

The important work of reconstruction will require the commitment of the Afghan government, the United Nations, and international aid agencies, with the help of the U.S. military in a peacekeeping role, providing assistance to disarmament and demobilization efforts. With greater security in the country, the other elements of nation-building could proceed under Afghan auspices.[12]

THE PROBLEM OF NATION-BUILDING

Nation-building will be particularly difficult in a country as poor and undeveloped as Afghanistan. There must be extensive commitments of resources and expertise, crisis management involving the warring factions and ethnic groups, and a sophisticated approach to dealing with the resentments of a historically xenophobic population that has never accepted an extended occupation. The failed British and Soviet experiences in Afghanistan in the nineteenth and twentieth centuries are sufficiently illustrative.

It is ironic that these problems are now at the doorstep of the Bush White House. During the election campaign, George W. Bush told a cheering crowd in Chattanooga, Tennessee, "Let me tell you what else I'm worried about: I'm worried about an opponent who uses nation-building and the military in the same sentence." A year later, however, President Bush told the West Point graduates that America "stands for more than the absence of war. We have a great opportunity to extend a just peace, by replacing poverty, repression, and resentment around the world with hope for a better day." But in January 2003 Defense Secretary Rumsfeld signed off on the closing of the Army War College's Peacekeeping Institute in Carlisle, Pennsylvania, the only government body specifically dedicated to the study of peacekeeping.

Afghanistan should have provided a lesson as we moved toward the invasion of Iraq. Unless the United States is prepared to fully commit itself to the difficult job of nation-building, it should hesitate to use force to achieve regime change or to assume that military force alone can achieve a permanent solution to a national or regional problem. The other alternative, one partially followed in Afghanistan, is to cede the task to an international organization, such as the United Nations. This demands that UN members have adequate will and resources to ensure success.[13]

The U.S. record in nation-building has not been encouraging, according to a long-term study by the Carnegie Endowment for International Peace. Of the fifteen cases involving U.S. participation, only two—frequently cited by the Bush administration—are cited as unambiguous successes: Germany and Japan following World War II. The study found that "[t]hree years following the withdrawal of American forces, democracy was considered functioning only in five of the fifteen cases . . . ; ten years after the departure of American forces, democracy was sustained in only four cases."[14] In addition to Germany and Japan, two very small nations, Panama and Grenada, were considered democratic successes. South Korea should be added to this short list.

Our major successes, Germany and Japan, provide lessons learned for assessing our chances of success elsewhere. Germany and Japan were both highly developed countries, with advanced infrastructures, civil societies, homogenous cultures, and centralized political systems. After the devastation of the war and their unconditional surrenders, both societies were willing to work with the United States in a transition process. The elites in both countries shared the U.S. aim of resisting communism and had the political sophistication to adapt to democratic government and rebuild their devastated infrastructures. In addition, the United States infused large amounts of money into their economies.

Many of the problems of nation-building in Afghanistan have plagued American efforts in other countries, particularly where there have been undeveloped economies and infrastructures, no democratic traditions, little civil society, and an insufficient commitment of outside resources. Previous failures include Cambodia, Cuba, Haiti, Nicaragua, and Vietnam.

Beyond the problem of nation-building, our invasion of Afghanistan and its complex aftermath question whether direct military invasion is the most effective way to deal with terrorism. While Afghanistan itself was unique, given the Taliban's close alliance with and protection of al Qaeda, it is clear that force alone is no solution. Much of the al Qaeda leadership slipped away, and many al Qaeda elements already were operating elsewhere. It is certainly neither possible nor desirable for the United States to invade the forty to sixty states that are sustaining terrorists in one manner or another. Thus, military force was needed in Afghanistan, but military force is a blunt instrument and does not provide a long-term or strategic answer.

Unfortunately, the Bush administration believes that it can introduce the values of democracy around the world at the point of a gun even in places that have little experience with it. Is the United States prepared to become not just a colonial empire, but one with such an impossible mission? As commentator Nicholas Lemann makes clear, "Democracy is a wonderful idea, but none of the countries in the Middle East, except Israel and Turkey, resemble anything that would look like a democracy to Americans. . . . [T]he very problem that democracy in the Middle East is meant to solve—rising Islamic radicalism . . . makes the prospect of elections dangerous, because anti-American Islamists might win."[15]

DANGERS OF INTERVENTION

A look at recent history shows the pitfalls of intervention without adequate follow-through. In Afghanistan, for example, the United States in the 1980s intervened through the CIA to overthrow the Soviet-dominated government. At the time it spent $3 billion to train and fund seven Afghan resistance groups—all strongly anti-American. When the Soviets withdrew in 1989, Americans were told that we had won a great victory. Robert M. Gates, former director of the CIA, called support of the mujahideen fighting the Soviets in Afghanistan, which included the transfer of Stinger ground-to-air missiles to the rebel forces, the CIA's "greatest success." Actually, the Soviets had decided to withdraw from Afghanistan before the first Stingers arrived.

Both the Central Intelligence Agency and the Pentagon had warned policymakers in Washington that supplying Afghan groups with Stinger missiles, which could end up in the hands of terrorists, could create a nightmare for U.S. interests. But the State Department convinced the Reagan White House to provide the Stingers; after the war the CIA spent considerable time and money trying to buy back many of the Stingers from the insurgents, but with incomplete success. Worse, even with the war over, the mujahideen training camps continued to operate and under Osama bin Laden became increasingly anti-American. The U.S. government, including Congress, overjoyed by the victory, was uninterested in such news and blissfully unaware that it had helped create the conditions for the emergence of the next major threat to U.S. security—al Qaeda.

After the departure of Soviet troops from Afghanistan, civil disorder and anarchy developed. The United States and the rest of the international community paid little attention. The force that filled the vacuum was the extremist Taliban faction. The Taliban provided a base of operations for bin Laden and al Qaeda; in return, bin Laden funded the Taliban regime.

Soon al Qaeda was targeting U.S. facilities in the Middle East and North Africa. The bombings of two U.S. embassies on the Horn of Africa occurred in 1998, followed by the attack on the USS *Cole* in October 2000 and then the attacks on the World Trade Center and the Pentagon in September 2001. The United States, having ousted the Soviet invader, allowed a far more corrupt and hostile power to establish itself.

The results of U.S. involvement in Iraq provided a more compelling lesson. In the late 1960s the United States engineered the coup against Saddam Hussein's predecessor, allowing the minority Ba'ath Party to come to power. In 1979 it endorsed Saddam Hussein as Ba'athist leader in order to secure an ally hostile to the Soviet Union and Iran and favorable to U.S. oil interests. In 1984 Donald Rumsfeld traveled to Baghdad to tell Saddam Hussein that the public criticism in the United States of Baghdad's use of chemical weapons would not derail the Reagan administration's efforts to improve U.S.-Iraqi relations. In each case, short-term tactical gains were accompanied by long-term strategic setbacks.[16]

THE WAR AGAINST TERRORISM

Shortly after September 11, President Bush announced, "Our war on terror begins with al Qaeda, but it does not end there. It will not end until every terrorist group of global reach has been found, stopped, and defeated." While this rhetoric may have appealed to a domestic audience, making the "war against terrorism" appear finite and winnable, it masked numerous contradictions and discontinuities. In both Pakistan and Saudi Arabia, for example, the governments cooperate with the United States while tolerating the continuing existence of terrorist infrastructures. As Nicholas Lemann explains, "The reason Pakistan's president, Pervez Musharraf, doesn't adhere more strictly to the Bush doctrine is that if he did he'd be overthrown by Islamists, and then Pakistan would be much less 'with us' than it is now."[17]

Meanwhile, the "war against terrorism" goes on with mixed results. Al Qaeda has been crippled but not destroyed. Many of its top leaders have been captured and many plans certainly disrupted. Its international funding has been slowed. Nonetheless, according to the draft of a UN report in 2003, "Despite the travel ban, members of the al Qaeda network have retained a high degree of mobility, and have been able to carry out and contribute to major terrorist attacks in several countries around the world," including Morocco, Saudi Arabia, and Indonesia.[18] Al Qaeda has tens of thousands of recruits it can call upon, a great deal of money, and operations in several dozen countries. With Saddam Hussein gone, Iraq has become another sanctuary for al Qaeda.

The history of terrorism demonstrates that increased intelligence and police operations are far more effective than massive military force and occupation. Success in Europe against terrorist groups such as Baader-Meinhof in West Germany, the Red Brigades in Italy, and the (Irish Republican Army) IRA in the UK indicates that good police work, intelligence, and negotiations were the tools that brought the success. Terrorism is a global phenomenon, not one confined to a few countries. In the 1970s there were terrorist attacks in Paris, Vienna, and the Olympics in Munich, as well as the seizure of American hostages in Tehran. In the 1980s there was an attack in London; the assassination of President Anwar Sadat in Egypt; suicide bombers at the U.S. embassies in Beirut, Lebanon, and Kuwait; the hijacking of a flight from Athens to Rome; bombings in Vienna and Rome; and the bombing of the Pan Am flight over Lockerbie, Scotland. The 1990s saw the bombings of the Israeli embassy in Argentina and the World Trade Center; the killing of U.S. troops in Mogadishu, Somalia; a nerve gas attack in Tokyo; the truck bombing in Oklahoma City; and the car bombing of the U.S. embassies in Kenya and Tanzania.

And this is only a partial list! While al Qaeda is one loose global network of Islamic extremists, there are many other dangerous terrorist groups. To combat terrorism, the United States must expand its work with the intelligence and police systems of countries all over the world. Most of our success against international terrorist organizations, including the arrests of top al Qaeda leaders, has involved cooperation with other intelligence services and police forces. We need to cement alliances and work out cooperative arrangements, not flaunt our power through unilateral actions.

We cannot stop terrorist attacks by invading other countries. On the contrary, our current situation suggests that, by creating a political vacuum in the wake of invasion, we create new conditions for breeding more terrorists. In the past conservatives and neoconservatives have been attracted to corrupt and brutal dictators such as Mobutu Sese Seko of

Zaire (now the Democratic Republic of Congo), Daniel arap Moi of Kenya, or Augusto Pinochet in Chile, where we have been responsible for terrible violence and terrorism against their own populations and have eventually made ourselves targets of hatred. There is a direct connection between the U.S. and UK overthrow of a democratically elected leader in Iran in 1953, the installation of the corrupt shah of Iran, and eventually the anti-U.S. Khomeini revolution in 1979.

The only means to prevent the creation of breeding grounds for terrorism is to provide stability and security and to infuse massive amounts of aid into the economies of these countries. By limiting economic assistance and relying on military force, the Bush administration has squandered its opportunity to address the systematic causes of terrorism and instability in Afghanistan and to deal humanely with the long-term sources of terrorism.

A DIFFERENT MODEL: EAST TIMOR

The security tasks for Afghanistan appear daunting, but it is useful to remember the violent situation in East Timor, an underdeveloped area beset by terrorist activists, which has become stabilized by multilateral efforts. The United States played only a secondary role in East Timor,[19] which can be considered a significant UN success under the brilliant leadership of Brazilian diplomat and UN representative Sergio Viera de Mello, who was tragically killed in the bombing of UN headquarters in Baghdad in the summer of 2003. De Mello, the UN high commissioner for human rights at the time of his death, had led UN peacekeeping missions for more than three decades.

Originally a Portuguese colony, East Timor was torn by civil strife between those who wished integration with Indonesia and those who favored independence. In 1976 Indonesia integrated East Timor as a province, although this act was never recognized by the United Nations. After continual conflict, the United Nations held a vote in August 1999, and the inhabitants of East Timor opted overwhelmingly for independence. Following the announcement, elements of the Indonesia security forces went on a rampage, killing, looting, and burning. The United Nations pressed Indonesia to act responsibly and rein in its military, and in September, with Indonesian cooperation on the surface, it put together a thirty-one-country peace force in which Australia took the lead and subsequently set up an international relief effort. The United States played a modest logistics and intelligence role when it was obvious that the Clinton administration had no stomach for another bout of peacekeeping.

In October 1999 the UN Security Council established a UN transitional administration for the country, and in December a meeting of international donors agreed to put up the funds. With majority East Timor representation, a council was set up during the transition period that began to put together basic buildings blocks for the creation of a civil society in the new country, such as a security system and legal and financial institutions. Continued UN pressure on Indonesia finally resulted in its cracking down on its terrorist military units. East Timor police and defense forces were developed, although, as pointed out by Brennon Jones, a former editor of *Afghan Update*, "bringing these forces up to international standards, and to the point where they have earned the respect of the local population, has taken more than three years of extensive training."[20] By 2001 an East Timor assembly had been voted in, a new Constitution adopted, and the framework for future elections and transition to full independence established.

East Timor was an important example of how the United Nations can act responsibly to deal with terrorism and nation-building; it is also an example of how the United States does not have to act unilaterally. To be sure, there are still difficult problems of governance ahead, in establishing full security, social and economic well-being, and justice and reconciliation after acts of terrorism. While security has been largely restored, there are budgetary shortfalls due to the loss of Indonesian subsidies and considerable economic distress. Long-term prospects are bright, however, due to the promise of East Timor oil production. The creation of an adequate legal system is proceeding slowly, as is the handling of crimes committed during Indonesian rule. Indeed, the motive of not wishing to antagonize Indonesia has caused the new state to hesitate in prosecuting war criminals—without an extradition treaty with Indonesia, the new country has no way to issue warrants for accused criminals outside the country—but East Timor is mostly handling these problems itself with increasing confidence.

This was a situation in which the United States sent virtually no ground troops, although it is making significant contributions in logistics, intelligence, military advisement, and support functions, such as police training, stimulating private investment, and civil education for independence. Its very presence as the world's only superpower carries enormous weight. It is, however, the international community and the citizens of East Timor who are primarily bearing the burden of peacekeeping and nation-building. A regional power, Australia, took responsibility for organizing the effort, which we are supporting.

This is a better model than Afghanistan or Iraq. Multilateral cooperation cements our relations with other countries, is less expensive, and ultimately models the interdependent world we live in. A cooperative relation with other countries in international peacekeeping suggests a number of possible involvements, such as the Congo, where over four million people have died. Another case is Liberia.

For decades the United States has opposed, and continues to oppose, the idea of a UN deployment force. The model of this force, developed initially in the 1950s by Dag Hammarskjold and Brian Urquhart, and most recently by Kofi Annan, would provide training for standby units drawn mainly from smaller nations, with larger powers, such as the United States, providing logistics and funding. In June of 2003 Donald Rumsfeld began talking about an international police force, trained and directed by the United States, without mentioning either the United Nations or NATO. Once again the United States, as it did after September 11, is speaking of multilateralism while insisting upon unilateral control. If our aim is to build viable nations, we should opt for arrangements and models that have a reasonable chance of success, not resort to policies that are not only doomed to fail but are likely to sow the seeds of increased stability, anti-Americanism, and even terrorism.

NOTES

1. Michael Dobbs, "Number of Wounded in Action on Rise," *Washington Post*, September 2, 2003, p. 1.

2. Bob Woodward, *Bush at War* (New York: Simon & Schuster, 2000), p. 30.

3. Sarah B. Sewall, "Confronting the Warlord Culture," *Boston Globe*, June 6, 2002. By relying on the Northern Alliance, the United States and its allies also allowed them to commit atrocities, such as the wanton killing of three thousand Taliban prisoners in unventilated truck convoys, according to the Boston-

based Physicians for Human Rights. See Babak Dehghanpisheh, John Barry, and Roy Gutman, "The Death Convoy of Afghanistan," *Newsweek*, August 26, 2002, p. 16, and Philip Smucker, "Afghan War Crimes a Low Priority," *Christian Science Monitor*, September 12, 2002, p. 6.

4. Editorial, "From Bonn to Baghdad: NATO Forces Join the War on Terror," *Wall Street Journal*, August 11, 2003, p.8. See also Thom Shanken, "NATO Agrees to Wider Role in Afghanistan beyond Kabul," *New York Times*, October 8, 2003, p. A14.

5. Amy Waldan, "NATO Takes Control of Peace Force in Kabul," *New York Times*, August 12, 2003, p. A9.

6. Study by Care International, reported by *Global Policy Forum*, June 18, 2003.

7. Joe Stephens and David B. Ottaway, "Post War Reconstruction Efforts Have Had Dicey History," *Washington Post*, April 28, 2003, p. A13.

8. Françoise Chipaux, "The Taliban Are Back in South Eastern Afghanistan," *Le Monde*, April 5, 2003. Mistakes are often made in targeting enemy forces, angering the local population. Also see Marc Kaufman, "U.S. Role Shifts as Afghanistan Founders," *Washington Post*, April 14, 2003, p. A10, and "Taliban Appears to Be Regrouped and Well Founded," *Christian Science Monitor*, May 8, 2003, p. 1.

9. Carlotta Gall and Amy Waldman, "Afghanistan Faces a Test in Democracy," *New York Times*, December 15, 2003, p. A6.

10. A *New York Times* editorial of November 17, 2003, declares, "Afghanistan is in danger of reverting to a deadly combination of rule by warlords and the Taliban, the allies and protectors of Osama bin ladan," p. A20.

11. See Michael Scherer, "The Return of the Poppy Fields," *Mother Jones*, May 19, 2003.

12. For a discussion of reforms for Afghanistan, see Mark Sedra, "Afghanistan: Between War and Reconstruction: Where Do We Go from Here?" *Foreign Policy in Focus* (March 2003), although Sedra waffles in recommending increased aid, then warning of the dangers of overdependence. For other sound studies of reform, see Human Rights Watch, "Afghanistan's Bonn Agreement One Year Later: A Catalog of Missed Opportunities," December 5, 2002, and "'Afghanistan: Are We Losing the Peace?' Chairmen's Report of an Independent Task Force Cosponsored by the Council on Foreign Relations and the Asia Society," June 2003.

13. For an excellent study of UN peacekeeping, see William J. Durch, ed., *UN Peacekeeping, American Policy, and the Uncivil Wars of the 1990s* (New York: St. Martin's, 1996).

14. See Minxin Pei and Sara Kasper, "Lessons from the Past: The American Record in Nation-Building," Carnegie Endowment for International Peace, May 1, 2002. The study does not grade Afghanistan or Iraq, as these are too recent. The study maintains that there are greater chances of success in nation-building if the United States cedes authority to an international agency, such as the United Nations, as it did in Bosnia and Kosovo.

15. Nicholas Lemann, "After Iraq," *New Yorker*, February 17, 2003, p. 70.

16. For the unintended effects of intelligence covert operations, see Melvin A. Goodman, "Espionage and Covert Action," in *National Insecurity: U.S. Intelligence after the Cold War*, ed. Craig Eisendrath (Philadelphia: Temple University Press, 2000). For the effects of U.S. intelligence operations on the United States, see Jack A. Blums, "Covert Operations: The Blowback Problem," in ibid. The present policy of a cease-fire agreement with the fifteen-thousand-member Mujahideen Khalq, or People's Holy Warriors, an Iranian terrorist group in Southern Iraq, as a hedge against Iran, carries a long-term blowback potential. See editorial, "A U.S. Deal with Terrorists," *Los Angeles Times*, May 1, 2003, p. B14.

17. Nicholas Lemann, "The War on What?" *New Yorker*, September 16, 2002, p. 36.

18. Susan Schmidt, "Trucker Pleads Guilty in Plot: Al Qaeda Brooklyn Bridge, D.C. Cited as Targets," *Washington Post*, June 20, 2003, p. A1.

19. Robert C. Orr, "Making East Timor Work: The United States as Junior Partner," *National Security Studies Quarterly* 7, no. 3 (Summer 2001); and "East Timor—UNTAET Background," prepared for the Internet by the Information Technology Section/Department of Public Information, United Nations, http://www.un.org/peace/etimor/UntaetB.htm.

20. Brennon Jones, "A Lesson for Baghdad," *New York Times*, September 13, 2003, p. A13.

CHAPTER THREE
GEOPOLITICAL COSTS AND RISKS OF THE IRAQI WAR

I think the burden is on those people who think [Saddam Hussein] didn't have weapons of mass destruction to tell the world where they are.

— Presidential press spokesman Ari Fleischer, July 9, 2003

There is no better example of the folly and reckless ambition of the Bush administration than the misguided decision to invade and occupy Iraq. An administration that wanted no part of nation-building is now preoccupied with the seemingly hopeless task of creating a democracy in an Islamic society that has had little experience with civil society, let alone free and democratic institutions. An administration that has declared a worldwide war against terrorism has committed half of its combat forces to a country that had no problem with terrorism until the United States invaded in March 2003. A secretary of defense who deplored the overuse of U.S. combat forces upon taking charge of the Pentagon is now consumed with plans for a forward-operating presence the world over as well as plans for using these forces more widely.

The war produced no evidence of Iraqi weapons of mass destruction (let alone plans to use them) or of Iraqi ties to terrorist organizations. As a result, the United States drew increased criticism from the international community, particularly those states that never believed there was a clear and present danger in the first place. Sadly, many more Americans have died and been wounded in the pacification stage in Iraq than during the war itself. In rolling the geopolitical dice with the use of force, President Bush demonstrated that he did not fully understand the regional implications of such high-cost and high-risk decision making.

Vice President Cheney and Secretary of Defense Rumsfeld began lobbying for the use of force before the dust had settled following the terrible attacks of 9/11. Cheney and Rumsfeld were obviously "spoiling for another war," Cheney to avenge the fact that Saddam Hussein survived Desert Storm in 1991 and Rumsfeld to demonstrate the military dominance of the new fighting forces of the Pentagon.[1] At a meeting of the National Security Council on September 12, 2001, Rumsfeld asked, "Why shouldn't we go against Iraq, not just al Qaeda?" And three days later Deputy Defense Secretary Wolfowitz told a meeting of the "war cabinet" at Camp David that "war against Iraq might be easier than against Afghanistan."

Only Secretary of State Colin Powell, who was chairman of the Joint Chiefs of Staff during Desert Storm, was concerned about the implications and consequences of a war with Iraq. Several days after 9/11, in a reference to the remarks of Rumsfeld and Wolfowitz, he asked army general Hugh Shelton, the chairman of the Joint Chiefs of Staff, "Can't you get these guys back in the box?" Powell also tried to convince the president that it was necessary to condition the invasion of Iraq on support from the United Nations. It was obvious from the start, however, that the president, vice president, and secretary of defense were committed to the use of force regardless of the UN position.

After the war Powell favored a major role for the United Nations in managing the transition period in Iraq, but Cheney and Rumsfeld again dominated the decision making, making sure that there was no international role for rebuilding Iraq. The neoconservatives became so impatient with Secretary of State Powell's efforts to be more conciliatory toward the international community that they leaked a story to the *Washington Post* in August 2003 describing Powell's alleged decision to leave the

State Department after the first term of the Bush administration. This willful act merely created embarrassment for the White House, and the Secretary and Mrs. Powell had to be invited to the Crawford ranch in Texas to demonstrate the secretary of state's good standing with the president. Several weeks later the president agreed to return to the United Nations for assistance for the reconstruction of Iraq.

Unlike the Vietnam War, when the incremental decision making of Presidents John F. Kennedy and Lyndon B. Johnson was responsible for U.S. involvement in Vietnam in the 1960s and 1970s, the decision to use force against Iraq developed quickly in the aftermath of 9/11. The Gulf of Tonkin Resolution in 1964, which authorized the president to use the armed forces of the United States to attack North Vietnam, was based on the misuse of intelligence that turned a provocative intrusion of U.S. naval forces in Vietnamese waters into a reason to go to war. Similarly, the Bush administration used and misused sensitive intelligence information to convince Congress and the American public to support the invasion of Iraq. Like the misuse of reporting on so-called Iraqi efforts to acquire enriched uranium in Niger, the Gulf of Tonkin Resolution involved the politicization of sensitive intelligence information in order to justify the use of force. The United States never lost a battle in Vietnam, but it could not militarily defeat the Vietnamese insurgency in South Vietnam. It is very likely that the United States, which swept through Iraq in less than two months, will be dealing with an Iraqi insurgency and instability for many years.

U.S. credibility has been compromised by the misuse of intelligence to justify the war, and President Bush was not helped by the remarks of neoconservative-in-waiting Michael Ledeen, resident scholar in the Freedom Chair at the American Enterprise Institute, which has become the bullpen for key appointments to the Bush administration. Ledeen, who was trying to "place the great victory [against Iraq] in its clearest perspective," remarked that "every ten years or so, the United States needs to pick up some crappy little country and throw it against the wall, just to show the world we mean business."[2] The international community justifiably fears that the United States has embarked on such a political use of military power around the world.

The case for war was controversial from the start. President Bush went to the United Nations in September 2002 to urge that "we work together to deal with the problem," but it was clear that the United States just wanted the international community to catch up with a decision the administration had already made. Prior to the speech, Bush met with his only close wartime ally, Prime Minister Tony Blair, in a "war summit"; several days later six hundred officers and enlisted men from the Central Command in Florida were sent to the Persian Gulf to establish a command structure for conducting the invasion. At this point the European allies were prepared to lend support to the pressure campaign against Saddam Hussein; French president Jacques Chirac called for a UN resolution that would give the Iraqi leader only three weeks to readmit the international inspectors. If Baghdad refused to comply, then Chirac favored a second resolution on intervention. Secretary of State Powell and even the White House appeared to indicate that it would support a new inspections regime, but the neoconservatives on Vice President Cheney's staff and in Secretary of Defense Rumsfeld's Pentagon were getting restless with what they considered delaying tactics. From the start, Cheney and Rumsfeld considered international inspections worthless; in the final analysis, the key European leaders correctly believed that UN inspections had worked in Iraq throughout the 1990s and could be made to work in order to avoid the use of military force.

In November 2002 the United Nations passed Resolution 1441, calling for the return of inspectors to Iraq with "immediate, unimpeded, unconditional, and unrestricted access" to anywhere and anyone. The inspectors were given the right to interview people outside the country and could demand a cessation of ground and air traffic in Iraq if they encountered suspicious activity. Sixty days after the start of their work, the inspectors were required to make an initial report to the Security Council. Chairman Hans Blix, who headed the inspection effort in the 1990s, was again asked to lead. Meanwhile, the United States made it clear that any interference with the inspection or any false Iraqi statement or omission would bring swift retribution, although the French and the Germans emphasized that nothing in the resolution made war automatic. In any event, the clock for both the carrot and the stick had begun.

In early 2003 the major difference between the five permanent members of the Security Council (the United States and Britain on one side and France, China, and Russia on the other) was over the specific time to be given to Saddam Hussein to account for his weapons of mass destruction. Secretary of State Powell's speech to the United Nations on February 5, 2003, was designed to make the case that Iraq held massive stockpiles of biological and chemical weapons, was reconstituting its nuclear program, and had links to al Qaeda terrorists. A vast majority of UN members believed that Powell made a good case for intensifying the inspections, but not for going to war, and that in any event a second resolution was needed before any war. In the wake of Powell's speech and the heavy international criticism of it, Saddam Hussein showed no sign of bowing to military pressure and seemed to believe that the United States and Britain would not resort to war in the face of international opposition. This was Saddam's final and fatal strategic miscalculation, one of many he had made over a twenty-year period.

The war began in March 2003 with no approving UN resolution. The United States launched a so-called decapitation strike that failed to kill Saddam Hussein or any of his senior staff. Within one week the invasion force had captured Iraq's southernmost port of Umm Qasr, secured Iraq's oilfields, and moved within fifty miles of Baghdad. U.S. forces captured the main airbases in Iraq's western deserts, from which Saddam had fired missiles on Israel during the 1991 war, and the United States airlifted special forces into Iraqi Kurdistan, north of Baghdad, after Turkey refused permission to allow U.S. forces to cross the Turkish border and enter northern Iraq. It was noteworthy that there were no humanitarian crises during the war that involved refugees or hunger, which the United States had anticipated and even planned for.

The second week of the war belonged to pundits and armchair generals who, dominating talk radio and cable news in the United States, exaggerated the significance of harassing actions against U.S. and British forces and even raised some inappropriate comparisons to the U.S. experience in Vietnam in the 1960s and 1970s and the Soviet experience in Afghanistan in the 1980s. In actual fact, by the third week of the war, U.S. armor was poised to enter Baghdad and, when it did so, there was little resistance of the type that had been anticipated by the armchair generals. There is still no authoritative count of Iraqi civilian casualties, but once again the reality was probably less than anticipated. Similarly, there were no examples of explosive outbursts of Arab nationalism in the key Arab capitals; the fact that Arabs viewed Saddam Hussein as a brutal and corrupt dictator mitigated the reaction to the U.S. invasion.

Six weeks after the start of the war, President Bush flew onto an aircraft carrier, the USS *Abraham Lincoln*, off the California coast and declared "mission accomplished," but his declaration was unfortunately premature. The sudden end of the war actually introduced the most serious challenges of the war: the failure to find evidence of weapons of mass distruction focused attention on the trumped up rationale for the American invasion, and the bungled handling of the postwar occupation of Iraq became increasingly apparent. It was particularly symbolic that every key government building in Baghdad was looted and sacked, except the oil ministry, which received overwhelming protection from U.S. forces. No protection was given to hospitals, generating a medical nightmare throughout the country, and no protection was given to the museums housing major Iraqi antiquities, which led to tragic losses of Iraq's legacy. European, Arab, and American archaeologists and historians had warned the Pentagon of the necessity to protect the museums and academic institutes, but U.S. commanding generals were unable or unwilling to protect the most important historical and cultural facilities in the country. Libraries lost books and universities lost research facilities, depriving Iraq of much of its cultural wealth.

In many ways the U.S. inability to protect these sites was symbolic of the occupation for which the United States was totally unprepared and for which the international community should have been consulted. As late as January 2003, only two months before the start of the war, there were only two Army officers assigned to Central Command to plan for the postwar period. They had no equipment and no budget, and the national security adviser who oversaw the operation, Elliott Abrams, had no expertise in the region and provided no leadership.

It is noteworthy that the United States, since the end of the Cold War, has engaged in a series of operations involving regime change and civil reconstruction but has devoted almost no attention to creating the military-civilian structure to plan for the most challenging phase of all, the period of internal reconstruction and reform. The Pentagon has the armor and infantry units to fight an almost casualty-free war in a short period of time but lacks the skill and equipment to repair the physical and psychological damage that it creates. The Iraqis actually had a decent civil society, but there is no indication that the U.S. occupation force knows how to put it to work. As a result, the occupation period will be very protracted and costly, doing far more damage to U.S. interests than the actual period of fighting.

Far more Americans have died in the pacification stage of the occupation than during the war itself, with no decline in casualties in the wake of the capture of Saddam Hussein in December 2003. During the war most deaths took place south of Baghdad; subsequently, many of the casualties occurred in Baghdad itself and many others were in the "Sunni triangle" between Baghdad and Tikrit, where there has been heavy resistance to U.S. reconstruction efforts. Since the war's end, nearly all the American deaths have been enlisted men from the army. Iraqi attacks on U.S. forces have become so commonplace that U.S. Central Command often does not announce casualties unless they have been accompanied by fatalities.[3] More than twice as many servicemen were wounded in Iraq in 2003 than during the Persian Gulf War in 1991.

There is no better example of the Pentagon's mishandling of the postwar Iraqi situation than its reliance on Ahmed Chalabi, the exiled leader of the Iraqi National Congress (INC) to dominate the transition period and become the first elected leader in Iraq's history. Chalabi was well known to State Department and CIA officials as a fraud and a faker who could not be trusted. But Chalabi was the "George Washington of Iraq" according to Deputy Undersecretary of Defense William Luti, and the obvious replacement for Saddam Hussein, according to Undersecretary of Defense Douglas Feith.[4] Chalabi was not only the Pentagon's candidate to create law and order in Iraq, but he was the source for most of the Pentagon's misbegotten intelligence regarding Iraqi weapons of mass destruction (WMD) and the expectations of an easy postwar transition. Even Judith Miller of the *New York Times*, who falsely claimed that the U.S. occupation force had found the "smoking gun" for making the case of Iraqi WMD, eventually conceded that her one and only unidentified source was Ahmed Chalabi.

The Pentagon even created a special unit, the Office of Special Plans (OSP), under Douglas Feith, to prepare finished intelligence analyses on Iraqi WMD and putative links to terrorism. Feith accepted Chalabi's recommendation to dismantle the Iraqi army and security agencies as soon as the war ended, which has contributed to the inability of U.S. forces to improve the security situation throughout most of the country. A former Pentagon intelligence analyst charged that the OSP "cooked the books" on intelligence for the war, reminiscent of the role of the National Security Council during the Iran-contra crisis in the Reagan administration in which the administration illegally used funds secured through arms sales in the Middle East to fund the covert war against the Sandinistas in Nicaragua. The OSP also had close links with the Defense Policy Board, whose members—particularly Richard Perle, former CIA director James Woolsey, and former Republican speaker of the House Newt Gingrich—peddled the OSP's disinformation to audiences at home and abroad.[5] The OSP was created in October 2002 when Secretary of Defense Rumsfeld became fed up with CIA analysis and ordered CIA Director Tenet to conduct an outside investigation of the agency's intelligence findings before and after the Iraqi war. The office was quietly abolished in 2003, and thus far the Republicans on the Senate Intelligence Committee have blocked efforts to investigate the intelligence chicanery at the OSP.

The failure of the Bush administration to do any genuine planning for the postwar situation means that the sudden collapse of the Saddam Hussein regime and the overwhelming success of U.S. military forces could not be exploited in a constructive manner. The neoconservatives who run the Defense Department, including Wolfowitz, Feith, Steve Cambone, and Jack Crouch, argued that U.S. forces would be met as liberators and that the Pentagon's man in Baghdad, Ahmed Chalabi, would be immediately installed to run a new Iraqi government. The Pentagon ignored the expertise of the CIA and the State Department, which argued that U.S. forces would not be welcomed in Iraq and that the postwar situation would be risky and protracted. Former army chief of staff retired general Eric K. Shinseki also testified that at least two hundred thousand American troops would be needed in Iraq in the postwar period, but his congressional testimony was demeaned and dismissed by Rumsfeld and Wolfowitz.

Once it was certain that Chalabi would have no political support in Iraq, the civilian leadership in the Pentagon had no backup plan for a transition government. Months after the war's end, there was no comprehensive plan for reconstruction of Iraq and no idea of the numbers and types of troops that would be needed for the future, according to a senior official from the Defense Department.[6] Unfortunately, the same civilian officials who planned the war and prepared the intelligence justification for going to war continued to orchestrate the transition. They are far more concerned with justifying the reasons for war than with the need for postwar stability. The regular losses of American servicemen that have undermined public support for Bush's war could pose the most daunting domestic problem of all for the administration. The Bush administration will certainly try to reduce U.S. military forces in Iraq before the election in November 2004, but the Pentagon has conceded that there will be a need for one hundred thousand U.S. troops there until 2006.

INTERNATIONAL OPPOSITION TO THE U.S. WAR AGAINST IRAQ

In addition to the terrible political and security problems that the United States faces in Iraq, the nation has squandered international respect and undermined its credibility. The most authoritative and respected poll of international attitudes toward the United States has been the annual poll of the Pew Global Attitudes Project, which released its most recent findings in the summer of 2003.[7] The study concluded that the war had widened the rift between the United States and western Europe, further inflamed the Muslim world, softened support for the war on terrorism, and significantly weakened global public support for the pillars of the post–World War II era—the United Nations and the North Atlantic alliance. Support remained strong for the fundamental economic and political values that the United States has long promoted, such as globalization, the free market, and democracy; this is accompanied, however, by a mostly negative picture of the image of America, its people, and its policies.

Pew surveys indicate that overwhelming majorities in such NATO member states as France, Germany, Turkey, Spain, and Italy support a stance on diplomatic and security affairs that is more independent of the United States. Opposition to the policies of the Bush administration became a major campaign issue in elections in many countries, and the Blair government in Britain—the only serious coalition partner in Iraq—was weakened over the issue of support for the American war against Iraq. The fact that the United States is no longer a status quo power, but is committed to preemptive military attacks against possibly threatening states, has disturbed elite European audiences. A study financed and supported by the Central Intelligence Agency's Directorate of Intelligence concluded, "Foreign audiences . . . frequently believe the United States does not act consistently with its stated values of political and economic liberalism."[8]

The United States has particularly angered the German policy and intelligence communities with its misuse of information supplied by the Bundesnachrichtendienst (BND), the German Federal Intelligence Service. The BND had supplied the information about mobile laboratories that were reportedly related to Iraqi production of biological weapons, a major part of Secretary of State Powell's speech to the United Nations in February 2003. But the Germans emphasized that they had "problems with the source" and no confidence with Powell's reference to émigré sources for the information.[9] The Germans eventually received corroboration of their own position in the summer of 2003 when analysts at the Defense Intelligence Agency and the State Department confirmed that the mobile laboratories were hydrogen-producing facilities for weather balloons to calibrate Iraqi artillery, which Baghdad had claimed all along. British sources became more aggressive in challenging their government's misuse of intelligence information in July 2003, following the suicide of Ministry of Defense biologist Dr. David Kelley, who argued that the Blair government had politicized intelligence on Iraq. U.S. inspector David Kay also concluded that the mobile labs have no connection to biological weapons programs.

German intelligence operatives have also testified in court that the United States had been given warning of the 9/11 attacks from an Iranian spy but chose to ignore the warning. The Iranian had been trained in an al Qaeda camp and worked in an Iranian department responsible for terrorists acts, so he had experience and credibility.[10] The White House and the U.S. intelligence community have denied allegations that they were forewarned of the 9/11 attacks.

The U.S. position in Europe became even more difficult because of the hard-liners in the Bush administration who went out of their way in the most undiplomatic fashion to insult and condescend to key European nations and prewar allies. Prior to the war Secretary of Defense Rumsfeld referred to France and Germany, the most vocal opponents of the war, as "old Europe" and described such newer members of NATO as Poland, Hungary, and the Czech Republic as "new Europe."[11] After the war Vice President Cheney admonished Germany and France, stating that neither country could expect oil or construction contracts from a new government in Iraq and that "perhaps, time will help in terms of improving their outlook."[12] Rumsfeld then delivered the most gratuitous shot of all, linking Germany with Cuba and Libya, with which the United States lacks formal diplomatic relations, for refusing to support the use of force against Iraq.[13] When Rumsfeld prevented France from taking part in a NATO air exercise in the United States in the spring of 2003, the major loser in this act of petulance was NATO.

Instead of reexamining the NATO security alliance, the Clinton and Bush administrations mindlessly expanded the alliance, ignoring Walter Lippmann's dictum that "an alliance is like a chain. It is not made stronger by adding weak links to it. A great power like the United States gains no advantage and it loses prestige by offering, indeed peddling, its alliances to all and sundry. An alliance should be hard diplomatic currency, valuable and hard to get, and not inflationary paper from the mimeograph machine in the State Department."[14]

The visit of Prime Minister Tony Blair to Washington in July 2003 added to the tension in international attitudes toward the United States and to a lesser degree Britain because of the obvious differences between London and Washington over the intelligence information that supported the war in Iraq. The United States had disavowed its claims that Iraq was trying to purchase enriched uranium from Niger and thus reconstitute its nuclear capabilities, one of its major selling points in the campaign to go to war. The British stood by their own sources but were unwilling to share these sources with the United States or their own constituents at home. The four-day Blair visit added to the general disarray between the two allies over the conduct of the war and the postwar transition and reminded many that the United States went to war even as the British were playing for time and seeking a second United Nations resolution to get greater support for war. The Blair visit also led to greater questioning of the reasons for going to war as well as to serious questioning of the so-called clear and present danger that Iraq presented in March 2003.

In addition to European opposition to U.S. national security policy, the CIA study found elite Asian audiences increasingly opposed to "U.S. unilateralism and heavy-handedness, especially regarding bilateral alliance management and transnational issues such as terrorism and illegal immigration."[15] As the United States pursues its counterterrorist policies in the area, it may create even greater tensions and increased opposition to the U.S. presence in the region.

South and Southeast Asian countries have generally pursued the policies that the United States ostensibly favors, such as globalization, liberalization, and democratization, but Washington's unilateral use of force and the Bush administration's barely concealed contempt for the United Nations have engendered a great deal of criticism.[16] The South Asian reaction to the Bush administration presents a similar dichotomy. These countries are democratic in nature for the most part, and they would have more confidence in U.S. efforts to introduce democracy into the Middle East if the Bush administration made greater efforts to introduce democratic reform to such allies as Egypt, Jordan, Morocco, and Saudi Arabia.

Despite the international opposition to the U.S. occupation of Iraq, the UN Security Council unanimously approved an American and British resolution in October 2003 that authorized an American-led multinational force in Iraq and marked a diplomatic triumph for the Bush administration. Nearly all of the countries that supported the resolution, including France, Germany, Russia, and Pakistan, wanted a more significant UN role in the political process in Iraq as well as a faster transition of political responsibility to the Iraqi people, but ultimately caved in to the U.S. pressure. The resolution also called for the Iraqi governing council to submit a timetable for creating a constitution and democratic government by mid-December, but that requirement was observed in a breach. Two months later the United States persuaded France and Germany to work with the Bush administration toward a substantial reduction of Iraq's massive debt.

The international community also believes that the United States is moving too slowly toward elections in Iraq because of the Bush administration's opposition to the Shiites and particularly their leader, Grand Ayatollah Ali al-Sistani. The Shiite community represents 60 percent of the Iraqi population, and Washington would like to delay its eventual electoral triumph by substituting a system of complicated caucus procedures. Sistani has reminded Washington, which fought its own "war for democracy," that direct elections must be held in 2004 for a new national provisional assembly.

GEOPOLITICAL CONSEQUENCES FOR TRANSNATIONAL ISSUES

The Bush administration's use of force in Iraq and the irresponsible use of ambiguous intelligence information will ultimately weaken international support for U.S. efforts to create an international coalition against terrorism, pursue arms control and disarmament, and stop the spread of WMD. President Bush's commencement address at West Point, where he endorsed a policy of preemptive attack against states and terrorist groups trying to develop WMD, produced an angry reaction abroad. U.S. plans for national missile defense, the U.S. withdrawal from the Anti-Ballistic Missile Treaty, and Washington's lack of support for the International Criminal Court added intensity to the reaction. A policy of preemption undermines the essential requirement of self-defense in any decision to use military force. Preemptive attack is also extremely dependent on the careful use of timely intelligence, which has been called into question by U.S. and UK distortions of intelligence information to justify the Iraqi war.

The Iraqi war is the first test of the Bush administration's belief that preemptive or preventive war can stop the proliferation of weapons of mass destruction. The neoconservatives of the Bush administration never accepted the notion that U.S. diplomacy had registered major successes in the former Soviet Union in destroying and dismantling strategic weapons or that international diplomacy would be effective in limiting the nuclear programs of Iran and North Korea. The case for war against Iraq was based in part on stopping the so-called reconstitution of Iraq's nuclear program in order to prevent possible proliferation of strategic weapons to third world states or nonstate actors. No evidence has been found of an Iraqi nuclear program, and the U.S. failure to conduct a timely inspection of the Tuwaitha nuclear reactor or search for documents at key nuclear facilities suggests that the United States did not expect to find evidence of a reconstituted nuclear capability or inexplicably did not prepare for an intensive search.

Furthermore, neoconservatives, such as Michael Ledeen of the American Enterprise Institute, recklessly believe that the case for war against Iraq can be applied to Iran or North Korea, where signs of nuclear programs are already in evidence. Both Iran and North Korea, however, possess genuine armies as well as the military arsenals to inflict damage on neighboring states. In the case of North Korea, Pyongyang's missiles could possibly hit parts of Alaska and Hawaii.

After the war and responding to heavy criticism at home and abroad, the United States created an Iraq Survey Group under former UN weapons inspector David Kay to search for documents. This indicated that the Bush administration had given up on finding the weapons and materials of a nuclear program and was focusing on archival materials in order to make a circumstantial case against Saddam Hussein. Kay's preliminary report in October 2003 indicated that there were no weapons of mass destruction to be found in Iraq, and in January 2004 Kay resigned from his position as the CIA's emissary in Iraq, concluding that Saddam Hussein "got rid" of his unconventional weapons long before the Iraqi invasion. Meanwhile, there were indications that both Tehran and Pyongyang had increased the pace of their respective programs in anticipation of U.S. coercive pressure. Bush's "axis of evil" may turn out to be a prime example of his administration's self-fulfilling prophecies.

If President Bush is serious about wanting to limit the WMD capability of nations in such a rough neighborhood as the Middle East, he will have to come to grips with the WMD capability of Israel, where two hundred nuclear warheads are believed to be stockpiled. Several Islamic countries already possess chemical weapons or weapons agents, including Egypt, Iran, Libya, and Syria, and the same countries have either biological weapons or at least research programs for such weapons.[17] These nations contend that their chemical and biological programs are a deterrent to a nuclear-armed Israel, which has instigated military force against Arab states in 1956, 1967, and 1982 and bombed an Iraqi nuclear reactor in 1981. It is unlikely that the military victory over Saddam Hussein will lead to progress in destroying or dismantling these programs; it is more likely that international diplomacy and such international agencies as the United Nations and the International Atomic Agency will have a more important role than U.S. force in counterproliferation strategy.

THE IRAQI LEGACY

The U.S. invasion of Iraq created a more difficult security situation in the Persian Gulf and worsened the security situations that the United States faces in Iran, Pakistan, and North Korea as it seeks to limit terrorism and the proliferation of weapons of mass destruction. The Iraqi legacy is particularly vexing because there has been no "smoking gun" in Iraq's program of WMD and no evidence of Iraqi ties to al Qaeda terrorists. Nearly

150,000 U.S. troops remain in Iraq, and U.S. officials, including the secretary of defense and the former commander of U.S. forces in the Central Command, indicate that large numbers of U.S. forces will be required for at least an additional four years. The cost of that presence reached $4 billion a month in 2003, which meant that prewar estimates of the size of the postwar occupation presence and the cost of that presence had been terribly underestimated. As it becomes clear that both U.S. forces and U.S. reconstruction efforts are inadequate, the price of the U.S. role will climb, as the head of the U.S. transition team in Iraq, Paul Bremer, has indicated. The bill for the occupation and rehabilitation of Iraq exceeded $150 billion, in September 2003, when President Bush requested an additional $87 billion for Iraq and Afghanistan, double the cost of the Desert Storm war.

Unfortunately, the postwar occupation was a disaster from the very beginning as the United States ignored the wisdom that "the first minute of war is the beginning of the peace." The Bush administration did not put an occupation and transition process into the planning stage until less than two months before the start of the war, and then it was a Pentagon-dominated process that did not rely on the interagency assets at the State Department and, more important, the Agency for International Development. None of the lessons of our experience in the Balkans, Haiti, southern Africa, or Afghanistan were put into play as the occupation effort was underfunded and understaffed. The assumption that building a civil society and conducting civil affairs could be turned over to the Pentagon was based on caprice and ignorance, and, as a result, the United States is paying a terrible price. As in Afghanistan, the United States is learning again that it cannot occupy other countries on the cheap. In both Afghanistan and Iraq inadequate resources and planning are creating resentment and fueling future problems, and continued attacks on U.S. forces have forced the United States to back away from ambitious initiatives to transform Iraq's political and economic systems.

We have also learned that the size and scope of government contracts awarded to American companies in connection with the war in Iraq are far greater than was previously disclosed, which is one of the reasons why the international community has opposed U.S. domination of the transition and has hesitated to get directly involved. Halliburton, the company formerly headed by Vice President Cheney, has won nearly $2 billion in contracts under Operation Iraqi Freedom and stands to make hundreds of millions more under an exclusive no-bid contract awarded by the U.S. Army Corps of Engineers.[18] Other companies with strong ties to the neoconservatives in the Bush administration, such as Kellogg, Brown and Root, and Bechtel, have acquired several billion dollars in contracts. In fact, independent contractors are receiving more than one-third of the monthly $4 billion cost of keeping U.S. troops in Iraq, and these contractors are such an integral part of the U.S. occupation that some of their employees dress in Army fatigues with civilian patches on their shoulders.

The overthrow of Saddam Hussein, moreover, has created a sanctuary or safe haven for terrorist organizations, including al Qaeda, whose members were not welcome in Iraq during the Ba'athist era. American and British forces and facilities are vulnerable to military attacks from Ba'athist Party members and foreign mercenaries, and presumably these guerrilla attacks will be used against the U.S. presence elsewhere in the Middle East. The bombing of the UN headquarters in Baghdad in August 2003, as well as successful attacks against oil and water pipelines, indicated that these guerrilla forces would concentrate on more vulnerable targets in order to demonstrate that the U.S. occupation force was not capable of protecting the country and restoring order. In November the CIA station in Baghdad predicted increased instability in Iraq; in December the station raised the possibility of a civil war.

The capture of Saddam Hussein in December 2003 did not significantly change the picture. Resistance to the U.S. occupation has been broad based, involving Hussein loyalists, Islamic guerillas, and foreign fighters. The loyalists with access to Hussein were probably a small group. For the most part, the resistance is highly decentralized, with most operatives choosing targets locally and controlling weapons that are close at hand.

The tactical military campaigns in Afghanistan and Iraq have been highly successful, but both have increased the logistical and security problems in the war against terrorism. One of the arguments against the war in Iraq from the outset was the possibility that such a war would prove to be a diversion from the more important war against terrorism. In Iraq the United States may find itself in a position that the Soviet Union inherited in Afghanistan, where a foreign invasion and occupation became a lightening rod for young Muslim militants to fight the "infidel" presence.

The war against terrorism has also been compromised by the U.S.

inability to find weapons of mass destruction and by the admission of the Bush administration in July 2003 that the Iraqi efforts to seek enriched uranium from Africa were exaggerated. This specious intelligence was known to the intelligence community and the National Security Council for nearly a year before the State of the Union address on January 28, 2003, when President Bush charged that the Iraqis were trying to obtain enriched uranium from Africa. Actually, the bulk of Iraq's nuclear infrastructure was either destroyed by allied bombs during the 1991 war or dismantled by international inspectors after the war, so there was never any evidence to sustain the charges of the Bush administration that Iraq had reconstituted its nuclear weapons program.

If President Bush, Vice President Cheney, and Secretary of Defense Rumsfeld were deliberately disingenuous when they made their charges of Iraq's nuclear activities, then they put American credibility at risk at a time when U.S. credibility is essential to forging a coalition against terrorism and proliferation. The tragic events of September 11, 2001, created excellent opportunities for creating a coalition against terrorism and proliferation and improving the international position of the United States, but the security policies of the Bush administration, particularly the war against Iraq, have squandered these opportunities.

Once again the United States needs the support of key nations in Europe, the Middle East, and Asia to deal with the problems of terrorism and proliferation that threaten international order. Instead of engaging regional centers of influence, the Bush administration has been applying unilateral use of force and diplomatic coercion to arrange solutions to problems. International cooperation had successfully contained Iraq before the war, and Saddam Hussein posed no threat to his neighbors, let alone the United States. Now U.S. military forces are overextended and at greater risk because of the use of force, and there is greater uncertainty over proliferation of WMD and the problem of terrorism. International cooperation is essential to anticipating the plans of terrorist organizations, but the United States has been antagonizing the international community by distancing itself from the International Criminal Court and violating the human rights of prisoners in the United States and Guantanamo Bay in Cuba. The United States must return to genuine power sharing in the global arena and must enlist other nations in burden sharing to manage key problems.

NOTES

1. Bob Woodward, *Bush at War* (New York: Simon & Schuster, 2002), p. 332.

2. Lewis Lapham, "Notebook: The Demonstration Effect," *Harper's* (June 2003): 11.

3. Vernon Loeb, "Number of Wounded in Action on Rise," *Washington Post*, September 2, 2003. p. 1

4. Franklin Foer, "Founding Fakers," *New Republic*, August 18 and 25, 2003, p. 17.

5. Jim Loeb, "War Critics Zero In on Pentagon Office," International Press Service News Agency, August 5, 2003.

6. Jonathan Landay, "No Real Planning for Postwar Iraq," KnightRidder News Bureau, July 12, 2003.

7. "Views of a Changing World 2003: War with Iraq Further Divides Global Politics," Washington, DC, Pew Research Center for the People and the Press, June 3, 2003.

8. Central Intelligence Agency, "Present at the Re-Creation: World Reactions to US Grand Strategy," Washington, DC, May 2003, p. iii.

9. *Die Zeit*, August 2003, cited in "Veteran Intelligence Professionals for Sanity," Press Release, August 22, 2003, http://www.commondreams.org/views03/0822-12.htm.

10. Ben Aris, "German Trial Hears How Iranian Agent Warned U.S. of Impending al Qaeda Attack," *Guardian*, January 24, 2004, p. 1.

11. James Chace, "Present at the Destruction: The Death of American Internationalism," *World Policy Journal* (Spring 2003): 1.

12. Lapham, "Notebook," p. 11.

13. Gerard Baker, "Tartuffe and the Shock-Jock Gird for War," *Financial Times*, February 13, 2003, p. 3.

14. Walter Lippman, cited in "On Alliances," *National Interest* (Summer 2003): 58.

15. CIA, "Present at the Re-Creation."

16. Karim Raslan, "A View from Southeast Asia," *Foreign Policy* (July/August 2002): 38.

17. See Joseph Cirincione, *Deadly Arsenals: Tracking Weapons of Mass Destruction* (Washington, DC: Carnegie Endowment, 2002).

18. Michael Dobbs, "Halliburton's Deals Greater Than Thought," *Washington Post*, August 28, 2003, p. 1.

CHAPTER FOUR
INTERNATIONAL DANGERS FOR AMERICAN SECURITY

T he war with Iraq was a major military success but may prove a long-term strategic disaster. It has complicated U.S. relations with its European allies as well as with key states in the Middle East and the Persian Gulf, and it has made it more difficult to gain international cooperation in the war against terrorism and the campaign to prevent the spread of weapons of mass destruction.

The war weakened U.S. standing throughout the international community, particularly because of the Bush administration's unwillingness to work with the United Nations and the mishandling of intelligence to justify the war itself. The absence of any evidence of Iraqi nuclear weapons or Iraqi ties to terrorist organizations has added to U.S. problems. The war, coupled with U.S. military deployments throughout the Horn of Africa, Central Asia and the Caucasus, and Southwest Asia, has overextended our military capacity. At home, U.S. defense spending is on course to reach $500 billion a year by 2008, and U.S. spending and tax cuts have produced record-level deficits and a vulnerable economy. The nonpartisan Congressional Budget Office projects $8 trillion in new deficits, moving the country from a projected $5.6 trillion surplus to a $2.3 trillion cumulative deficit. In this context it is difficult to argue that going to war with Iraq has actually improved the U.S. security position.

DANGERS OF THE BACK BURNER

The war and the controversial occupation of Iraq have placed far more dangerous situations on the geopolitical back burner, with the potential for serious consequences for our security. Iran, North Korea, and Pakistan play significant regional roles and have deployed or may be developing nuclear weaponry. U.S. relations with all three have been troubled. We have had no diplomatic relations with North Korea for more than fifty years or with Iran for twenty-five years. The continued unwillingness of the Bush administration to conduct a strategic dialogue with Tehran and Pyongyang exposes an ostrichlike U.S. stance that assumes if we cannot see the problem then perhaps it will go away. Pakistan, for its part, may well be a failing state whose nuclear weaponry could fall into terrorist hands. There has never been a greater need for dialogue and openness with these three states. Preoccupied with Iraq, however, our attention has faltered and opportunities for negotiation and possible resolution have been missed.

North Korea

U.S.–North Korean relations have never recovered from the American occupation of South Korea after World War II. The decision to divide Korea at the thirty-eigth parallel was driven by military necessity: the Soviet Red Army was poised to move down from Manchuria and occupy the entire peninsula, whereas the United States was not in position to move an occupation force quickly into the South. The decision was seen as tactical and expedient but soon became part of U.S. long-term strategy. As diplomatic historian Robert H. Ferrell noted, "No one at the time, certainly not the military commanders on the spot, anticipated a division of the world between communists and noncommunists, and the consequently unfortunate results for Korea."[1]

From the beginning of the division of the Korean peninsula, North Korean strongman Kim Il-Sung was anxious to unify the two Koreas and convinced both the Soviets and the Chinese that the United States was not in position to mount a significant opposition to an invasion. Kim's arguments were unwittingly buttressed by the remarks of leading U.S. officials, including Secretary of State Dean Acheson and U.S. commander of forces in Japan Gen. Douglas MacArthur, which removed South Korea from the U.S. defense perimeter in the Far East. The lack of preparedness of U.S. military forces was well advertised, and the initial success of North Korean forces at the outbreak of the Korean War in 1950 was no surprise. President Harry Truman's use of UN sanctions and participation produced huge diplomatic advantages and should have been a model for President Bush in the buildup to war in the Persian Gulf against Iraq nearly fifty years later. Unlike Bush, Truman cobbled together a coalition of nineteen states that sent forces who fought courageously beside their U.S. ally.

The war was fought to a bloody stalemate over a three-year period, with campaign names such as Operation Killer and Operation Ripper, and fifty years later there has been no negotiation of a peace treaty. There have been numerous flash point situations between North Korean and U.S. forces, particularly in 1968 and 1969, when Pyongyang captured a U.S. naval communications ship (the *Pueblo*) and shot down a U.S. EC-121 reconnaissance airplane in territorial waters off the North Korean coast, respectively. One of the worst incidents was the "Ax Murder Incident" in 1976, when several American and South Korean soldiers entered a forbidden neutral area of the demilitarized zone without prior approval from North Korea in order to trim a poplar tree that was blocking surveillance northward.[2] North Korean soldiers intervened, grabbed an ax from one of the Americans, and killed two U.S. soldiers. As in the EC-121 case, B-52s were dispatched from Guam and skirted close to North Korean airspace, but there was no further confrontation.

The current crisis between the United States and North Korea is the most serious since the Korean War because it involves Pyongyang's possible development of nuclear weapons for a military arsenal that includes intermediate-range missiles and a regime that has helped other nations develop short- and intermediate-range missiles. The Central Intelligence Agency believes that Pyongyang has developed the technology to make nuclear warheads small enough to fit the nation's growing arsenal of missiles, thus placing Japan and the sixty-thousand American troops based in Japan at risk. American satellite reconnaissance vehicles reportedly have identified an advanced nuclear testing site that suggests the North Koreans have learned to miniaturize their nuclear weapons.[3] North Korean testing of a third-stage capability for its missile force suggests that its weapons could reach the southernmost Aleutian Islands and Hawaii, with the possibility that this capability could be increased should North Korea resume testing of longer-range missiles.

North Korea has not yet tested a nuclear weapon, nor has U.S. intelligence detected signs of the krypton gas that is released into the atmosphere when nuclear fuel rods are converted into weapons-grade plutonium. In August 2003, however, North Korea threatened to test a nuclear weapon. Even before this, Pyongyang's ouster of international inspectors in 2002 and the resumption of activity at its reprocessing facilities in January 2003 had created concerns in the United States, South Korea, Japan, and China. The North Koreans have claimed that they have produced enough plutonium to make six nuclear bombs and that they intend to weaponize the materials they have produced.[4] Unlike Iraq, which spent the past two decades hiding strategic materials from the United States, North Korea has brazenly informed the United States of its strategic progress. North Korea has facilities that Iraq could never claim and may be several years ahead of Iran.

The Bush administration continues to refer to possible military options to meet the North Korean threat, but many government and academic analysts believe that the Pyongyang government is searching for a dialogue with the United States and that the nuclear activities are bargaining chips to gain U.S. diplomatic recognition and economic assistance.[5] Former secretary of defense William Perry, who negotiated a major freeze of North Korean nuclear weapons in 1994, believes, moreover, that the United States is "losing control" of the situation and that the continued absence of negotiations could lead to war.[6] Many experts on counterproliferation favor negotiations with North Korea to freeze plutonium production and to establish confidence-building measures. Even a hard-liner such as Rep. Curt Weldon (R-PA) believes that Pyongyang is practicing nuclear diplomacy only to get the United States to accept direct negotiations.

In 1994 the United States and North Korea concluded a nuclear freeze agreement, known as the Agreed Framework, which froze operations at the Yongbyon reactor and reprocessing plant, although it did not stop construction of two larger reactors. North Korea made it clear at that time that the framework did not cover missiles and that the dismantling of the Yongbyon facilities depended on future U.S. behavior. Pyongyang emphasized that it would surrender its nuclear option "once and for all only after the United States fully normalizes relations and no longer poses what Pyongyang considers to be a military threat."[7]

Nearly a decade later, the North Koreans continue to tie their nuclear weapons program to U.S. security guarantees, including the removal of land mines from the demilitarized zone and significant economic aid, particularly energy supplies and agricultural products. The United States and Japan want an unconditional end to the North Korean nuclear program before making any commitments; the Chinese and the Russians believe that the Bush administration must be more forthcoming and more conciliatory. Beijing and Moscow argue that Pyongyang's primary objective is to normalize relations with Washington and not to possess nuclear weapons.

Again, the neoconservatives have taken advantage of these differences to block progress toward negotiations, arguing that direct talks with Pyongyang would be giving in to nuclear blackmail and that there should be no concessions. On the eve of six-power talks (North and South Korea, Russia, China, Japan, and the United States) in Beijing to stabilize the situation on the Korean penninsula and end the North Korean nuclear program in August 2003, the neoconservatives forced the resignation of U.S. negotiator Charles L. Pritchard, who favored a more moderate approach toward North Korea. Pritchard, the most senior U.S. diplomat on Korean matters, had angered Sen. Jon Kyl (R-AZ), who called for "corrective action" in letters to Vice President Cheney and Assistant Secretary Bolton.[8] The talks themselves, in any event, marked neither progress nor greater acrimony, and there was an agreement to meet in 2004 at the six-power level.

At the very least, the United States could be instrumental in arranging greater dialogue between North and South Korea in order to stabilize the peninsula and increase contacts between the two states. A regional dialogue needs to be formalized as well, and the United States is the only nation in a position to bring China, Russia, and Japan into the picture. There have been positive signals from Beijing, Moscow, and Tokyo; North Korea, moreover, appears to have dropped its demand for bilateral talks with the United States, but the Bush administration has given conflicting signals about its willingness to take part in anything less than full multilateral discussions and has insisted on major North Korean concessions before even considering its demands.

The Europeans have increased their political and diplomatic stability with the use of institutional arrangements, such as the European Union and the World Trade Organization, for discussing political and economic differences. With the exception of the Association of Southeast Asian Nations, the Asian theater lacks many of these arrangements, but the key states in the region would benefit from any multilateral framework that offers a forum for dialogue and debate. The United States must abandon its unilateralist approach in order to allow the United Nations and UN secretary general Kofi Annan to play a bigger role in effecting such a forum. Unfortunately, the preoccupation with Iraq has allowed the North Korean situation to spiral out of control.

Iran

The end of Operation Iraqi Freedom found the neoconservatives of the Bush administration applying the case for war against Iraq to the situation in Iran. High-level administration spokespersons began discussing the development and deployment of weapons of mass destruction in Iran; the support and sanctuary for terrorists, including providing them WMD; and violation of international agreements on strategic weapons, particularly the Nonproliferation Treaty of 1968. The leading voices of the propaganda war against Iran, including President Bush, Vice President Cheney, Secretary of Defense Rumsfeld, and National Security Advisor Condoleezza Rice, emphasized that Iran's development of nuclear weapons would be intolerable and that Iranian dissidents should be supported in their campaign against the Iranian government and the Iranian clergy. In the wake of the Iraqi war, the administration demanded that Tehran turn over key al Qaeda figures to the United States but ignored Tehran's demands for a similar arrangement for members of the Mujahideen Khalq, an anti-Iran terrorist organization, being held by the United States.

The international community, fearing that the Bush administration was making another case for going to war, began to distance itself immediately from the pressure tactics of the neoconservatives. It appeared that, once again, the president's reference to the "axis of evil" (Iraq, Iran, and North Korea) in the State of the Union speech in 2002 was becoming a self-fulfilling prophecy that would lead to the use of force. Britain and Russia, both with strong economic ties to Iran, pressed for a diplomatic track for dealing with U.S.-Iranian differences and specifically called for a greater role for international arms agencies, such as the International Atomic Energy Agency (IAEA), to engage in more intrusive inspections of Iranian nuclear facilities.

Similar to the U.S.–North Korea impasse, the differences between the United States and Iran can be traced to events five decades ago, in this case the covert involvement of the United States and Great Britain in the overthrow of the government of Mohammed Mossadegh and the installation of the shah of Iran, which severely weakened and embittered the progressive middle class in Iran. The shah himself was overthrown twenty-six years later by a revolutionary force that branded the United States as the "great Satan." U.S.-Iranian relations have never recovered from the revolution led by Ayatollah Khomeini, and the seizure of the U.S. embassy that lasted more than a year probably caused the defeat of President Jimmy Carter in his reelection bid in 1980. There are numerous political and economic differences between the United States and Iran, but, as in the North Korean case, the major dispute is over Iran's possible development of nuclear warheads for its nascent missile force. North Korea's covert assistance to the Iranian missile program, which has helped Iran develop missiles in the thirteen-hundred-kilometer range, has added to U.S. tensions with both countries and was partly responsible for President Bush's branding of Iran, Iraq, and North Korea as the "axis of evil" in his State of the Union message.

The war planners for the invasion of Iraq appeared to believe that military success would allow the United States to encircle Iran with U.S. forces and U.S. allies. There is no good geopolitical reason to believe that such diplomatic and military pressure would work against the revolutionary leaders in Tehran. The Bush neoconservatives have dismissed Iran's relatively stable regional and international position and have totally underestimated Iran's support from such key European states as Russia, France, and even Britain. Many of the advisers to the Pentagon, particularly former Pentagon official Richard Perle and former CIA director James Woolsey, are cold warriors who resent the strategic loss of Iran in the 1979 revolution and want to redeem U.S. interests in the Persian Gulf.

The Iranian situation does present a serious problem because Tehran has pursued the development of nuclear weapons for the past decade. The government has imported uranium and constructed two large nuclear facilities, a massive uranium processing plant at Natanz, south of Tehran, and a heavy-water production plant at Arak. In July 2003, UN nuclear inspectors detected traces of enriched uranium at Natanz, which pointed to the secret production of nuclear weapons, and in August Iran admitted for the first time that it had received considerable foreign help in building the Natanz plant.[9] Tehran refused to identify the country, but the International Atomic Energy Agency believes that Pakistan was the source of critical technology to enrich uranium for Iran, North Korea, and other nations.

Production of nuclear weapons by Iran would be a direct violation of the Nuclear Nonproliferation Treaty, to which Iran is a signatory, which provides an opening for U.S. participation in a diplomatic solution to the problem. The United States also is concerned that the one-thousand-megawatt nuclear plant at Bushehr on the Persian Gulf, which is being built with Russia's assistance, will help to make Iran independent of foreign fuel suppliers for its nuclear reactors and capable of producing its own weapons-grade fuel. Iran also has not permitted IAEA inspectors to take environmental samples at the Kalaye Electric Plant, which may be a cover site to enrich uranium or other nuclear materials. Leading members of the European Community and Russia have persuaded Iran to accept more intrusive inspection of these facilities to meet their legitimate concerns. What they most emphatically do not want is the unilateral application of U.S. pressure or force, with unintended consequences possibly far worse than those in Iraq.

There are other issues that separate the United States and Iran, but these could be addressed and resolved through negotiations. Iran began testing a medium-range surface-to-surface missile (the Shahab-3) in the summer of 2003, meaning that the ballistic missile was ready to be delivered to Iranian armed forces. The Shahab-3 is modeled after the North Korean Nodong-1 missile but has reportedly been improved with assistance from Russia.[10] The development of a missile that could target Israel and the fact that Iran may be developing its own completely indigenous nuclear fuel cycle have created diplomatic tensions between the United States and Iran as well as between the United States and Russia.

Unlike the United States, the governments of Britain and Russia have used diplomacy to press Iran to accept greater international scrutiny of its nuclear sites, including a protocol to the Nuclear Nonproliferation Treaty that would allow additional inspections and even surprise inspections. Iran also agreed to suspend temporarily a program of uranium enrichment and to give the IAEA a full account of past nuclear activities. Russia has some leverage in Iran because of Moscow's assistance in building the $1 billion nuclear power plant in Bushehr that will become operational in 2004.

There is probably some international diplomatic leverage in this situation. Iran presumably realizes that if it were to obtain even a modest nuclear capability, its bilateral relations with all its neighbors, including Russia, Turkey, and the nations of central Asia and the Caucasus, would worsen. Tehran has made a significant effort in the past ten years to develop stable diplomatic ties throughout Europe and the states of the former Soviet Union, and Iran is not isolated in the way that Iraq and North Korea have been. Tehran's moderates presumably would not want to put these diplomatic ties at risk. But the United States needs to signal a serious interest in improving relations with Iran, perhaps ending its policy of economic isolation that has included opposition to the development of energy pipelines through Iran and Iran's application to join the World Trade Organization. Certainly, Washington's across-the-board hostility toward Iranian policies has been counterproductive.

Just as the United States must lead the way in arranging for a dialogue of North Asian states, including North and South Korea, there must be a more formal arrangement for a dialogue among the states of the Persian Gulf—principally Iran, Iraq, and Saudi Arabia—to work out the details of energy shipments. These states need a diplomatic process that uses the energies and initiatives of the indigenous states of the Persian Gulf and relies less on the presence of foreign forces, particularly those of the United States, which is increasingly perceived to be using force to strengthen its own national interest. It is unlikely that the United States can be successful in stabilizing the situation in Iraq without establishing normal relations with Iran and Syria, as well as stable Iraqi relations with its neighbors. As a result of the failure of the Bush administration to accommodate international concerns in the postwar Iraqi situation, the international community will be critical of any U.S. unilateral efforts to apply pressure on Iran and Syria.

Both European and Asian nations, for example, are hesitant to commit forces to peacekeeping missions in the Gulf. They have been crit-

ical from the start of American unilateralism in going to war in Iraq and
have been especially mindful of the way that Secretary of Defense Rumsfeld and the Pentagon dominated the planning in both the prewar and
postwar situations. The Bush administration should have relied on the
State Department to canvas its allies and encourage the states of the
region to develop their own principles, rules, and confidence-building
measures for avoiding friction and flash point situations.

Pakistan

The United States and Pakistan have had an uneven and often difficult
diplomatic relationship since the creation of Pakistan in 1947, but Islamabad's willingness to take on difficult and significant missions for various
Washington administrations led the United States to ignore serious problems, including Pakistan's development of nuclear weapons. Over the
years, Pakistan provided a base and logistics support for the then highly
secret U-2 reconnaissance aircraft that conducted the clandestine collection of intelligence over the Soviet Union (1950s); a secret platform for
the conduct of sensitive diplomacy with China that ultimately led to an
exchange of diplomatic relations between China and the United States
(1979); and covert assistance to the mujahideen forces that were responsible for the ouster of Soviet forces from Afghanistan (1980s). As a result,
the United States has been willing to ignore a series of authoritarian
regimes in Islamabad, Pakistani support for terrorism in the disputed territory of Kashmir and even India, and the development of nuclear
weapons since the 1980s with the support of China and North Korea.

U.S. and European intelligence agencies believe that Pakistan has
supplied weapons technology to countries trying to acquire fissile material.[11] It is possible that Pakistan sold nuclear centrifuge designs to Iran in
the 1980s and to North Korea in the late 1990s. These disclosures have
weakened Geneal Musharraf's standing with the hard-line Islamic parties
that accuse the Pakistani president of cooperating with Western intelligence agencies.

Of the various potential flash point situations in the world today,
moreover, none is more serious than the specter of a failing state in Pakistan, where there are nuclear weapons and materials that could easily fall
into the hands of nonstate terrorist organizations. Pakistan in recent years

has been combating a series of political, economic, and social problems; widespread corruption has eroded public confidence in the government. None of these problems points to an imminent collapse of the Pakistani state, but it probably rules out for the near term the establishment of a democratic government in Islamabad, where military regimes have ruled for more than half of the past fifty years. As a result, fifty years after its birth, Pakistan remains a "nation in the making."[12]

The weakness of Pakistan and the government led by Gen. Pervez Musharraf calls into question the regime's ability to safeguard its nuclear arsenal and to make sure weapons and components do not fall into the hands of terrorist elements that roam freely in Pakistan. Pakistani weapons are probably more vulnerable to accidental detonation than those weapons in the inventories of the United States, Russia, China, and even India. There were two major assassination attempts against Musharraf in late 2003, which points to the fundamental instability of the Pakistani situation.

The risk of a conventional clash between India and Pakistan going nuclear is always present, and the absence of a strategic dialogue between the two nuclear states is particularly worrisome. The two nations have not discussed confidence-building and security-building measures since the Lahore summit meeting in 1999. Musharraf and Prime Minister Atal Bihari Vajpayee need to become better partners, and recognize the need for a strategic dialogue, and the United States needs to institutionalize arrangements for a more regular dialogue with both of them.

The Clinton administration had an active policy designed to prevent the spread of weapons of mass destruction through two presidential terms, but the Bush administration has not developed a strategic approach to counterproliferation or a strategy for dealing with nuclear inventories in India and Pakistan. Pakistan has reportedly been providing technical assistance and materials to assist nuclear programs in North Korea and Iran, which is another provocative situation that needs to be addressed. North Korea, Pakistan, and Iran have developed a covert dialogue over the past decade to exchange nuclear technology and materials.

Efforts by Pakistan and India to ease the tension in their bilateral relations suffered a temporary setback in August 2003 when two powerful bombs killed 45 people and wounded at least 135 more in the heart of Bombay. No group has taken responsibility for the attack, but Indian officials suspect the Students Islamic Movement, which works closely with the Pakistan-based Islamic militant group Lashkar-e-Taiba. Increased tension between India and Pakistan always has the potential to escalate into a military confrontation.

Pakistani instability also has permitted Taliban and al Qaeda forces to maintain sanctuary in the disputed northwestern territories of Pakistan and then cross into southeastern Afghanistan. The Taliban has reconstituted some of its military capabilities in the southeastern province of Afghanistan as a result of the porous border, and al Qaeda forces are crossing back and forth between Pakistan and Afghanistan. The United States continues to pressure the Musharraf government to close down these safe havens, but the dual loyalties of the Pakistani army and intelligence services, some of which support Muslim extremist causes, often dictate a hands-off approach to these terrorist activities. This is, of course, another indication of the weakness of the central government.

The increased tensions between India and Pakistan presumably led their leaders, Prime Minister Atal Vajpayee and General Musharraf, to issue a joint statement in January 2004 and to agree to a "composite dialogue" in February. Musharraf assured Vajpayee that he would not "permit any territory under Pakistan's control to be used to support terrorism in any manner," and Vajpayee noted that the "resumption of the composite dialogue will lead to a peaceful settlement of all bilateral issues, including Jammu and Kashmir."[13]

A MAJOR BREAKTHROUGH IN LIBYA

The Bush administration registered a major success in December 2003 when Libya agreed to give up its nuclear, chemical, and biological weapons programs, following nine months of secret diplomacy.[14] Libyan leader Col. Muammar Qadhafi apparently initiated secret talks with the United States and Britain nine months ago, just as the U.S.-U.K. invasion was about to begin. Inspectors from the International Atomic Energy Agency will monitor the dismantling of all Libyan facilities, which Qadhafi had never acknowledged until now. President Bush and Prime Minister Blair immediately claimed that the Libyan concession was a direct result of the use of force against Iraq, but critics of the war emphasized the role of diplomacy in gaining Qadhafi's renunciation of all weapons of mass destruction.

THE MIDDLE EAST PEACE PROCESS AND THE "ROAD MAP"

There has never been an Israeli movement toward negotiations with the Arabs or a settlement of Arab-Israeli issues without significant U.S. involvement and willingness to apply pressure to Israelis and Arabs alike. U.S. blandishment and pressure were important to Israeli withdrawal from the Sinai Peninsula after the 1956 war, an end to Israeli cease-fire violations during the end game of the 1973 war, and the step-by-step negotiations that followed the 1973 war. Equally, the United States has applied pressure to those Arab states that have not recognized the legitimacy of Israel or indicated a willingness to engage in normal diplomatic or commercial relations. After the Persian Gulf war in 1991, the administration of George H. W. Bush promised to get involved in the Palestinian-Israeli peace process but failed to do so. The Israelis and Palestinians established their own secret dialogue in Oslo, Norway, that ultimately led to the Camp David summit of July 2000. The two sides were closer to a final settlement of outstanding issues at Camp David than at any time in the past five decades. Rather than try to regain the momentum begun in Oslo, however, the administration of George W. Bush virtually ignored the Israeli-Palestinian problem for almost two years, during some of the worst violence between the two sides.

Key members of the Bush administration have tried to rationalize the war with Iraq as a first step toward an Israeli-Palestinian settlement as well as toward democratizing the entire Middle East. President Bush and both Deputy Secretary of Defense Wolfowitz and Undersecretary of Defense for Policy Feith have stated that a war with Iraq could help bring democracy to the Arab Middle East and that Iraq "would serve as a dramatic and inspiring example of freedom for other nations in the region."[15] Professor James Chace has noted that "such a task would be Herculean, and, I suspect, quixotic."[16]

Nevertheless, one of the few initial benefits of the war in Iraq was a renewed U.S. interest in a two-state solution to the crisis between Israel and the Palestinian Authority that would follow UN Security Council Resolutions 242 and 338. These resolutions envision a secure Israel returning to the pre-1967 war borders, which would require abandoning settlements, and a viable Palestine on the West Bank and Gaza, coupled with the end of Palestinian terrorism. Both Russia and the European Union have supported the efforts of the Bush administration to make its "road map" work, and such key Arab states as Egypt, Saudi Arabia, and Jordan appear prepared to apply pressure on the Palestinians to be more forthcoming in their dealings with Israel.

Prime Minister Tony Blair convinced the Bush administration that a U.S.-UK coalition could be successful in Iraq but that long-term progress in the region required a solution to the Israeli-Palestinian problem that only the United States could manage. As a result, President Bush publicly supported the idea of a Palestinian state but, in deference to the Israelis, stated that the United States would not negotiate with Yasir Arafat. The installation of Mahmoud Abbas marked an initial success for U.S. diplomacy, permitting the Bush administration to open direct talks with the Palestinians. His resignation in September 2003 seemed to be a major setback, but his successor, Ahmed Qurie, participated in the Oslo Accords and is also considered a moderate.

Only several months after the Iraq war's end, however, it was obvious that the war was going to pay no diplomatic dividend in the Israeli-Palestinian crisis. If anything, the crisis worsened, and the United States was far too preoccupied in Iraq to play a major role. Indeed, terrorist incidents in Israel and the occupied territories increased during 2003, with more than forty innocent lives lost in the summer, prompting more vows of retaliation. Suicide bombers have penetrated the Middle Eastern landscape for the past twenty years, but the bombing of a city bus in Jerusalem in August was particularly violent and brought Israeli forces back to their occupation positions in the West Bank and Gaza. The underlying weakness of the U.S. hand in the crisis was graphically demonstrated by Secretary of State Powell's call for Yasir Arafat, the preeminent Palestinian leader but a pariah to Washington, to try to stabilize the crisis. Until then the United States had been honoring Prime Minister Sharon's demand to ignore Arafat, who, the Israelis claim, tolerated and even encouraged terrorism.

If the peace process is to pick up its lost momentum, Washington must convince the Palestinians to halt the terrorist attacks by Hamas and other terrorist organizations in Israel; at the same time, it must convince the Israelis to stop the installation of a security barrier on the West Bank, to pull its military forces back from the West Bank, and to dismantle or at least freeze settlements on the West Bank and in Gaza. The Bush administration has impressed many watchers of the peace process with the decision to make direct assistance payments to the Palestinian Authority instead of allowing Israel to be a conduit for such payments and to threaten to reduce guaranteed loans to Israel if it continues to build a security fence on the West Bank that increasingly isolates Palestinian villages, although it has not followed through on these threats.

The "road map" for peace can have no meaning without reciprocal progress in these areas. Signs of progress could still lead to creation of a Palestinian state as early as 2005, according to Phase III of the road map, which is designed to resolve borders and the status of Jerusalem, refugees, and the settlements. Phase I requires the Palestinians to "undertake an unconditional cessation of violence," while Israel "freezes all settlement activity" and "immediately dismantles settlement outposts erected since March 2001." Phase II would create an "independent Palestinian state with provisional borders" by December 2003, but only if the mutual security measures of Phase I were implemented. It will be difficult for the Bush administration to be successful if the Palestinian Authority does not challenge the terrorist activities of Hamas and Islamic Jihad who seem "intent on destroying the road map" and if Israeli prime minister Ariel Sharon continues to support settlements, sanctions the killing of civilians in assassination attempts against terrorist leaders, and adds to the Israeli "separation fence" that runs along the 1967 border in some areas but penetrates deeply into the West Bank in other areas.[17]

It is possible that the United States, Israel, the Palestinians, and the Arab states, in dragging their heels on a settlement for nearly four decades, have waited too long to effect one now. But most Middle Eastern experts still believe that the only long-term solution to the problem of terrorism that the United States faces at home and abroad is in the establishment of an independent Palestinian state. A number of independent variables remain to thwart a solution, including the impact of unpredictable terrorist actions by Hamas and Hezbollah on the negotiation process, plus the support of Syria and Iran for these organizations. There are also indications that moderate Arab states will find it difficult to work closely with the United States because of the mounting opposition in their countries to the U.S. occupation of Iraq that will be more long-lived than the Bush administration initially believed. Saudi Arabia has already taken steps to remove the U.S. military presence from the kingdom, and Egypt and Jordan are getting restless with the unwillingness of the Bush administration to apply pressure on Israel. Unlike the 1991 war, when Islamic jurists in Egypt and Saudi Arabia issued *fatwas* (legal decrees) to sanction the use of foreign troops to liberate Kuwait, there were no such *fatwas* in support of military force against Saddam Hussein in 2003.

Prior to the 2003 war, the Bush administration sent a series of political signals to the Middle East that suggested that it would have no interest in intense involvement in the process. The first act of the administration regarding the region was the firing of the two Americans most experienced and most engaged in the Arab-Israeli dialogue, the State Department's Dennis Ross and Aaron Miller, who were well known and respected in both Israel and the key Arab capitals. The naming of pro-Israeli lobbyist Elliott Abrams as the national security advisor on the Middle East sent a strong signal to the Muslim world that President Bush was going to favor Israeli interests in any negotiating process. Abrams was an early critic of Secretary of State Powell's efforts to alleviate differences between Israel and Palestine and has not been an enthusiastic supporter of the road map. Additional criticism of the road map has come from Deputy National Security Advisor Stephen Hadley, who appears to be Vice President Cheney's man on the NSC, and from Undersecretary of Defense Feith. The close ties between many members of the Bush administration and the hard-line Likud Party as well as President Bush's reference to Sharon as a "man of peace" certainly do not resonate well in Arab communities.

Israeli and Palestinian impatience with the inability or unwillingness of their leaders as well as the United States to press for a genuine Middle East peace has once again led private individuals to create a detailed agreement between the two sides. Like the Oslo peace process a decade earlier, the current Geneva Accord would give explicit Palestinian recognition of Israel as the Jewish state and would outline a reasonable solutioin for Jerusalem and the Palestinian refugees. A majority of Israelis and Palestinians favor such an agreement, but their leaders have been opposed to any serious steps to move forward. President Bush has been critical of

Palestinian heel dragging but has virtually ignored the continued construction of illegal settlements on the West Bank and the Israeli use of overwhelming military force in the occupied territories.

Another reason why it is difficult to believe that the Bush administration is genuinely prepared to press for peace and stability in the Middle East is the lack of any genuine movement or opening toward Syria, which has been the key to preventing another major Arab-Israeli war in the region ever since Israel and Egypt exchanged full diplomatic relations in the Camp David peace process in 1979. Indeed, in the immediate wake of the Iraq war, the United States went out of its way to create tensions with Syria; U.S. forces actually crossed the Syrian border in June 2003, wounding five Syrian border guards and delaying their release to Syrian authorities. Since then U.S. planes and helicopters have routinely violated Syrian airspace, and U.S. forces continue to fire at Syrian villagers.

The United States issued a series of warnings and threats to the Syrians in the immediate wake of the war with Iraq, accusing Damascus of allowing Iraqi officials to flee to Syria, permitting the transfer of military equipment across the Syrian-Iraqi border in both directions, and even warehousing Iraqi weapons of mass destruction. The charge regarding WMD was particularly improbable, but the Bush administration persisted. In a short period of time, Washington squandered the goodwill that had been established over the past decade from Syrian support for Desert Storm in 1991, assistance in tracking down Islamic extremists, and endorsement of UN Security Council Resolution 1441, which the United States used to justify the 2003 war against Iraq.[18] If the Bush administration is serious about stabilizing the Israeli-Arab front, then a place must be made for Bashar Assad's regime at the negotiating table. Unfortunately, the neoconservatives in both the United States and Israel prefer confrontation in lieu of diplomacy with Syria and elsewhere.

In gratuitously picking a fight with Syria, the neoconservatives are antagonizing a poor country with little military capability that is a threat to no nation in the region. Syria may have had broad regional ambitions twenty years ago, but no Syrian action today justifies U.S. or even Israeli military action. Oil interests account for much of the U.S. interest in Iraq, but it is hard to identify the issues that are drawing the ire of the Bush administration toward Damascus.

The United States should have learned from the Israeli example that military superiority is not the answer to stopping terrorist activities and bringing stability to the region. Israel is a military superpower, with more than 160,000 military personnel under arms and one of the world's most active and sophisticated reserve systems. Israel is the only nation in the region with nuclear weapons and the ability to deploy some of the most sophisticated and lethal conventional weapons. The Palestinian Authority is no match for the Israeli Defense Forces (IDF), but the IDF has not found the answer to stopping the acts of terrorism that emanate from the West Bank and Gaza. Increased Israeli military actions against the Palestinians only bring greater acts of revenge and defiance, and the pattern that has been long familiar to Israeli-Arab relations is now replicating itself in Iraq, where U.S. forces are unable to guarantee stability despite an occupation force of about 130,000 military personnel. If Israel cannot guarantee security in its own state, which is the size of New Jersey, then it appears increasingly unlikely that the United States will be able to police and monitor Iraq, which is the size of California.

THE GEOECONOMIC DIMENSION

The Bush administration has adopted international economic policies that have worsened social and economic conditions in the third world, thus creating additional breeding grounds for terrorism. In the last decade of the twentieth century, total world income increased by 2.5 percent annually, but the number of people living in poverty increased by almost one hundred million.[19] This disparity was due in part to the policies of the developed nations, particularly the United States, which imposed terms of trade that put the developing world at a distinct disadvantage. High tariffs on the goods of the developing world, particularly such agricultural products as cotton, sugar, or tobacco, and high subsidies for farmers in the developed world have created huge imbalances. At the same time, the demand that developing countries import manufactured goods without protective tariffs has increased debt, weakened currencies and banking systems, and cut living standards.

The International Monetary Fund, set up at the end of World War II under the direction of the great British economist John Maynard Keynes, was designed to assist countries in this condition by creating greater demand for goods and thus stimulating economic recovery. Keynes wanted to put money into the hands of the classes most likely to consume—the poor and working classes. Since 1971, however, the IMF and the International Bank for Reconstruction and Development (World Bank), which report to the central banks and finance ministries of the developed countries, have pursued different policies from those suggested by Keynes. These policies, which benefit the financial interests of the United States and others, do not succor the poor and disadvantaged peoples of the third world.

The IMF has imposed conditions, called the "Washington consensus," that do not create internal demand, including

- raising interest rates,
- raising taxes,
- lowering wages,
- eliminating unions,
- curtailing government credits to farmers and businessmen,
- stopping unemployment benefits,
- closing government programs,
- privatizing industries and government programs,
- eliminating tariffs and other trade barriers, and
- subsidizing banks and protecting private loans even if they are irresponsible or speculative.

Under IMF policies, countries receive loans desperately needed to pay off debts and stabilize currencies only if these "neoliberal" conditions are met. Since banks and ministries within the developing countries share the IMF's loyalty to the financial community, it is relatively easy to impose these terms. The results have been disastrous for over three decades, particularly for the poor.

At the same time that the United States benefits from its trade policies, it has become increasingly tightfisted in extending economic aid and assistance, currently ranking dead last among the sixteen most developed nations. Our insistence on "free trade" and our pride in our "compassionate conservatism" abroad are comfortable myths that do not conform to third world realities.

If we are to fight terrorism effectively, these economic policies must be reassessed. Changes must be gradual so that U.S. farmers and other groups that have been dependent on tariffs and subsidies are not destroyed. At the same time, the government must be sufficiently independent of lobbyists and special interest groups in order to embrace policies that are in the long-term interests of the United States and the international economy.

Unfortunately, the invasion and occupation of Iraq has made it extremely difficult to address more serious situations elsewhere. President Bush's doctrine of preemptive war has both frightened and angered the international community, and it has become more difficult to cobble together the international coalitions that are needed to resolve the crises in Iran, North Korea, Pakistan, the Middle East, and elsewhere. U.S. deployment of a national missile defense, abrogation of the ABM Treaty, and retreat from the Kyoto Protocol, the Comprehensive Test Ban Treaty, and the International Criminal Court have left the international community in a quandary regarding U.S. tactics and policies. The unilateral use of force and economic policies that create economic distress in the third world have increased rather than diminished the threat of terrorism. The dominance of the neoconservative movement in the Bush administration has convinced the member states of the United Nations that the United States is determined to go it alone in the international arena regardless of the consequences. In only two years, President Bush has managed to exhaust the world's sympathy and support in the wake of 9/11 and create an international community that must scrutinize everything the Bush administration says and does. The result is a world that is considerably less safe than it was before the Bush administration took office.

NOTES

1. Robert H. Ferrell, *American Diplomacy: A History* (New York: W. W. Norton, 1969), p. 766.

2. Selig Harrison, *Korean Endgame: A Strategy for Reunification and U.S. Disengagement* (Princeton, NJ: Princeton University Press, 2002), p. 199, the most authoritative account available on U.S.–North Korean relations and negotiations.

3. David E. Sanger, "CIA Said to Find Nuclear Advances by North

Koreans," *New York Times,* July 1, 2003 p. A1. National intelligence estimates since 1999 indicated that North Korea already possessed one or two weapons.

4. David E. Sanger, "North Korea Says It Has Made Fuel Atom Bombs," *New York Times*, July 15, 2003, p. 1.

5. Harrison, *Korean Endgame*, p. 225.

6. Thomas E. Ricks and Glenn Kessler, "U.S., North Korea Drifting toward War, Perry Warns," *Washington Post*, July 15, 2003, p. 14.

7. Harrison, *Korean Endgame*, p. 224.

8. Christopher Marquis, "Top U.S. Expert on North Korea Steps Down," *New York Times*, August 26, 2003, p. 8.

9. Joby Warrick, "Iran Admits Foreign Help on Nuclear Facility," *Washington Post*, August 27, 2003, p. 17.

10. Reuters, "Iran Competes Testing of Long-Range Missile," *Washington Post*, July 8, 2003, p. A14.

11. William Broad, "Inquiry Suggests Pakistanis Sold Nuclear Secrets," *New York Times*, December 22, 2003, p. 1

12. See Shahid Javed Burki, *Pakistan: A Nation in the Making* (Boulder, CO: Westview Press, 1986).

13. "India and Pakistan: Back to Jaw-Jaw," *Economist* (January 10, 2004): 35.

14. David Sanger and Judith Miller, "Libya to Give Up Arms Programs," *New York Times*, December 20, 2003, p. 1.

15. Elisabeth Bumiller, "The President: Bush Says Ousting Hussein Could Aid Peace in Mideast," *New York Times*, February 27, 2003, p. A1; George W. Bush, "In the President's Words: 'Free People Will Keep the Peace of the World,'" *World Policy Journal* (Spring 2003): 4.

16. James Chace, "Present at the Destruction: The Death of American Internationalism," *World Policy Journal* (Spring 2002): 4.

17. Edward R. F. Sheehan, "The Map and the Fence," *New York Review of Books*, July 3, 2003, p. 8. Jonathan Cook, an American journalist living in Israel, wrote in the *International Herald Tribune* that the "security wall will cage in more than two million Palestinians."

18. See Martha Kessler, "Avoiding the Road to Damascus," *Los Angeles Times*, April 18, 2003, p. 17.

19. See Joseph E. Stiglitz, *Globalization and Its Discontents* (New York: W. W. Norton, 2002). See also Elisabeth Becker and Ginger Thompson, "Poorer Nations Plead Farmers' Case at Trade Talks," *New York Times*, September 11, 2003, p. A3.

CHAPTER FIVE
THE FAILURES
OF INTELLIGENCE

*. . . make no mistake; we simply cannot win the war [on terrorism]
without enthusiastic international cooperation, especially
on intelligence.*

— Former national security advisor General Brent Scowcroft,
August 15, 2002

The tragic events of September 11, 2001, and the misuse of intelligence to justify the use of force against Iraq in March 2003 demonstrated a serious failure of the intelligence community and the government itself. Despite numerous warnings and a flurry of earlier terrorist attacks overseas, the United States lacked strategic warning and was completely unprepared for the attacks on the World Trade Center and the Pentagon. Despite the absence of significant intelligence on weapons of mass destruction in Iraq, the Bush administration convinced Congress to go to war in 2003. Our massive intelligence apparatus, which now spends nearly $40 billion annually, was not able to protect us from terrorism or the questionable use of military force.

The leaders of the Bush administration and Congress have thus far responded in classic bureaucratic fashion, throwing lots of money at the problem in hopes of finding a solution. But what will we get for these large increases in spending and what are we doing to improve our intelligence capability—the "eyes and ears" of our efforts to prevent terrorism and to assess threats? Once again, we are satisfying the needs of the military services, the defense contractors, and their allies in Congress—Eisenhower's military-industrial complex.

9/11 AND THE FAILURE OF INTELLIGENCE

One week after the attacks on the Pentagon and the World Trade Center, National Security Adviser Condoleezza Rice told the press corps, "This isn't Pearl Harbor." No, it was worse. Sixty years ago the United States did not have a director of central intelligence or thirteen intelligence agencies or a combined intelligence budget of $40 billion to provide early warning of enemy attack. And just as intelligence was divided and diffuse on the eve of Pearl Harbor, there was no genuine intelligence collaboration on the eve of September 11, 2001.

Less than two weeks after the surprise attack on Pearl Harbor, President Franklin D. Roosevelt appointed a high-level military and civilian commission to determine the causes of the intelligence failure. Following the September 11 attacks, however, President George W. Bush, CIA Director George Tenet, and the chairmen of the Senate and House Intelligence Committees were adamantly opposed to any investigation or postmortem. The president's failure to appoint a statutory inspector general at the CIA from January 2001 to April 2002 deprived the agency of the one individual who could have started an investigation regardless of the director's opposition.

The eventual Senate and House Intelligence Committees' joint investigation of the September 11 failure, which began in June 2002, was mishandled at the outset. The original staff director for the investigation, former CIA inspector general L. Britt Snider, had the stature and experience for the job, but he was soon forced out by former Senate Intelligence Committee chairman Richard Shelby (R-GA), a staunch critic of CIA Director Tenet. The staff itself seemed too small and inexperienced to do the job seriously.

The August 2002 decision of the chairmen of the Senate and House Intelligence Committees, Sen. Bob Graham (D-FL) and Rep. Porter Goss (R-FL), to order an aggressive FBI investigation of the joint committee, ostensibly to uncover leaks of classified information, marked a blatant violation of the separation of powers between the executive and legislative branches. Much time was lost as senators and representatives debated whether committee members should submit to unprecedented polygraph examinations, a move designed to placate the Bush administration.

President Bush never wanted an investigation of September 11, neither congressional nor independent, and established roadblocks to a more general investigation of the intelligence community. He did not permit his secretaries of state and defense to testify to the joint congressional investigation in public session and wanted any investigation to be quick and dirty. According to Senator Shelby, the administration has "delayed cooperating fully, knowing it [the committee] has a deadline to meet."[1] The White House has blocked any release of information that would determine the kind of intelligence the president received from the CIA and significantly delayed the release of findings of the joint congressional investigation. Bush's heel dragging for eight months begged the question whether the White House may have had some warning to pursue preventive measures against a terrorist attack.

To make matters worse, the congressional oversight process has broken down, and there is no sign that the appropriate committees are willing to scrutinize the intelligence community. In various intelligence failures over the past ten years, particularly the failure to monitor the weakness and collapse of the Soviet Union, the oversight committees have not been "junkyard dogs" in monitoring the activities of the intelligence community, particularly the CIA. Sen. Charles Grassley (R-IA) says, "Everyone's in awe of them [intelligence agencies]. Everyone just melts in their presence, and so they have always gotten a long leash." Rep. David Obey (D-WI) agrees, adding that congressional oversight has been "miserable." Rep. Saxby Chambliss (R-GA) conceded that the congressional intelligence committees have a "share in the blame for not providing better oversight."[2] The intense squabbling between the Republican chairman of the Senate Intelligence Commitee, Pat Roberts, and the ranking Democratic member, Jay Rockefeller, has hindered the congressional investigation.

Nevertheless, the preliminary report of the joint intelligence committee did an excellent job of ferreting out evidence documenting the failures at the CIA and the FBI.[3] The report describes a director of central intelligence who declared a war on terrorism in 1998 but allocated no additional funding or personnel to the task force on terrorism, an intelligence community that never catalogued information on the use of airplanes as weapons, and a Central Intelligence Agency that never acknowledged the possibility of weaponizing commercial aircraft for terrorism and prepared its last national intelligence estimate on terrorism six years before 9/11.

We now know from the preliminary report that the timely use and distribution of intelligence data would have provided some warning of the terrible terrorist acts of 9/11. At the very least, the CIA would have been more open to the possibility of a terrorist attack in the United States, and the FBI would have appreciated that there were terrorist assets already in the United States that had such capabilities. The refusal of the White House and the CIA to declassify the information provided to the president before the attacks, some of which has already been reported in the international press, makes it almost impossible to learn what types of sensitive intelligence made its way to the highest levels of government.

Two days after the preliminary report was published, the Bush administration reversed itself, bowed to pressure, and endorsed the creation of a separate, independent commission to study not only the intelligence failure but the full range of government responses and policies for dealing with terrorism.[4] The initial appointment of former secretary of state Henry A. Kissinger to head the commission to probe the intelligence and security flaws that allowed the September 11 terrorist attacks was a cynical and dangerous maneuver. The Bush administration's explanation that "you need someone like a Kissinger because of his security clearances" was a puerile rationalization for an investigative position that calls for character and integrity.

Kissinger's government career was marked by significant lapses of judgment and calculated efforts to circumvent bureaucratic and even constitutional limits on the use of force and power. The secret bombing of Cambodia avoided constitutional checks and balances in order to expand the war in Southeast Asia, using a clandestine dual reporting system that was hidden from Congress, the public, and even most of the Pentagon for nearly five years. The secret bombing nearly became an issue in Richard M. Nixon's impeachment inquiry in 1974 when the Senate Armed Forces Committee conceded that it still had not learned how the dual book-keeping system originated. The same week that the government of Prince Sihanouk was overthrown in Cambodia, a direct result of the secret bombing, Kissinger approved a covert action to undermine the democrat-ically elected government of Salvador Allende in Chile. Kissinger told the secret committee that approved all covert actions: "I don't see why we need to stand by and watch a country go communist due to the irrespon-sibility of its own people."[5]

Fortunately, the criticism of Kissinger and his unwillingness to take the actions needed to avoid conflicts of interest as chairman of the investiga-tion led Kissinger and his deputy, former senator George Mitchell, to resign their posts before the work of the commission was underway. The Bush administration then appointed former New Jersey governor Thomas Kean to head the commission, placing the sensitive position in the hands of a man without experience in the fields of intelligence or international secu-rity. Governor Kean immediately appointed Philip Zelikow as staff director, although Zelikow was a political operative for the administration of President George H.W. Bush and was instrumental in the 1990s in using the influence of Harvard University's Kennedy School of Government to cover up the CIA intelligence failure to monitor the decline of the Soviet Union. Zelikow, in turn, appointed a former CIA official, Douglas MacEachin, who was the senior official in the directorate of intelligence on the Soviet Union and thus central to the failure, to head the committee staff investigating the CIA. The appointment of former representative Lee Hamilton (D-IN), who played a major role in the Iran-contra investigation in the 1980s, does provide some needed balance to the independent inves-tigation, but the sudden resignation of former representative Max Cleland (D-GE), the most agressive Democrat on the commision, did not auger well for the commission's final report. Despite the real possibility that the White House may have had some general warning to pursue preventive measures against terrorist attack, there was no reason to believe that either the Senate or House Intelligence Committees were prepared to do a rigorous investi-gation, particularly one embarrassing to the Bush administration.

FAILURES OF INTELLIGENCE

The failure to anticipate an act of terrorism in the United States is merely the latest in a long series of CIA blunders, consistently matched by the inability of the intelligence committees to conduct rigorous oversight. The 9/11 intelligence failure points to the need for reform and supervision of the entire intelligence community, but, over the past half century, U.S. presidents have been derelict. They have probably accepted the poor performance of the CIA in order to cover up their own involvement in covert action and because the agency offers a clandestine and relatively inexpensive instrument of American foreign policy. President Eisenhower employed the CIA in a series of covert actions in Guatemala, Iran, and Cuba that contributed to instability in these countries. The Bay of Pigs in 1961 and Iran-contra in the 1980s, in which funds were illegally provided to the contra rebels in Nicaragua from profits gained by selling arms to Iran, were directed from the White House. In the field of intelligence analysis, there was no warning for the 1973 October War, the 1982 Israeli invasion of Lebanon, or the 1983 terrorist bombings that killed 250 U.S. marines and destroyed the U.S. embassy in Beirut. Intelligence missed the Iranian revolution and the fall of the shah in 1979, Iraq's invasion of Iran in 1980, and the Iraqi invasion of Kuwait in 1990.

In the 1980s CIA director William Casey politicized the intelligence analysis of the CIA and orchestrated the Iran-contra scheme that seriously embarrassed the Reagan administration. Following Casey's death in 1987, Deputy Director Robert Gates failed to receive confirmation as CIA director because the Senate Select Committee on Intelligence did not believe his denials of knowledge of the Iran-contra affair, which flouted the will of Congress to ban assistance to the contra forces in Nicaragua. Casey and Gates were directly responsible for the CIA's poor analytical record in dealing with Soviet issues throughout the 1980s, from the failure to foresee the Soviet collapse to the revelation that CIA clandestine officer Aldrich Ames had been a Soviet spy for nearly a decade, the greatest intelligence failures in the history of the agency until the terrorist attacks in 2001. In an unguarded moment in March 1995, Gates admitted that he had watched Casey on "issue after issue sit in meetings and present intelligence framed in terms of the policy he wanted pursued."[6]

There has never been a better definition of politicization by a director of central intelligence.

The performance of the intelligence community did not improve in the 1990s. When the CIA missed Indian underground nuclear testing in 1998, Director George Tenet stated, "We didn't have a clue."[7] This failure to monitor Indian testing and Tenet's inexplicable testimony that the CIA could not guarantee verification of a nuclear test ban led to the Senate's unwillingness to ratify the Comprehensive Test Ban Treaty. The CIA also underestimated the progress of the North Korean missile program, which added a third-stage capability in 1998, leading to congressional calls in the United States for a national missile defense.[8] Since 1998, when the Rumsfeld Commission issued a report that exaggerated the missile threat to the United States, CIA analysis of this threat has taken on a worst-case flavor, politicizing the intelligence data. The CIA's exaggeration of Iraqi WMD fits into the larger picture of the agency's distortion of the missile threat to the United States.

The CIA has been particularly weak on the issue of terrorism. In 1986 Casey and Gates created the Counter-Terrorism Center (CTC), believing that the Soviet Union was responsible for every act of international terrorism (it wasn't), that intelligence analysts and secret agents should work together in one office (they shouldn't), and that the CIA and other intelligence agencies would share sensitive information (they didn't). The CIA and FBI provided no warning of terrorist attacks on the World Trade Center in 1993, the U.S. military barracks in Saudi Arabia in 1996, the U.S. embassies in East Africa in 1998, or the USS *Cole* in 2000. There was very little useful intelligence analysis by the CTC during this period, which was one of the major reasons for the CIA's failure to anticipate the terrorist attacks in New York City and Washington in 2001. Similarly, the CTC was late in linking al Qaeda to acts of terrorism against the United States and in linking Khalid Sheikh Mohammed, the planner of the World Trade Center attack in 1993, to Osama bin Laden and the al Qaeda organization.

The CIA's Counter-Terrorism Center and the FBI's terrorism experts never understood the connection between Ramzi Ahmed Yousef, the coordinator of the 1993 World Trade Center attack, and the al Qaeda organization until it was too late. The CTC expected an attack abroad, not at home. Not even the foiled plot to bomb the Los Angeles International Airport in December 1999 led the CIA and the FBI to heighten concerns over the ability of al Qaeda to strike inside the United States.[9] President Bill Clinton's national security advisor, Samuel Berger, told the joint intelligence inquiry in September 2002 that the FBI repeatedly assured the White House that al Qaeda lacked the ability to launch a domestic strike.

The September 11 attack exposed the inability of analysts and agents to perform strategic analysis, challenge flawed assumptions, and share sensitive secrets. No agency in the intelligence community could imagine a terrorist operation conducted inside the United States using commercial airplanes as weapons, although al Qaeda had planned such operations in the mid-1990s in Europe and Asia. The CIA was tracking al Qaeda operatives but never forwarded their names to be placed on the immigration service watch list; the FBI failed to track Arab men attending flight schools who were behaving in a suspicious fashion.

The CIA often has been slow to pass along sensitive information to other intelligence agencies because of the risk of releasing information that could be embarrassing. In this case, the CIA placed the needs of agency security (protecting sources and methods) over the national need to counter terrorism. The CIA actually received sensitive information from the Malaysian intelligence service on two hijackers, who then lived openly in San Diego, but the CIA was slow to pass names to the FBI, and FBI officials assigned to the Counter-Terrorism Center apparently failed to catch the names as well. One of the hijackers was listed in the San Diego phone directory, and the other used a credit card in his own name; both were active at the San Diego Islamic Center and actually lived with a FBI informant. Either one of these hijackers could have led the FBI to at least eleven of the nineteen hijackers and the plan to hijack and weaponize commercial airliners. The CIA never informed the State Department that one of these men, Khalid al-Midhar, held a multiple-entry visa to get into the United States and should be placed on the watch list to prevent future reentry. Nevertheless, without the benefit of classified information and foreign liaison, the Congressional Research Service of the Library of Congress and University of Pennsylvania professor of political science Stephen Gale did anticipate the hijacking of commercial aircraft and warned both the CIA's National Intelligence Council and the Department of Transportation.[10]

The final report of the joint panel of the House and Senate Intelligence Committees, which was finally released on July 24, 2003, had serious flaws. It did not hold any senior officials responsible for the 9/11 failure and directed the inspectors general of the various intelligence agencies to assess the responsibility of these agencies. Important information on the special U.S. and CIA relationship with Saudi Arabia was redacted from the final report, blocking information on the Saudi funding of terrorist organizations, including al Qaeda. The final report of the joint intelligence committees contained twenty-eight blank pages dealing with alleged Saudi ties with terrorist organizations. The report did acknowledge the need for an overall intelligence chief to oversee the analytical efforts of the entire intelligence community, but the Bush administration has demonstrated no interest in an intelligence czar.

Tenet's inability to coordinate and arbitrate sensitive intelligence differences within the community was finally revealed in January 2003 in the wake of President Bush's State of the Union address. The speech itself resorted to spurious and fabricated intelligence to charge Iraq with seeking to purchase enriched uranium from Niger and thus reconstitute its nuclear capabilities. The CIA director claims not to have read the draft of the speech and was unaware of a special emissary that his directorate of operations had sent to Niger in March 2002 to pursue the Iraq-Niger story. Seven months later Tenet's national intelligence officer for proliferation released a national intelligence estimate that also charged Iraq with trying to obtain enriched uranium in Africa, thus ignoring the fact that the relevant intelligence was highly questionable. (Tenet himself briefs the president on intelligence matters on a daily basis but apparently never informed the president of the false claims linking Iraq to a possible purchase of Niger's uranium.) Curiously, in October 2002 he did tell the deputy national security advisor to the president, Stephen Hadley, that the intelligence on Iraq and Niger could not be used in a presidential speech scheduled that month in Cincinnati.

The White House initially criticized Tenet and the CIA for not vetting the speech, then praised Tenet and the CIA for "darned good intelligence." This reversal of opinion pointed to the politicization of intelligence at the highest levels and begged serious questions about the actual role of the CIA in presenting unbiased intelligence to the White House and the National Security Council. It called into question all the intelligence community's reporting on the reconstitution of Iraq's nuclear program, which had been used to justify the invasion of Iraq in March 2003.

In December 2003 the President's Foreign Advisory Board (PFIAB) concluded that the White House should share the blame with the CIA for allowing spurious intelligence in the State of the Union speech. The PFIAB, chaired by former national security advisor Scowcroft, said there was "no deliberate effort to fabricate" a story but that the White House clearly disregarded warnings from the intelligence community that the Niger claim was questionable.[11] The inspectors general of the CIA, the Pentagon, and the State Department are also investigating the matter, as well as the Senate and House Intelligence Committees. The findings of the PFIAB and David Kay's Iraq Survey Group clearly point to the CIA's intelligence failure and the White House's mishandling of sensitive intelligence material.

At the same time the White House and the CIA were spinning the intelligence on Iraq, the Blair government was doing the same in London. British intelligence experts told a public inquiry in September 2003 that a year earlier they had complained that the Blair government was "exaggerating a public dossier on the threat posed by weapons of mass destruction in Iraq."[12] The Bush and Blair governments were intentionally exaggerating the likelihood of Iraq having and deploying WMD, with political aides in both governments dictating language in finished intelligence products.

STRUCTURAL FLAWS

One reason for the consistent failures of the intelligence community is the organizational disarray at both the CIA and the FBI. The CIA has an operational mission to collect clandestine intelligence and conduct covert action; it also analyzes and publishes national intelligence estimates. The agency cannot perform both missions well, and the operational demands of the agency have often politicized the intelligence analysis. This has happened in such regions as Central and South America, where the CIA supported right-wing dictators and covered up human rights abuses, and Pakistan, where the agency covered up intelligence on Islamabad's strategic weapons programs in order to protect the role of Pakistan as an aid conduit to the Afghan mujahideen in their fight in the 1980s against the Soviet occupation. The operational demands of the Counter-Terrorism Center meant that analytical tasks were often placed on the agency's back burner.

The FBI also suffers from a bipolar mission. Its traditional law enforcement mission involves reacting to crimes that have already occurred. Its counterterrorism mission, by contrast, requires an active role, ferreting out threats to national security before they occur. Under former FBI director Louis Freeh, the FBI remained hostile to the inexact world of analysis and intelligence that is the basis of any investigation of international terrorism. Walter Lippmann reminded us seventy years ago that it is essential to "separate as absolutely as it is possible to do so the staff which executes from the staff which investigates."[13]

Turf issues abound. The protection of "sources and methods" has been an obstacle to information sharing, with the CIA and the FBI having a long history of poor communication. Intelligence agencies and the Pentagon often lock horns. The director of central intelligence (DCI) is responsible for foreign intelligence but lacks control and authority over 90 percent of the intelligence community, including the National Security Agency (NSA), the National Geospatial-Intelligence Agency (NGA), and the National Reconnaissance Office (NRO), which are staffed and funded by the Department of Defense.

The priorities of the DCI and those of the Pentagon are quite different. Previous DCIs, particularly Gates and John Deutch, harmed the CIA by de-emphasizing strategic intelligence for policymakers and catering instead to the tactical demands of the Pentagon. The CIA, as a result, produces fewer intelligence assessments that deal with strategic matters and emphasizes instead intelligence support for the warfighter. Gates ended CIA analysis of controversial military issues in order to avoid contentious analytical struggles with the Pentagon; Deutch's creation of the National Imagery and Mapping Agency at the Department of Defense (DoD) enabled the Pentagon to be the sole interpreter of satellite photography.* In its short history, NGA has been responsible for a series of major intelligence disasters, including the failure to monitor Indian nuclear testing in 1998, the bombing of the Chinese embassy in Belgrade in 1999, and the monitoring of missile programs in North Korea and Iran.

The Pentagon uses imagery analysis to justify the defense budget, to gauge the likelihood of military conflict around the world, and to verify

---

*The National Imagery and Mapping Agency was renamed the National Geospatial-Intelligence Agency (NGA) in December 2003.

arms control agreements. In creating NIMA, Deutch abolished the CIA's Office of Imagery Analysis and the joint DoD-CIA National Photographic Interpretation Center, which often challenged the analytical views of the Pentagon and monitored arms control agreements that would not have been feasible without the CIA's capability to do so. Meanwhile, policy-makers and congressional leaders are denied intelligence analysis free from a policy bias in significant areas.

Worst of all, the Bush administration has referred to a "marriage" between the Pentagon and the CIA, which in the present climate confirms that the key intelligence agency is subordinate to the Pentagon. The CIA's worst-case analysis on global issues is being used to justify the highest peacetime increases in defense spending since the record-level increases of the Reagan administration as well as the construction of an untested national missile defense system. In justifying the use of force against Iraq, it appears that the policy community made sure that CIA Director Tenet referred to links between Iraq and Saddam Hussein on the one hand and Osama bin Laden and al Qaeda on the other. In cases where CIA intelligence has not been helpful to policy, the Bush administration has turned to Secretary of Defense Rumsfeld, who appointed his own undersecretary of defense for intelligence, presumably to supply the kind of information that supported the policy interests of the Bush administration.

MISUSE OF COVERT ACTION

One of the CIA's major missions, covert action, remains a dangerously unregulated activity. There are no political and ethical guidelines delineating when to engage in covert action, and previous covert actions have harmed U.S. strategic interests, placing on the CIA payroll such criminals as Panama's Gen. Manuel Noriega, Guatemala's Col. Julio Alpirez, and Chile's Gen. Manuel Contreras. Although President Bush, like every other president since Gerald Ford, had initially signed an executive order banning political assassination, exceptions were made in writing for the unsuccessful pursuit of Iraqi president Saddam Hussein prior to the U.S. invasion and former Afghanistan prime minister Gulbuddin Hekmatyar, who received CIA assistance in the 1980s and was targeted by the CIA in 2001. In another instance, a CIA-operated Predator unmanned surveillance plane in 2002 destroyed a car in Yemen that was carrying several alleged al Qaeda operatives and a naturalized American citizen. U.S. unilateralism and fear of such CIA exploits are major components of the anti-Americanism that is sweeping across Europe, the Middle East, and Southwest Asia.

In 1998, U.S. operatives used the cover of the UN and the UN Special Commission (UNSCOM) to conduct a secret operation to spy on Iraqi military communications as part of a covert action to topple Saddam Hussein. This intelligence was used to support military operations in the Iraqi no-fly zones. Neither the UN nor UNSCOM had authorized the U.S. surveillance, which Saddam Hussein cited as justification for limiting the activities of UN monitors. As a result, the inspection process was compromised, and the United States and the UN lost their most successful program to monitor and verify Iraq's nuclear, chemical, and biological weapons programs.

THE MISUSE OF INTELLIGENCE TO GO TO WAR

President Bush and Vice President Cheney have been the most persistent supporters of the notion that Iraq was "reconstituting" its nuclear weapons program, which was cited to justify the urgency to use military force. Bush, Cheney, and National Security Advisor Rice consistently raised the "smoking gun that would appear as a mushroom cloud" in order to gain congressional and public support for going to war. They went to great efforts to misuse bad intelligence and to ignore good intelligence in order to make their case. Secretary of State Powell's speech to the United Nations on February 5, 2003, which was designed to make the case for war against Iraq, was prepared by the CIA and contained extremely controversial and often unsubstantiated charges, particularly regarding current Iraqi strategic programs and so-called links between Iraq and al Qaeda.

Critics of the war, particularly the Germans and the French, were consistently skeptical of the U.S. insistence on a clear and present danger. And prior to the White House statement of July 7, 2003, even the Pentagon announced that it was withdrawing the U.S. task force that had been sent to Baghdad to search for WMD, acknowledging that no chemical, biological, or nuclear materials had been found. In December 2003, U.S. military forces released nearly all of the captured Iraqi scientists which indicated that the Pentagon no longer believed there was anything to be gained from additional interrogations.

The allegation that Iraq was trying to purchase nuclear materials from Niger deepened the scandal. The Bush administration was forced to concede the error in the State of the Union speech because of an op-ed article in the *New York Times* from a former ambassador, Joseph Wilson, who was sent to Africa in February 2002 to investigate reports of the so-called purchase and determined that Niger would not sell uranium to Iraq and that, in any event, Niger could not do so without being detected.[14] A four-star general from the Pentagon's Joint Chiefs of Staff reported similar findings to the military chain of command, and the U.S. ambassador in Niger similarly informed the State Department. The Department of Energy and the Department of State as well as most CIA analysts never believed the charges in the fabricated documents. It is mind-boggling that the president of the United States, his national security advisor, the director of central intelligence, and the secretary of defense claimed to know nothing of Ambassador Wilson's trip to Niger until after the State of the Union speech. Similarly, no policymaker claimed to have knowledge of the marine general's trip, and even the chairman of the Joint Chiefs denied receiving any briefing on the findings.

White House anger with Wilson's revelations led administration sources to reveal to syndicated writer Robert Novak that the ambassador's wife was employed by the Central Intelligence Agency in an undercover position. The "outing" of a CIA operative is a violation of a federal law and, as a result, eventually led to an FBI investigation. A special counsel has been appointed to head the investigation, and Attorney General John Ashcroft has recused himself from the case, but there has been no success in identifying the White House sources responsible for the leak and no indication that anyone in the Bush White House is taking seriously the "outing" of a CIA operative. A grand jury began hearing testimony in January 2004.

The international community now has good reason to believe that the so-called clear and present danger of weapons of mass destruction that President Bush cited to justify the invasion simply did not exist, and that the claims of the president, Vice President Cheney, Secretary of Defense

Rumsfeld, and even CIA Director Tenet were vastly exaggerated or simply false. If so, there are serious consequences for the interests of the United States.

- Any distortion of evidence of Iraqi WMD makes it harder to gain international cooperation in the war against terrorism and the campaign to prevent the spread of WMD. These efforts require international support. Information from foreign intelligence services has been essential in the capture of all al Qaeda terrorists thus far; any success in stopping the strategic weapons programs of Iran and North Korea, both more advanced than those of prewar Iraq, will require international help.
- Any misuse of intelligence by the White House or politicization of intelligence by the CIA weakens the key instrument in preventing further terrorist acts and thus undermines U.S. national security interests. The misuse of intelligence during the Vietnam War prolonged a brutal and costly war. The manipulation of intelligence during Iran-contra in the 1980s led to political embarrassment for the Reagan administration. Any administration's use of intelligence for political ends is simply unacceptable.
- Finally, one of the worst possible scenarios for U.S. security interests, and those of the international community, would be learning that WMD materials had been looted or smuggled from Iraqi weapon sites. As former White House spokesman Ari Fleischer noted during the Iraqi war: "[WMD] is what this war was about and is about. And we have high confidence that it will be found." We lost an opportunity to verify any remnants of WMD in Iraq in the spring of 2003 when the U.S. military occupation made no attempt to investigate possible WMD sites, not even Tuwaitha, where Iraqis previously stored supplies of enriched material. The only way to ensure that such sites were not looted of old materials is to deploy international inspectors who had examined these sites in the 1990s.

Ari Fleischer was also responsible for one of the more Orwellian remarks in the postwar period when he remarked on July 9, 2003, "I think the burden is on those people who think he didn't have weapons of mass destruction to tell the world where they are."[15] The burden of proof is on the Bush administration, which insisted on going to war even while UN inspectors were doing their job—and obviously doing it well. It was the international agencies, and not U.S. military power, that effectively destroyed Iraqi weapons of mass destruction.

WHAT IS TO BE DONE?

What the CIA and the intelligence community should be, what they should do, and what they should prepare to do are more at issue today than at any time since the beginning of the Cold War. Throughout the Cold War, the need to count and characterize Soviet weapons systems and the search for indications of surprise attack focused the efforts of the CIA. These goals disappeared with the collapse of the Berlin Wall in 1989 and the dissolution of the Soviet Union in 1991.

It is essential that the intelligence community provide an independent source of intelligence to the decision-making community. Currently, the uniformed military dominates the collection and analysis of sensitive technical intelligence, which means that the CIA is no longer a check on the military bureaucracy as it was during the Vietnam war and throughout the arms control decision-making process in the 1960s and 1970s. In these years, civilian analysts were a more objective and balanced source of intelligence than their military counterparts in assessing threats to the United States and the military capabilities of foreign threats. Since the Gulf War in 1991, the CIA has not played a major role in military intelligence affecting national security. According to former senior CIA analyst Richard Russell, "The absence of an independent civilian analytic check on military intelligence threatens American civilian control of the military instrument for political purposes."[16]

Retired general Brent Scowcroft, the head of the President's Foreign Intelligence Advisory Board, has conducted a comprehensive review of the intelligence community for President Bush and favors transferring budgetary and collection authority from the Pentagon to a new office that reports directly to the Director of Central Intelligence.[17] Scowcroft believes that such an office would monitor such agencies as the National Security Agency, which conducts worldwide electronic eavesdropping; the National Reconnaissance office, which designs spy satellites; and the

National Imagery and Mapping Agency or the National Geospatial-Intelligence Agency, which analyzes satellite photography. Secretary of Defense Rumsfeld opposes this transfer and has created a new position, undersecretary of defense for intelligence, to preempt such reform. Congressional approval of this new position ensured preservation of the status quo and closed the narrow window of opportunity for extensive reform proposals under consideration by the joint intelligence committees of the House and Senate.

At the very least, Scowcroft or some senior statesman with vast experience in the Washington bureaucracy should be asked to investigate the Niger issue to determine who was responsible for fabricating intelligence, who actually received the information, and who pressed for introducing flawed intelligence into the State of the Union address. This investigation should be expanded to examine all types of intelligence on weapons of mass destruction in Iraq in order to determine how the CIA and the intelligence community handled the various aspects of the problem and the information that the White House actually received on sensitive weapons matters. In fact, there needs to be a full investigation of the intelligence community on all aspects of intelligence and policy, not merely those issues that relate to the Iraqi war. The British have managed to hold a public inquiry, but the United States is unable to do so. It is very possible that intelligence documents showing that Iraq was developing weapons of mass destruction were prepared in the CIA's Directorate of Operations.

It is crucial that the CIA and other intelligence agencies strengthen their links in order to share intelligence. Unfortunately, these agencies often place too much emphasis on the compartmentalization of intelligence and the "need to know," which are obstacles to intelligence sharing. The failures at Pearl Harbor in 1941 and the 9/11 terrorist attacks might have been prevented with genuine sharing of sensitive intelligence information. As in 1941, before the creation of the intelligence community, this information moves vertically within each of the intelligence agencies instead of horizontally across them. The FBI and the CIA have never been effective in sharing information with each other or with such key agencies as the Immigration and Naturalization Service, the Federal Aviation Agency, the Border Guards, and the Coast Guard, which are on the front lines in the war against terrorism. There is no guarantee that the CIA and the FBI will share raw reporting on terrorism with the new Department of

Homeland Security, which has no genuine capability for collecting or even analyzing intelligence relating to terrorism, despite its mandate to centralize intelligence related to terrorism. Paul Redmond, a former CIA expert on counterintelligence, was asked to create such a capability at Homeland Security and lasted in the job less than two months. More than a dozen intelligence officers have turned downed the opportunity to be Redmond's successor. Several other senior officials from the department have also resigned, creating an image of disarray in the organization.

Even if the thirteen agencies and departments of the intelligence community were willing to share information, the obsolescent computer systems of many of these agencies would not allow it. The FBI computer system is particularly anachronistic, unable to store and recall basic data, because former director Louis Freeh believed that computer technology was overrated and too expensive. The State Department computer system is from another age, which means that American embassies overseas regularly issue visas to likely terrorists because consular officials cannot obtain up-to-date information. And State Department computers are not linked to the CIA, the FBI, or the Immigration and Naturalization Service. The inability to share and transfer data between these agencies contributed significantly to the watch list problems that allowed the September 11 terrorists to enter the United States on multiple-use visas.

To prevent the politicization of intelligence analysis, the CIA's clandestine operations and finished intelligence production should be placed in two separate agencies. The director of the CIA should be responsible for the clandestine operations. A new director of national intelligence should be responsible for national intelligence estimates and all other intelligence analysis. This division is necessary because of the fundamental differences between the two major functions of the CIA. The Directorate of Operations is responsible for all clandestine activities, including clandestine collection of intelligence and covert action. This should be under the direction of the CIA. It relies on secrecy, hierarchy, and the strict enforcement of information on a need-to-know basis. And it is involved in the policy-making process. The Directorate of Intelligence is devoted to analysis, which helps set the context for people who formulate policy, and it should not be involved in the making of policy. This should be under the new director of national intelligence. The FBI also should be split into two agencies, one which performs its traditional role and the other, a Domestic Counter-Terrorism Service, reporting directly to the director of central intelligence.

The intelligence community, moreover, could learn a great deal from the State Department, where foreign service officers cannot advance through the system or receive prestigious positions without mastering foreign languages. The chronic shortage of language experts in the intelligence community is the Achilles' heel of all collection and analytic agencies. The FBI lacked the means to translate documents found in the wake of the murder of Rabbi Meir Kahane that could have provided significant intelligence on the role of al Qaeda. (A vigorous pursuit of the Kahane case might not have prevented both attacks on the World Trade Center, but it would have alerted the FBI and the CIA to ties between al Qaeda and terrorist acts in the United States.) The National Security Agency lacked the means to translate important messages that were intercepted on the eve of September 11 that mentioned "Tomorrow is zero hour." The CIA has been improving its language capabilities, but it should not be forgotten that there was only one Farsi speaker in the embassy in Tehran when the embassy was seized in 1979.

THE NEED FOR *GLASNOST*

CIA Director Tenet has reversed the modest steps toward greater openness that were instituted by several of his predecessors. At his confirmation hearings in 1997, Tenet promised to continue the policy of openness, but he also emphasized that it was time for the agency to stop looking over its shoulder at its critics and to increase its clandestine role in support of national security. Accordingly, he withheld thousands of sensitive documents detailing covert operations in Chile that took place three decades ago, despite demands for openness by former president Bill Clinton and secretary of state Madeleine Albright. Tenet argued that releasing these documents would compromise covert sources and methods; more likely, he feared that declassification would embarrass the United States both by revealing the efforts of the Nixon administration to overturn a constitutionally elected government and by exposing the details of the murders of former Chilean foreign minister Orlando Letelier and his assistant, Ronnie Moffitt, on the streets of Washington, DC, during the Ford administration. The CIA's intelligence failure regarding 9/11 and the politicization of intelligence regarding the Iraqi war indicate that Tenet is not capable of coordinating or arbitrating intelligence analysis throughout the community and will not carry tough and unpopular messages to the president and the policy community.

Tenet, in fact, has no control over the intelligence community, most of whose agencies are under Pentagon control, and has made no attempt to block the formation of a separate intelligence department in the Department of Defense, the Office of Special Plans, which carried its own messages to the White House and the National Security Council. The Office of Special Plans cultivated its own sources among the Iraqi exile community and used these sources to collect disinformation that supported the Bush administration's drive toward war in the winter of 2002–2003. At the State Department, Undersecretary of State for Arms Control Bolton ran his own intelligence program, providing "white papers" on WMD that lacked support within the intelligence community and testimony to congressional committees that exaggerated the WMD programs in Syria and Cuba. In July 2003, during the brouhaha over the Niger documents, Bolton was prepared to tell a House of Representatives International Relations subcommittee that Syria's WMD program had "progressed to such a point that it posed a threat to stability in the region."[18] In 2002 Bolton was responsible for a similar controversy involving the misuse of intelligence data when he falsely asserted that Cuba had a biological weapons program.

Recent CIA directors have helped the "old boy network" to survive. Former CIA director Gates (1991–1993) did not share with the White House the fact that a CIA operative, Aldrich Ames, had compromised every agency operation aimed at the former Soviet Union. Former CIA director James Woolsey (1993–1995) never punished those officials who failed to monitor Ames. Former director Deutch (1995–1997), in an attempt to avoid embarrassment for the CIA, upheld a decision to revoke the security clearance of Richard Nuccio, the State Department whistle-blower who tried to expose CIA lying when he revealed a suspected murderer on the CIA's payroll in Guatemala. Current CIA director Tenet withheld documents on Chile to avoid embarrassment to former DCI Richard Helms, who lied to a congressional committee regarding the CIA's role there. Tenet defended the CIA's intelligence on 9/11 and made no serious attempt to coordinate and arbitrate differences at the CIA regarding intelligence on Iraq prior to the war.

These egregious performances demonstrate the need for congressional oversight and public knowledge of the CIA performance record. But the U.S. Senate, led by Senator Shelby, then director of the Senate Intelligence Committee, aggravated the situation in September 2000 when it passed a bill that would have criminalized the disclosure of all "properly classified" information, thus creating an official secrets act. It is already a crime to disclose classified information about nuclear weapons codes, intelligence communications, and the names of covert agents. The CIA initially convinced the Senate to criminalize all leaks of classified information, and President Clinton's Justice Department was persuaded to support the measure.

Far too much information is classified, and "properly classified" information is too broad a category. Even the Pentagon Papers were "properly classified," and recent disclosures of the CIA's role in Chile demonstrated that intelligence is often classified to cover up government embarrassments and CIA misdeeds. Opposition to the bill to criminalize the leak of all classified information was bipartisan, but when the House of Representatives did not block it in a House-Senate conference, the threat of another "torment of secrecy" akin to the worst days of the Cold War was anticipated. Fortunately, President Clinton vetoed the bill in November 2000, choosing to protect his legacy and the public's right to know rather than endorse the zeal of his CIA director.

Former senator Daniel Moynihan's 1995–1996 Commission on Secrecy concluded that the American public both needs and has a right to a full accounting of the history of U.S. covert operations. A presidential executive order to extend openness to intelligence material is required along with congressionally mandated limits on the intelligence community's prerogative to conceal information. Senator Shelby, minority director of the Senate Intelligence Committee, accused the CIA and the intelligence community of slowing the flow of information to the congressional investigation of September 11.[19] The Bush administration is blocking any attempt to balance the interest of the public and national security in the declassification of intelligence materials and the release of information under the Freedom of Information Act.

The CIA should not be able to hide behind its secret budget and remain in violation of Article I, Section 9 of the Constitution, which demands that a "regular Statement and Account of the Receipts and Expenditures of all public Money shall be published from time to time." The overall intelligence community budget (now nearly $40 billion) has been declassified only in 1997 and 1998, but the CIA budget (more than $4 billion) has never been declassified. The CIA absurdly maintains that, because of the openness in those two years, the release of old budget figures would "help identify trends in intelligence spending" that may permit correlations "between specific spending figures and specific intelligence programs."[20]

The intelligence community, particularly the CIA, faces a situation comparable to that of fifty-five years ago, when President Harry S. Truman created the CIA and the National Security Council. As in 1947–1948, the international environment has been recast, the threats have been altered, and as a result the institutions created to fight the Cold War must be redesigned. If steps are not taken to improve the intelligence community, we can expect more terrorist operations against the United States. Certainly the FBI's and the CIA's unwillingness to investigate the intelligence and operational failures of the collapse of the Soviet Union, the espionage careers of Aldrich Ames and Robert Hanssen, and the terror attacks of September 11 does not auger well for the future of intelligence in the United States.

NOTES

1. James Risen, "White House Drags Its Feet on Testifying at 9/11 Panel," *New York Times*, September 13, 2002, p. 10.

2. Ibid.

3. *Joint Inquiry Staff Statement, Part I, Joint Inquiry Staff*, September 18, 2002, http://www.911investigations.net/document1152.html.

4. James Risen, "CIA's Inquiry on Qaeda Aid Seen as Flawed," *New York Times*, September 23, 2002, p. 1.

5. Gregory F. Treverton, *Covert Action: The Limits of Intervention in the Postwar World* (New York: Basic Books, 1987), p. 11.

6. Melvin A. Goodman, "Who Is the CIA Fooling? Only Itself," *Washington Post*, December 19, 1999, p. B1.

7. "Desert Blasts," *Wall Street Journal*, May 13, 1998, p. 22.

8. Ronald E. Powaski, *Return to Armageddon: The United States and the Nuclear Arms Race, 1981–1999* (New York: Oxford University Press, 2000), p. 226.

9. Risen, "CIA's Inquiry on Qaeda Aid Seen as Flawed."

10. Steve Fainaru, "Clues Point to Changing Terrorist Tactics," *Washington Post*, May 19, 2002, p. A9.

11. Walter Pincus, "White House Faulted on Uranium Claim," *Washington Post*, December 24, 2003, p. 1.

12. Glenn Frankel, "British Experts Protested Iraq Dossier," *Washington Post*, September 4, 2003, p. 10.

13. Walter Lippmann, *Public Opinion* (New Brunswick, NJ: Transaction Publishers, 1997), p. 386.

14. Joseph C. Wilson, "What I Didn't Find in Africa," *New York Times*, July 6, 2003, p. D9.

15. Dana Millbank and Mike Allen, "Bush Skirts Queries on Iraq Nuclear Negotiations," *Washington Post*, July 10, 2003, p. A18.

16. Richard Russell, "CIA's Strategic Intelligence in Iraq," *Political Science Quarterly* 117, no. 2 (2002): 207.

17. John Deutch, "The Smart Approach to Intelligence," *Washington Post*, September 9, 2002, p. A17.

18. Warren Strobel and Jonathan Landay, "CIA: Assessment of Syria's WMD Program," Knight Ridder Newspapers, July 15, 2003, http://www.miami .com/mld/miamiherald/6310763.htm..

19. Allison Mitchell, "In Senate, a Call for Answers and a Warning on the Future, *New York Times*, September 10, 2002, p. 1.

20. John Harris, "Conservatives Sound Refrain: It's Clinton's Fault," *Washington Post,* October 7, 2002, p. 16.

PART TWO
FOUNDATIONS OF FAILURE

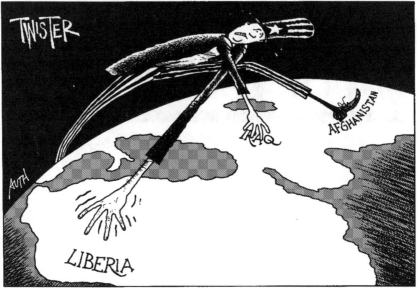

CHAPTER SIX
MILITARIZING AMERICAN SECURITY POLICY

In the councils of government, we must guard against the acquisition of unwarranted influence, whether sought or unsought, by the military-industrial complex. The potential for the disastrous rise of misplaced power exists and will persist.
— President Dwight D. Eisenhower, January 17, 1961

It is not in the American national interest to establish preemption as a universal principle available to every nation.
— Former secretary of state Henry A. Kissinger, August 11, 2002

The Bush administration has placed the Pentagon at the top of the decision-making ladder on national security policy, thus weakening the role of the Department of State and other agencies dealing with foreign policy. As a result, the long-term security interests of the United States have been put in peril, weakening the international coalition against terrorism and compromising the pursuit of arms control and counterproliferation. The actions of the administration often have not been discussed with congressional committees or debated in the foreign policy community, and many of these moves have reversed major tenets of American foreign policy.

Prior to World War II, the military rarely influenced foreign and national security policy. The Cold War and the 1947 National Security Act made the military an integral part of national security policy in peacetime and in war. The National Security Act created the position of chairman of the Joint Chiefs of Staff (JCS), and successive amendments and reforms enhanced the power of the chairman and weakened the influence and leverage of the civilian secretaries of the army, navy, and air force. The Goldwater-Nichols Act of 1986 made the chairman the "principal military advisor to the president, the National Security Council, and the secretary of defense." The stature of JCS chairman Colin Powell in the early 1990s added to the leverage of the position, and the authority of regional commanders of forces in major regional areas (previously known as commanders in chief or "Cincs") was also strengthened, thus weakening the stature of assistant secretaries of state for the regions and key ambassadors in the field. In her book *The Mission: Waging War and Keeping Peace with America's Military*, Dana Priest refers to the regional commanders as "proconsuls to the empire."[1]

The unprecedented statutory authority of the regional commanders has given them greater influence in the budget process, foreign policy formulation, and national security decision making, including the debate over the transformation of the military in the twenty-first century. These commanders, backed up by the secretary of defense, have prepared regional engagement plans around the world without proper consultation with the State Department, resulting in the overuse of U.S. forces. In May 2003, several weeks after the end of the war in Iraq, the U.S. military conducted a raid on the Palestinian diplomatic mission in Baghdad without consulting any civilian official in Iraq. An official in the Bush administration explained that "marines don't get paid to worry about any flags other than the Stars and Stripes, and this unit carried out its disarmament mission with relish and Semper Fi."[2]

The gradual militarization of the intelligence community has been even more profound. Nearly 90 percent of the $40 billion budget for the intelligence community is allocated and monitored by the Pentagon, and more than 90 percent of all intelligence personnel report to the Pentagon.

The Pentagon now controls the tasking, collection, and analysis of all satellite photography. Such key intelligence agencies as the National Security Agency, the National Geospatial-Intelligence Agency, and the National Reconnaissance Office are designated as "combat support" agencies. This is exactly what President Harry Truman was trying to avoid in 1947 when he created the Central Intelligence Agency. Secretary of State Rumsfeld has gone even further in an effort to control intelligence reporting. He created the position of undersecretary of defense for intelligence as well as an Office of Special Plans, which misused intelligence data in order to justify the war against Iraq and mishandled the transition process in the postwar period. The Senate Armed Forces Committee fully funded the new undersecretary position without any input from the Senate Select Committee on Intelligence, which severely weakened the oversight role of this committee on intelligence matters.

Some of the blame for this dangerous trend of militarization lies with President Clinton, who entered office with an aversion to the use of force and a suspicion of both the military and the intelligence community. Coming to office with the reputation of a draft dodger and a critic of the Vietnam War, his relations with the Pentagon were tenuous from the start. Clinton immediately alienated the military by suggesting in a press conference that he would allow homosexuals to openly serve in the military. When Clinton ultimately backtracked from the policy and adopted the cynical stance of "don't ask, don't tell," the uniformed services realized that they could challenge the authority of the commander in chief with impunity.

Congress, moreover, has become an even stronger advocate of the Pentagon's interests and has rarely challenged a weapons system favored by the Pentagon or the huge increases that have been introduced into the defense budget in recent years. Fewer members of Congress have performed military duty than in previous decades, and only one child of a senator or representative served in the war against Iraq. There is little congressional familiarization with the inner workings of the Pentagon in Washington and with forces in the field. President Bush (and nearly all of his key advisers) also avoided the draft during the Vietnam War, but he has deferred to the military and never suffered the personal slights that confronted President Clinton.

THE LESSON OF THE USS *COLE*

The attack on the USS *Cole* in 2000 illustrated how the Pentagon's influence over foreign policy can lead to disastrous results. Before the attack on the USS *Cole* off the coast of Yemen, the U.S. Department of State and the Central Intelligence Agency had warned American officials and tourists against travel to Aden, the Yemeni capital. State Department advisories were made more urgent after the kidnapping of sixteen tourists, including two Americans, and the killing of four of them. CIA advisories became increasingly explicit as the agency collected sensitive intelligence describing the administrative network that al Qaeda had developed in Aden.

Aden had long been known as a hub for terrorists in the region as well as a busy port for international arms sales, and in 1991 Yemen had refused to join U.S. allies in the 1991 Persian Gulf War against Iraq. Concern over the possibility of terrorist attacks in Yemen had prompted then U.S. ambassador to Yemen Barbara Bodine to veto several planned military ship visits to the country because of heightened sensitivity to terrorism. But Chairman of the Joint Chiefs of Staff Henry Hugh Shelton and leaders of the Central Command wanted a web of support bases and facilities around the Persian Gulf in case of another war against Iraq.

Despite the concerns of the State Department and the CIA, marine general Anthony Zinni, then commander in chief of U.S. forces in the Persian Gulf, made an agreement with Yemen that allowed U.S. warships to refuel there. This pact was an effort to improve U.S. relations with Yemen—the type of job usually left to career diplomats. Zinni had been given other unusual diplomatic assignments, including defusing tensions between nuclear-armed India and Pakistan and negotiating Jordan's handover of terrorists to the United States.

The refueling contract led to disaster in 2000 when two men in a dinghy full of explosives rowed up to the destroyer and blew a one-thousand-square-foot hole in the hull of the ship, killing seventeen American sailors.

The tragedy pointed to the Pentagon's influence over political-military decision making. The increasing domination of the Pentagon over the decision-making process in American national security policy has reached crisis proportions in the administration of President George W.

Bush. The operational tempo of the U.S. military has not been greater since the end of the Vietnam War, and U.S. national security policy has become increasingly dependent on its military leadership. This development comes at a time when U.S. policymakers, congresspeople, and journalists know less and less about the doctrine and capabilities of U.S. forces as the Pentagon uses secrecy and nondisclosure to maintain a free hand in the formulation of policy.

MILITARIZATION OF FOREIGN POLICY

Despite the decline in the strategic threat to the United States since the collapse of the Berlin Wall and the Soviet Union, military influence over national security policy has grown substantially. Too often the United States has walked away from international negotiations in areas of arms control and disarmament to satisfy the Pentagon's concerns about possible constraints on U.S. forces or the use of force.

The Pentagon has been a consistent opponent of arms control treaties for the past forty years, starting with its heavy-handed opposition to President John F. Kennedy's negotiation of a Partial Test Ban Treaty in 1963, which banned the testing of nuclear weapons on land, at sea, and in the atmosphere. Military brass, particularly air force chief of staff Gen. Curtis LeMay, opposed Kennedy's diplomatic solution to the Cuban missile crisis and believed that the test ban represented an additional concession to Moscow. President Richard Nixon had to override Pentagon opposition to the Strategic Arms Limitation Talks (SALT) Treaty in 1972, which stabilized mutual deterrence on the basis of parity and equal security, and the Anti-Ballistic Missile (ABM) Treaty in the same year, which limited antiballistic missile sites in the United States and the Soviet Union to two sites, and eventually one, and thus prevented the deployment of a nationwide or comprehensive antiballistic missile system.

In 1975 then secretary of defense Donald Rumsfeld convinced President Gerald Ford to ignore the advice of Secretary of State Henry A. Kissinger and not pursue a follow-up agreement to SALT I, which delayed strategic arms control for fifteen years. The opposition of the Pentagon to a ban on mobile intercontinental ballistic missiles and multiple reentry vehicles on ICBMs delayed bans on these destabilizing strategic systems as well. Presidents Ronald Reagan and Mikhail Gorbachev negotiated the Intermediate-Range Nuclear Forces (INF) Treaty in 1987, which banned intermediate-range missiles in Europe and led to the resignations of Secretary of Defense Caspar Weinberger and Assistant Secretary of Defense Richard Perle, who were consistent critics of détente and arms control and who are among the leading neoconservative supporters of the Bush administration. The arms control successes from 1987 to 1991 pointed to the key roles played by Secretary of State Shultz in the Reagan administration and General Scowcroft in the Bush administration. The Clinton administration lacked a heavyweight manager for national security issues.

CLINTON ADMINISTRATION: DEFEAT OF THE CTBT AND THE INTERNATIONAL CRIMINAL COURT

In 1998 the Senate rejected the Comprehensive Test Ban Treaty (CTBT) in a vote that reflected strong Pentagon influence and Clinton's inept management. It was the first rejection of a significant multilateral security agreement since the Treaty of Versailles, which established the League of Nations more than eighty years ago.

The Comprehensive Test Ban Treaty had support from Democratic and Republican administrations for two decades, but after the impeachment of President Clinton, the Republicans decided to embarrass the White House by forcing a vote on ratification. Ironically, the Republicans were aided in their effort by the failure of the Central Intelligence Agency and the Pentagon's National Geospatial-Intelligence Agency (NGA) to predict five Indian nuclear tests in March 1998. If the intelligence community could not monitor the activities of India, the opposition argued, then how could it monitor a "comprehensive" test ban.[3]

The defeat of the Comprehensive Test Ban Treaty marked the first time that civilian agencies could not prevail over the Pentagon's resistance to an arms control or disarmament treaty. Students of the CTBT's defeat argued that the failure to ratify the treaty "may well have been a turning point in American statecraft if not in world politics, marking at the least a setback for the efforts to regulate weapons through detailed arms control treaties, and possibly their end."[4] (See chapter 7 for the Bush administration's retreat from arms control.) The defeat of the CTBT was particularly costly because India and Pakistan, two of the three nuclear states outside the Nonproliferation Treaty, had agreed to join the counter-proliferation regime in return for U.S. support of the test ban.

The following year the United States, in an unusual alliance, joined hands with so-called rogue states such as Iran, Iraq, Libya, and Sudan to vote against the International Criminal Court (ICC) because of the Pentagon's resistance to the agreement. The ICC was consistent with U.S. international behavior since the Nuremberg trials to bring human rights violators to justice. Every member state of NATO and the European Union favors the ICC, and the Clinton administration did as well, particularly in the wake of successful war crimes tribunals dealing with the former Yugoslavia and Rwanda. But the Pentagon resisted exposing U.S. soldiers to international justice, claiming that the court would allow countries with specific political motivations to prosecute U.S. military personnel without the consent of the United States. The Pentagon's interpretation of the ICC charter was misguided, since the ICC would allow such personnel to be tried in U.S. courts; nonetheless, its opposition drove U.S. policy and eventually forced the Clinton administration to oppose the ICC, which is now functioning with 139 member states but not the United States.

The debate over the ICC was not the only place where the interests of the Pentagon have pushed the United States to join the less civilized nations in supporting dubious policies. The United States has been out of step in the campaign to ban the use of land mines, which the Pentagon opposes because of its deployment of mines in the demilitarized zone between North and South Korea. Several retired chairmen of the Joint Chiefs of Staff have lobbied Congress on behalf of the land mines ban, and human rights groups have argued that antipersonnel mines, unable to tell the difference between a combatant and a child, have maimed and killed hundreds of thousands of innocents in Afghanistan, Angola, Bosnia, Cambodia, El Salvador, Iran, Iraq, and Mozambique. But the regional commanders have made land mines part of the deterrent against numerically larger North Korean forces, ignoring the possibility of using increasingly sophisticated weapons that would not create havoc with innocent civilians.

Perhaps the low point for the Clinton administration took place in 2000 when the United States voted against UN efforts to ban using child soldiers under the age of eighteen in combat. Nearly two hundred nations voted in favor of the ban, and only Somalia, which for all practical purposes had no viable government at the time, joined the United States in casting an opposing vote. The Pentagon's opposition was particularly gratuitous in view of the fact that fewer than three thousand of the 1.4 million Americans in uniform are under the age of eighteen.

MAKING THE WORLD MORE PERILOUS

President Bush has taken the militarizing of U.S. foreign policy to a new and unprecedented level. One of his first national security decisions was to cut funding for the Nunn-Lugar Cooperative Threat Reduction Act, which the Clinton administration had used successfully to denuclearize the non-Russian republics of the former Soviet Union (see chapter 7).

The only arms control treaty that the Bush administration has negotiated with Russia, the Strategic Offensive Reductions Treaty of May 2002, calls for no specific reductions before 2012, contains no process for verification or monitoring, and allows missiles and warheads taken off the front line to be placed in storage rather than destroyed or dismantled. The treaty preempts any real disarmament agreement rather than advancing disarmament.

The Bush administration has taken no steps to prevent the theft or sale of weapons of mass destruction or weapons materials in Russia or to prevent desperately poor Russian nuclear physicists or engineers from offering their services to countries with nuclear ambitions. During their summit meeting in Russia in May 2003, Bush and President Vladimir Putin did nothing to reduce the risk of accidental or unauthorized launch of their tens of thousands of nuclear warheads. The United States has done nothing to reduce the readiness of its strategic submarine forces, keeping half of its Trident nuclear submarines at sea, including regular patrols near the Russian coast. Russian submarines were rarely on patrol in international waters prior to 2002, although they could launch missiles from their moorings at Russian bases. The Bush administration has also taken several doctrinal steps that will increase opportunities for the use of force and could even lead to the use of weapons of mass destruction. In calling for a policy of preemptive attack against states and terrorist groups trying to develop weapons of mass destruction, the president abandoned the policy of deterrence that had been successful against the former Soviet Union as well as against Iraq.

The president's remarks produced an angry reaction in Europe, where opposition had been mounting to U.S. plans for a national missile defense, the withdrawal from the Anti-Ballistic Missile Treaty of 1972, and Washington's lack of support for the International Criminal Court. Key European leaders, particularly in France and Germany, view the declaration of war on terrorism and the doctrine of preemption as an insidious effort to place the United States on a course of permanent war, thus marking the abandonment of the collective security regimes developed during the presidencies of Woodrow Wilson and Franklin D. Roosevelt and maintained until the presidency of George W. Bush.

The Europeans are particularly concerned that the United States now sanctions the use of WMD in preemptive attacks, even the use of nuclear weapons against nonnuclear states, which would be a violation of the Nuclear Nonproliferation Treaty. A policy of preemption increases the possibility of confrontation by removing predictability, undermines the importance of the use of military force only as a last resort and only in self-defense, and makes military planners overly dependent on so-called actionable intelligence, that is, intelligence geared to support military action, in deciding when force is required. European commentary has been highly critical of the swagger of the Bush administration on military matters, particularly the concept of preemption.

The danger of basing a preemptive or preventive attack on "actionable" intelligence was demonstrated by the run-up to war in Iraq when strategic intelligence was heavily politicized by the United States and Britain to justify the invasion in March 2003. The misuse of intelligence created a political crisis for Prime Minister Tony Blair's government in London. It also compromised the credibility of U.S. policy and the integrity of U.S. intelligence. A British inquiry established in August 2003 that Prime Minister Blair was personally involved in the distortion of intelligence materials in order to make the case for war, but it is still not clear how involved key U.S. leaders were in distorting the evidence in Washington.[5]

Several months after the 2002 West Point commencement address, the White House issued a thirty-three-page report, *The National Security*

Strategy of the United States, that discarded the policy of détente and containment and endorsed preemptive or preventive military actions against states with which we were at peace.[6] Ominously, the report warned that the United States would "make no distinction between terrorists and those who knowingly harbor or provide aid to them."

In the section about strengthening alliances to defeat global terrorism, it stated:

> We will not hesitate to act alone, if necessary, to exercise our right of self-defense by acting preemptively against such terrorists, to prevent them from doing harm against our people and our country.

In the section dealing with weapons of mass destruction, the strategy stated:

> The United States has long maintained the option of preemptive actions to counter a sufficient threat to our national security. The greater the threat, the greater the risk of inaction—and the more compelling the case for taking anticipatory action to defend ourselves, even if uncertainty remains as to the time and place of the enemy's attack. To forestall or prevent such hostile acts by our adversaries, the United States will, if necessary, act preemptively.

The tone of the new strategy was clearly confrontational.

The *National Security Strategy* was based on a series of provocative assumptions, including the option of "regime change" and the preemptive use of force as the means of securing peace through international acceptance of U.S. hegemony. The 2002 strategy statement was an excellent example of American triumphalism in the wake of the end of the Cold War, emphasizing the universality and nonnegotiability of U.S. values and the American public's acceptance of "deep, costly, lengthy engagements." The latter assumption may have had some validity in the wake of the 9/11 attacks, but is not likely to survive the disarray of the postwar situation in Iraq. The emphasis on "regime change" is particularly dangerous in view of the current problems that the United States has created in Afghanistan and Iraq; it indicated that current U.S. leaders learned nothing from the Vietnam experience in the wake of the assassination of

South Vietnamese leader Ngo Dinh Diem or the Chilean experience following the CIA-assisted coup against Salvador Allende.

The *National Security Strategy* and particularly the *Defense Planning Guidance* of 2002 essentially reiterated the 1992 draft of the *Defense Planning Guidance*, which was drafted by then undersecretary of defense Paul Wolfowitz. The draft guidance was designed to respond to the fundamentally new geopolitical situation in the wake of the unexpected collapse of the Soviet Union and the discrediting of Communist ideology. Instead of designing a new security architecture for the postcontainment era, however, the draft *Guidance* for the years 1994–1999 was a bellicose document that required the United States to "prevent any hostile power from dominating a region whose resources would be sufficient to generate global power."[7]

Prior to the *Defense Planning Guidance*, the Department of Defense had issued its *Quadrennial Defense Review Report* in September 2001, which projected an indefinite future of continuous and worldwide war. The report focused on U.S. efforts, without allied consultation or support, and argued for anticipating conflicts rather than waiting for them to occur. The Bush administration had not yet withdrawn from the Anti-Ballistic Missile Treaty, but the report called for a multitiered missile defense system and space-launched weapons banned by the treaty. The Joint Chiefs of Staff's *Joint Vision 2020,* also published in 2001, placed overwhelming emphasis on forward-based forces and served as a primer for the war in Afghanistan in 2001 and Iraq in 2003. It promoted the "importance of basing military assets abroad and/or in gaining temporary access to facilities in foreign countries, and the growing role of special operations forces in the fight against terrorism."[8]

The Pentagon released its *Nuclear Posture Review* in 2002, which projected a nuclear threat from Iraq that had no basis in fact and called for "improved earth penetrating weapons (EPWs) to counter the increased appearance of hardened and deeply buried facilities." Nuclear EPWs and nuclear testing were endorsed, although the United States and the rest of the world had not conducted nuclear tests since 1992. The most startling aspect of the *Review,* which was leaked to the press, was the possibility that the United States would employ nuclear weapons in the event of an Iraqi attack on Israel, a North Korean attack on South Korea, or a Chinese attack on Taiwan. Iran, Syria, and Libya were also mentioned as potential nuclear battlegrounds. For the first time in U.S. history the United States had declared a readiness to use nuclear weapons preemptively against nonnuclear states, a clear violation of the Nonproliferation Treaty.

Several international commissions have concluded that the "possession of nuclear weapons by any State is a constant stimulus to other States to acquire them." Nonetheless, instead of seeking ways to limit the strategic arsenals of the nuclear powers and to effectively destroy reserve nuclear forces, the Bush administration has sanctioned greater uses for nuclear weapons and even the first use of such weapons. An unworkable national missile defense is now the most costly single weapons system in the Bush defense budget.

The Nuclear Posture Review of 2002 lowered the threshold for using nuclear weapons, and the 2003 defense bill eliminated restrictions on researching low-yield nuclear weapons. The bill provided additional funds for research on high-yield nuclear bombs for use against deeply buried targets and for reducing the preparation time for the resumption of underground nuclear testing. Although funds to the final bill were cut in the House of Representatives, they were not eliminated, permitting the beginning of a research program. Funds for this purpose are a very small part of the $400 billion defense budget, but there will be more money spent on developing, testing, and manufacturing nuclear weapons in this decade (at least $6.4 billion annually) than during the worst days of the Cold War (average of $4.2 billion annually).[9] Furthermore, using nuclear weapons against buried caches of weapons of mass destruction will vent these materials into the atmosphere.

The uniformed military has traditionally sought ways to reduce dependence on the nuclear stockpile because of the risks of safeguarding such weapons and fighting on a nuclear battlefield. The Bush administration, however, particularly the civilian leadership of the Defense Department, is searching for more ways to use nuclear weapons. In the final analysis, conventional precision-guided bombs and missiles are capable of destroying all targets in any conceivable scenario requiring U.S. military action. The head of the U.S. Strategic Command, Adm. James O. Ellis Jr., favors the use of special forces on the ground to guide air attacks on bunker sites or mountain redoubts, which was done in Afghanistan in 2001 and Iraq in 2003. This could not be accomplished with nuclear weapons without endangering U.S. forces because of radioactive fallout.[10] Unfortunately, Ellis is so enamored with his idea that he has commissioned studies to place conventional weapons on intercontinental ballistic missiles, instead of dismantling or destroying these missiles as planned by two previous administrations.

In addition to shelving the Comprehensive Test Ban, the Bush administration has declined to be part of a protocol setting a verification process for the Biological and Toxin Weapons Convention and has abandoned the inspection system negotiated during the presidencies of Ronald Reagan and George H.W. Bush. The administration devoted significant energy to removing the head of the international organization to implement the Chemical Weapons Convention and has proposed no measures to improve the convention's inspection regime. Unlike the Clinton administration, the Bush White House has maintained the right to veto "challenge inspections" on U.S. soil and to prevent the taking of samples abroad for rigorous laboratory testing.

GLOBAL DOMINION

As part of a major realignment of U.S. military forces overseas, the Bush administration also created a network of far-flung bases designed for the rapid projection of power against terrorists and hostile states in its worldwide and continuous war.[11] Bases are being built or expanded in Qatar in the Persian Gulf, Kyrgyzstan in central Asia, and Bulgaria. Forward operating bases in Bahrain, Kuwait, Oman, and the United Arab Emirates will replace the huge facilities previously existing in Saudi Arabia from which nearly all U.S. forces have been withdrawn.

The United States stationed forces throughout central Asia and obtained access to bases in Uzbekistan and Kyrgyzstan and airspace in Tajikistan, Kazakhstan, and Turkmenistan, a region that had been Moscow's geopolitical backyard for more than a century. Kazakhstan, which will be one of the world's top five producers of oil by 2012, has particular importance to the United States and China as an alternate source for oil, with U.S. oil giants ExxonMobil and ChevronTexaco investing billions of dollars in Kazakh oilfields. The United States also carved out a position in the Caucasus, creating a military assistance program in the Republic of Georgia, the site of a pipeline route for energy from the Caspian basin, and conducted operations and exercises in West Africa, the Horn of Africa, Southwest Asia, and the Philippines.

Senior U.S. military officers have been publicly discussing the role of "combination warfare" (i.e., financial and trade warfare, resource warfare, and legal warfare, in addition to traditional military confrontation), although this issue has not been addressed in military doctrine.[12] In any event, only several years after the United States decided that it could not afford the military concept of two major-theater wars, it was endorsing a force to confront contingencies "across the spectrum of possible conflict," reminiscent of Charles de Gaulle's *tout azimut,* or full-spectrum nuclear policy.

Secretary of Defense Rumsfeld even wants to move the sophisticated base structure in western Europe to new bases in eastern Europe, a move designed to "punish" old Europe and "reward" the countries of new Europe for their positions toward the war in Iraq. The fact that such a move would create massive logistical and infrastructure problems does not seem to be a concern to the secretary of defense and his neoconservative advisers. The theory is that forward operating bases maintained by small, permanent support units will be located in a new "arc of instability" that U.S. defense officials have drawn from the Andean region in the Southern Hemisphere to North Africa and the Middle East and even Southeast Asia. These forward units will replace many of the major bases in Turkey, Germany, and South Korea. The problem is that very little preplanning has been done for the location of these new facilities and that sensitive diplomatic and political issues almost certainly will create problems for a long-term U.S. presence.

The new U.S. strategy seemed deliberately provocative, particularly in the wake of the 2002 State of the Union address that referred to Iran, Iraq, and North Korea as the "axis of evil."[13] Following the war against Iraq, the United States resorted to a campaign of pressure and intimidation against Iran, North Korea, and Syria in order to signal that the policy of preemption was not just a one-time orchestration of military power. National Security Advisor Condoleezza Rice explained that the "threat must be very grave" for a policy of preemption to be pursued and the "risks of waiting must far outweigh the risks of action," but this has not been adequate reassurance to Damascus, Tehran, and Pyongyang in view of the absence of a clear and present danger in Iraq.[14] President Bush called attention to international situations that would "not be tolerated" by the United States and, in the words of Undersecretary of State John Bolton, placed "all options on the table."[15] In other words, one might surmise, the United States will do what it wants to do.

IRAQ: TEST CASE FOR THE NEW STRATEGY

The Bush doctrine of preemption essentially overrides the UN Charter's Article 51, which emphasizes the "inherent right of individual or collective self-defense if an armed attack occurs." Instead, the United States merely needs to issue a unilateral determination that allows the use of force in response to any undefined future threat that might be acquired or developed in a way that challenges U.S. national interests.

The first target on the Bush list for preemption was, of course, Iraq, where intelligence was cited as sufficient evidence that Iraq had reconstituted its nuclear capabilities in violation of a series of UN resolutions. In using intelligence to make the case for preemptive or preventive attack against Iraq, President Bush and Vice President Cheney misused bad intelligence on weapons of mass destruction and ignored good intelligence that described the destruction of WMD under UN aegis from 1991 to 1998. The United States also abandoned a policy of containment that had been in place for more than a decade and that had successfully kept Saddam Hussein from extending power beyond Iraqi borders. Director of Central Intelligence Tenet informed Congress in October 2002 that the CIA did not expect that Iraq would use its weapons of mass destruction unless the United States were to invade, and Secretary of Defense Rumsfeld told Congress that he did not expect Saddam Hussein to use WMD in any scenario because "wise Iraqis will not obey his orders to use WMD."[16] *The National Security Strategy* argued that the "greater the threat, the greater is the risk of inaction," but the failure to find weapons of mass destruction in Iraq and evidence of Iraqi links to such terrorist organizations as al Qaeda led to serious political opposition to the governments of President Bush and Prime Minister Blair, who had virtually guaranteed large-scale findings of WMD before the onset of war.

The US blitzkrieg war against Iraq was based on speed, maneuverability, flexibility, and surprise against a third world country that had no air force, no navy, no air defense, and virtually no army. According to the Bush administration, the invasions of Afghanistan in 2001 and Iraq in 2003 were examples of a "new American way of war" relying on precisionfirepower, special forces, and combined-arms operations to overwhelm the enemy.

While the United States easily won the war, President Bush and Secretary of Defense Rumsfeld do not dwell on the difficulties of capturing Osama bin Laden and other top terrorists in Afghanistan; the problems with locating Iraqi WMD; or the fact that the United States now has responsibility for two chaotic security situations in Afghanistan and Iraq, where American forces are taking losses. U.S. forces did not face significant problems or obstacles in either wartime confrontation, but there is no indication that the United States has a "silver bullet" to stabilize Afghanistan or Iraq, much less to improve the standing of the United States throughout the Islamic world. The postwar instability includes the return of the Taliban to the southeastern part of Afghanistan and the creation of a safe haven for foreign terrorists, including al Qaeda, in Iraq. The bombing of UN headquarters in Baghdad in August 2003 demonstrated that the United States had "taken a country that was not a terrorist threat and turned it into one."[17] There is no better example of a self-fulfilling prophecy.

ASSASSINATION

In addition to the greater use of overt military force, President Bush lifted the ban on covert CIA assassination plots in order to target not only Saddam Hussein but any number of shadowy figures that allegedly had links to international terrorist organizations. Following the war in Afghanistan, U.S. forces and the CIA combined in a covert action ostensibly against Afghan Taliban forces that, in fact, annihilated numerous members of an Afghan village celebrating a wedding ceremony. In December 2002 a Predator reconnaissance aircraft, armed with Hellfire antitank missiles, destroyed a vehicle in Yemen that was carrying an al Qaeda agent as well as three other individuals, including an American citizen. Previous CIA assassination plots against Fidel Castro, Patrice Lumumba—the first prime minister of the Republic of Congo, who was killed in 1961—Prime Minister Diem, and others complicated U.S. security interests and led President Gerald Ford and all his successors (except Bush) to ban such actions.

RAISING THE DEFENSE BUDGET

The Bush administration has endorsed policies that are responsible for the greatest peacetime increases in defense spending since the Reagan administration, which led to record levels of deficit spending and domestic economic problems in the late 1980s and the early 1990s. At current rates, the United States will be spending $500 billion for the defense budget by the end of this decade. According to the Congressional Budget Office, the cost would exceed the peak of spending at the height of Reagan's Cold War buildup and would reach the levels of spending during the Korean War.[18] Secretary of Defense Rumsfeld claims that he is conducting a transformation of the military for the twenty-first century, but he is actually adding new programs and weapons systems to the old structure without abandoning old missions. Many military budget experts, such as analysts at the Center for Strategic and Budgetary Assessments, contend that upgrading "existing systems . . . might cost substantially less," without sacrificing defense requirements.

There is no indication that Congress is willing to oppose the Bush administration on any issue involving increased defense spending and weapons procurement. Congress has gone along with huge increases in the Pentagon's request for Tomahawk cruise missiles for the navy, begging the question of how many wars will have to be fought in the next several years to justify the production of nine hundred Tomahawk missiles per year. Congress has also supported the deployment of a national missile defense in Alaska and California, although there is no evidence that the system works, and the Pentagon is no longer sharing NMD weapons testing and evaluation data as required by law. (See the appendix for a fuller discussion of the NMD problem.) The Senate also has approved the construction of new attack submarines for no obvious mission; these submarines are produced in Virginia and Connecticut, the home states of the chairman of the Senate Armed Forces Committee, John Warner, and the ranking Democrat on a key subcommittee, Joseph Lieberman.

The huge increases in military and intelligence spending came at the expense of investment in American diplomacy. The State Department budget of $2.5 billion is smaller than spending for the Central Intelligence Agency, and the operational spending for all diplomatic activity, including assessments to international organizations, disaster relief, and food aid, is $27 billion, much less than the budget for the intelligence community (around $40 billion).[19] Because diplomatic activity is not considered part of the national security budget, diplomacy must compete with such agencies as the Commerce and Justice Departments to gain additional funds. All domestic departments are facing downward spending trends, and such congressional stalwarts as Rep. John Kasich (R-OH) have targeted the "150 Account" or diplomatic account for continued cutbacks.

The spending problem at the State Department is so bad that a form of "sovietization" is taking place at Foggy Bottom. The State Department is lacking foreign service officers for more than three hundred overseas positions and has had to move officers from other agencies and departments into State Department slots. Similarly, there are more military attachés than political officers in the U.S. embassy in Moscow. The State Department has also been forced to close more than thirty consulates and United States Information Agency libraries around the world. When the former Soviet Union faced a similar budget problem in the late 1970s and 1980s, the KGB began to assign its personnel to fill foreign ministry slots overseas. Mikhail Gorbachev, the last Soviet leader, moved smartly in 1985, his first year in power, to correct this situation, but the Clinton and Bush administrations and their Offices of Management and Budget have done nothing to reverse this trend. Secretary of State Powell has been a disappointment in this particular area; his popularity on Capitol Hill was supposed to improve the situation, but Congress continues to ignore the problem of the underfunded State Department.

IS MILITARY POWER ENOUGH?

In *The Paradox of American Power*, Joseph Nye asks whether it is desirable and efficient for the United States to express its de facto supremacy by a policy of dominance based on military power.[20] His answer is that the United States should rely less on traditional measures of power and more on the so-called soft power that derives from the appeal of its culture, values, and institutions. This culture has supported diplomacy, international law, and bilateral cooperation, but President Bush has demonstrated little interest in diplomacy, treaties, or such cooperative measures as the Nunn-Lugar Cooperative Threat Reduction Act, which provided funding for the denuclearization of the former Soviet Union. In the Bush *National Security Strategy* of 2002, only one sentence was devoted to the need to "enhance" diplomatic instruments.

The paradox of American power, according to a British observer, is that the United States is too powerful "to be challenged by any other state, yet not great enough to solve problems such as global terrorism and nuclear proliferation" on its own.[21] Washington must find a way to strengthen its international ties or Americans now and in the future will bear the costly consequences of the reliance on force. The European response to Bush's national security strategy came from the European Community's representative for foreign and security policy, Spain's Javier Solana, who acknowledged the primary threats of terrorism and WMD but stressed the importance of multilateral diplomacy and a law-based international order.[22] Many key European security analysts, such as Solana, see the need to constrain the United States as a major security concern.

The United States already has established that overwhelming unilateral force cannot assure the stabilization and rehabilitation of Afghanistan or Iraq, guarantee that there will be no proliferation of strategic weapons, or prevent the spread of terrorism around the world. The systemic causes of these problems require international cooperation, international law enforcement, and intelligence sharing. When the use of force is required, it is essential to create an international consensus for providing assistance and resources to deal with the consequences of military power. Samantha Power, the author of *A Problem from Hell: America and the Age of Genocide*, warned before the invasion of Iraq that a "unilateral attack would make Iraq a more humane place, but the world a more dangerous one."[23] In fact, the consequences have been worse.

THE DANGERS OF MILITARIZATION

Since the end of the Cold War, many of America's closest allies have complained about the rise of American unilateralism and militarism, particularly the tendency for Washington to make decisions without regard for the interests of its allies or the rest of the world. America's partners have been offended by the restrictions that the United States has tried to apply to trade with Cuba and Iran, often in violation of international law. The United States has not funded its fair share of the budgets of the United Nations, the International Monetary Fund, and the World Bank. The United States acted alone in denying Boutros Boutros-Ghali a second term as UN secretary general in 1996, and has weakened international arms control by rejecting the Comprehensive Test Ban Treaty as well as treaties banning small arms, land mines, and biological weapons.

The Europeans have been concerned with American militarism since the war in Kosovo in 1999 when the United States bombed the Yugoslav capital, Belgrade, and the Chinese embassy there. France and Germany, which opposed the war in Iraq, took major exception to America's strategic bombing in Serbia, particularly the attacks on the bridges across the Danube River and Serbia's economic infrastructure. The British general in charge of NATO forces in Kosovo actually disobeyed a reckless order from NATO's supreme commander, U.S. general Wesley Clark, who unwisely wanted to evict Russian troops after their surprise takeover of the main airfield in Serbia at Pristina. As a result, the Europeans have gradually moved toward the creation of their own rapid reaction force and have looked for ways to restrict America's unilateral use of military power.

Today, the charge of unilateralism goes even deeper. The Bush administration has abandoned the security architecture that the United States built to wage and win the Cold War. U.S. allies have become particularly concerned with the size of U.S. military forces, the increased influence of the military in the making of foreign policy, and the use of military force as the first and only resort in decision making since the collapse of the Berlin Wall and the dissolution of the Soviet Union.

Diplomatic solutions to major problems elude the United States when it resorts too quickly to the use of military instruments of policy. Twelve years after Desert Storm in the Persian Gulf, the United States invaded Iraq despite the absence of a clear and present danger to U.S. national interests. President Bush announced on an aircraft carrier in May 2003 that the mission in Iraq had been accomplished, but American soldiers and marines continue to die there in combat. Two years after the invasion of Afghanistan, there were still nearly 11,500 U.S. combat forces in that country and no end in sight to the battles with Afghan warlords and Taliban guerilla fighters. At the same time, the Bush administration is ignoring far more serious scenarios involving the deployment or possible development of nuclear weapons in Iran, North Korea, and Pakistan. And the green light for a national missile defense and a red light for the Comprehensive Test Ban and Anti-Ballistic Missile treaties point to the possibility of another arms race in the not too distant future.

These are signals that reliance on militarization and use of force as a first option does not work. The United States is demonstrating that "if the only tool in the toolbox is a hammer, than all of our problems will soon look like nails." By so doing, we are multiplying problems for this country and the world. We do have other tools, and, to create a safer world, we need to use them.

NOTES

1. Dana Priest, *The Mission: Waging War and Keeping Peace with America's Military* (New York: W. W. Norton, 2003).

2. Patrick E. Tyler, "U.S. Civilians Not Told of Raid on Palestinians," *New York Times*, May 31, 2003 p. A6.

3. President Jimmy Carter failed to gain ratification of the SALT II Treaty in the wake of the CIA's failure to monitor a so-called combat support regiment in Cuba. Unlike the case of the CTBT, however, Senate Republicans agreed to withdraw the treaty from the ratification process in order to avoid an embarrassing vote denying ratification.

4. Terry L. Deibel, "The Death of a Treaty," *Foreign Affairs* 81, no. 5 (September/October 2002): 143.

5. Warren Hoge, "Inquiry Shows How Blair's Inner Circle Made Case for Use of Force in Iraq," *New York Times*, August 24, 2003, p. A11.

6. *National Security Strategy of the United States* [hereafter NSS] (Washington, DC: Office of the President, September 2002).

7. Patrick E. Tyler, "Pentagon Plan to Prevent the Re-Emergence of a New Rival," *New York Times*, March 8, 1992, p. A14.

8. See Hugh De Santis, "The Emerging Future and the Bureaucratic Mind," *World Policy Journal* (Summer 2002): 56–69.

9. Stephen I. Schwartz, "Quietly Expanding Our Nuclear Budget," *New York Times*, June 1, 2003, p. D12.

10. Walter Pincus, "Future of U.S. Nuclear Arsenal Debated," *Washington Post*, May 4, 2003, p. A6.

11. Vernon Loeb, "New Bases Reflect Shift in Military," *Washington Post*, June 9, 2003, p. 1.

12. James Callard and Peter Faber, "An Emerging Synthesis for a New Way of War," *Georgetown Journal of International Affairs* (Summer 2003).

13. President George W. Bush, State of the Union Address, Washington, DC, January 29, 2002.

14. Condoleezza Rice, "A Balance of Power That Favors Freedom," Wriston Lecture, New York City, October 1, 2002.

15. David Sanger, "Two Nuclear Weapons Challenges," *New York Times*, June 21, 2003, p. A3.

16. Secretary of Defense Donald Rumsfeld, testimony before the Congress, House Armed Services Committee, September 18–19, 2002; Director of Central Intelligence George Tenet, letter to the Senate Armed Forces Committee, October 17, 2002.

17. Jessica Stern, "How America Created a Terrorist Haven," *New York Times*, August 15, 2003, p. 21.

18. Walter Pincus, "Defense Bills Expected to Pass Quickly," *Washington Post*, May 19, 2003, p. A4.

19. Melvin A. Goodman, "Shotgun Diplomacy," *Washington Monthly* (December 2000): 49.

20. Joseph S. Nye, *The Paradox of American Power: Why the World's Only Superpower Can't Go It Alone* (Oxford: Oxford University Press, 2002).

21. Sebastian Mallaby, "A Mockery in the Eyes of the World," *Washington Post*, January 31, 1999, p. B5.

22. Javier Solana, "A Secure Europe in a Better World," speech before the European Council, June 20, 2003.

23. Katha Pollitt, "War: What Is It Good For?" *Nation*, April 7, 2003, p. 9.

CHAPTER SEVEN
THE END OF ARMS CONTROL AND DISARMAMENT

A rms control and disarmament emerged as major goals of U.S. foreign policy only after World War II and the widespread deployment of U.S. and Soviet nuclear missiles. Arms control was designed not as an idealistic instrument in the U.S. national security arsenal but as a major policy initiative to blunt Cold War suspicions, reduce tens of thousands of nuclear warheads on alert in the arsenals of the two major superpowers, and limit the spread of nuclear weapons to other countries. The American public wanted such controls, and the U.S. Congress wanted some means of limiting military spending.

Over three decades of intense and difficult negotiations, Washington and Moscow reduced their nuclear arsenals, addressed the danger of inadvertent war, tried to stop the proliferation of weapons of mass destruction, limited conventional weapons, and experimented with confidence-building regimes and transparency measures in order to reduce the risk of war. International institutions played a major role in the process, particularly the United Nations, the International Atomic Energy Agency, and various verification and monitoring associations.

The Bush administration now has taken a series of steps that have effectively ended the international arms control process, which had been institutionalized over the past four decades by both Democratic and Republican administrations. This comes at a time when the problem of proliferation of weapons of mass destruction has worsened because of the risk that such weapons might fall into the hands of terrorist organizations or states that may resort to terrorism.

President John F. Kennedy was the first president to give a huge boost to the importance of arms control in the nuclear era, and every president since then, with the exception of President George W. Bush, has made a significant contribution to reduce the nuclear threat. Kennedy's arms control advisor, John J. McCloy, convinced the president that the executive branch needed its own agency to provide expertise and advise on the crucial questions and problems of arms control. The creation of the Arms Control and Disarmament Agency (ACDA) in 1961 was the result. The Kennedy administration negotiated two major arms control agreements with the Soviet Union in the wake of the Cuban missile crisis of 1962. The first, the Hot Line Agreement, established a direct communications link between the world's only nuclear powers during times of crisis. The second, the 1963 Limited Test Ban Treaty, banned nuclear weapons tests in the atmosphere, outer space, and on the earth's surface. The Limited Test Ban Treaty was strengthened in 1974 when Washington and Moscow concluded a Threshold Test Ban Treaty to limit the size of weapons being tested underground.

In 1967, during the Johnson administration, the United States and the Soviet Union finally agreed to a ban on placing nuclear and other weapons of mass destruction in space, after nearly a decade of negotiations. The Soviets had wanted such a ban in the 1950s in order to prevent the militarization of space. The United States argued that, since offensive strategic ballistic missiles transited space during their flight trajectory, a comprehensive agreement on intercontinental missiles was required.

The success of the Limited Test Ban and Outer Space treaties led directly to the 1968 Nuclear Nonproliferation Treaty (NPT), following the efforts of the Soviet Union to convince the Johnson administration of the importance of preventing Germany and Japan from developing and deploying nuclear weapons. The NPT committed states that had not exploded a nuclear device to forfeit the right to build nuclear weapons, obligated nuclear weapons states to eliminate their own weapons, and prevented the transfer of nuclear technology to nonnuclear states. The NPT regime was unsuccessful in including India, Pakistan, and Israel in its program, but it persuaded more than a dozen nations with nuclear programs to stop and reverse course. It achieved the denuclearization of South Africa, which dismantled a small nuclear arsenal, as well as the denuclearization of Brazil and Argentina, which abandoned their nuclear weapons programs in 1990 and allowed mutual inspections that were coordinated with the International Atomic Energy Agency (IAEA). The entire continent of South America, in accord with the Treaty of Tlatelolco, has declared itself nuclear free; the nations of the South Pacific have made the same decision. France has reduced its nuclear testing program as well.

Many officials associated with the NPT and the IAEA believe that the United States could get North Korea to give up its nuclear weapons program if Washington entered direct negotiations with Pyongyang and offered it a nonaggression treaty. These officials also believe that U.S. ratification of the Comprehensive Test Ban Treaty (CTBT) could bring India and Pakistan into the NPT and that U.S. pursuit of "negotiations in good faith" on nuclear disarmament would strengthen the NPT regime.

The Soviets tried to use the NPT in the early 1970s to get the United States to agree to a "no first use of nuclear weapons" agreement. Washington and its allies rejected the "no first use" concept because they preferred the notion of using a nuclear deterrent to a nonnuclear threat or attack by the Soviet Union, which had a quantitative conventional advantage in Europe. Moscow also pursued a Soviet-American agreement in the early 1970s to counter any "provocative" attempt to provoke a war between the United States and the Soviet Union, but Washington rebuffed this démarche as a not so subtle attempt to arrange an alliance against China.

Détente in the 1970s between the two major nuclear powers—the United States and the Soviet Union—led to a series of arms control agreements designed to lessen the uncertainty of the nuclear era. In 1971 President Richard M. Nixon and Soviet leader Leonid Brezhnev completed the Agreement on Measures to Reduce the Risk of Outbreak of Nuclear War between the United States of America and the Union of Soviet Socialist Republics. The agreement was formally signed in Washington. It was designed to guard against accidental or unauthorized use of nuclear weapons and provided that the superpowers would notify and consult each other in the event of any such occurrence and would seek to reduce misunderstanding in situations involving unexplained nuclear incidents. In that same year, the two sides upgraded the "Hot Line" communications by switching to a satellite communications system.

The following year, 1972, the superpowers concluded both the Strategic Arms Limitations Talks (SALT) Treaty, which imposed caps on the future development of offensive strategic nuclear systems, and the Anti-Ballistic Missile (ABM) Treaty, which imposed strict limits on current and future strategic defensive capabilities. The ABM Treaty led to a major battle inside the Pentagon, with Secretary of Defense Cyrus Vance taking on the Joint Chiefs of Staff and those congressional barons who strongly favored missile defense. The treaty was ratified by an overwhelming margin, with only two dissenting votes.

The next major round of Soviet-American disarmament agreements began in the mid-1980s during the Reagan administration. The two sides agreed to jointly staff nuclear risk reduction centers and to remove all of their intermediate-range missile systems from Europe. The idea for a risk reduction center came from Sen. Sam Nunn (D-GE); the Pentagon and hard-liners in Congress led the opposition. Nunn and his cosponsor, Sen. John Warner (R-VA), wanted joint U.S.-Soviet military manning of risk centers in Washington and Moscow, but the Pentagon objected to the concept of jointness. The fallback solution was the creation of a simpler communications channel to exchange information and notifications required by various arms agreements in order to reduce the risk of miscalculation or misunderstanding.[1] The agreement was signed in September 1987, marking the first arms control agreement concluded by the Reagan administration.

The Intermediate-Range Nuclear Forces (INF) Treaty, also signed in 1987, redefined the East-West security relationship. In banning all intermediate-range land-based nuclear missiles, it became the first and only disarmament treaty to eliminate an entire class of nuclear weapons. The INF Treaty essentially ended the Cold War and led directly to President Mikhail Gorbachev's surprise announcement in 1988 that the Soviet Union would remove hundreds of thousands of Soviet troops from central Europe and the Sino-Soviet border. This move, the most important step in Moscow's strategic retreat from 1986 to 1991, caught the U.S. policy and intelligence communities off guard.

These agreements were followed by the Treaty on Conventional Forces in Europe (CFE) in 1990, which provided for deep reductions and significant restructuring of all East-West military forces between the Atlantic and the Urals. The CFE Treaty prescribed much greater troop reductions for the Soviets than for the West and presented the United States with a decided military advantage in Europe. While the discrepancy did not pose a problem of real military significance to the Soviet Union, the perception of a one-sided Soviet retreat contributed to Mikhail Gorbachev's political problems; an abortive coup d'état against him in August 1991 led eventually to his removal from the Kremlin in a "constitutional coup d'état" in December of that year.

Fortunately, several months before the challenge to Gorbachev, the United States and the Soviet Union had signed the Strategic Arms Reduction Treaty (START I), which cut their long-range nuclear forces from a Cold War high of between eleven thousand and twelve thousand warheads to between six thousand and seven thousand for each side. Later in the year President George H.W. Bush and Gorbachev each made unilateral commitments to withdraw most of their land- and sea-based tactical or short-range nuclear weapons.

After the Soviet Union dissolved and Boris Yeltsin became president, the United States and Russia negotiated START II, which registered an additional 50 percent cut in strategic nuclear forces—down to thirty-five hundred warheads for each country. Bush and Yeltsin signed this treaty in January 1993, marking another landmark in the history of arms control. The nuclear arsenals of the two superpowers had been reduced by two-thirds from their Cold War highs, and the two sides established a total "de-MIRVing" or prohibition on land-based missiles with multiple warheads. Ironically, the final ratification of this treaty by the U.S. Congress and the Russian Duma occurred in 2002, under the administrations of Presidents George W. Bush and Vladimir Putin.

When the Russians did not move quickly enough to dismantle and destroy the strategic weapons in the former Soviet republics (Russia, Ukraine, Kazakhstan, and Belarus), Sen. Sam Nunn (D-GE) and Richard Lugar (R-IN) passed the Cooperative Threat Reduction Act to tackle the problem of "loose nukes." Their Cooperative Threat Reduction Program (CTR) was responsible for the destruction of thousands of ICBMs, ICBM silos, strategic submarines, and submarine-launched ballistic missile

(SLBM) launchers during the Clinton administration in the 1990s. The CTR program provided hundreds of kilometers of "quick fix" security fencing and associated sensor systems at warhead storage sites in Russia and secured transport of Russian warheads from deployment to storage and then to dismantlement sites.[2] The U.S. Department of Defense has provided funding for specialized railcars for warhead transport, and there have been six or seven shipments per month on average. Nunn-Lugar funding also secured chemical and biological weapons stockpiles, with the installation of microwave sensors and fencing around storage buildings, as well as the demilitarization or destruction of buildings at chemical weapons production sites. The CTR also played a vital role in the denuclearization of weapons arsenals in Kazakhstan, Ukraine, and Belarus, the three former non-Russian members of the Soviet Union that had nuclear weapons after the Soviet collapse. One of the first acts of the new Bush administration in 2001 was the inexplicable decision to cut CTR funding for the former Soviet Union.

THE END OF ARMS CONTROL AND DISARMAMENT: PLACING AMERICA AT RISK

Reversals in the Clinton Administration

The bipartisan U.S. arms control consensus of the Cold War era did not survive the Cold War. After the fall of the Berlin Wall in 1989 and the collapse of the Soviet Union in 1991, the United States took steps that weakened the disarmament consensus at home and abroad, increased the motivation of nonnuclear states to acquire their own weapons of mass destruction, and ignored the Nuclear Nonproliferation Treaty. The Clinton administration mishandled the ratification process for the Comprehensive Test Ban Treaty (CTBT) in 1999 by failing to secure Senate Republican support. This failure represented a major turning point in the international campaign to stop the proliferation of nuclear technology. In October 1999, on the eve of the fateful vote on the CTBT, Prime Minister Tony Blair, President Jacques Chirac, and Chancellor Gerhard Schroeder published a joint editorial in support of ratification.[3] They correctly identified nuclear proliferation as the "principal threat to world safety" and argued that U.S. rejection of the CTBT would undermine the arms control regime and lead to nuclear proliferation. Two years later, the terrorist attacks in Washington and New York City awakened the United States to the specter of greater horrors if international terrorists actually had access to fissile materials or nuclear weapons.

Clinton also failed to stop Sen. Jesse Helms (R-NC) from abolishing the Arms Control and Disarmament Agency and folding its personnel into the State Department. The dissolution of the ACDA virtually ended the professional careers of those public servants who had devoted their careers to international disarmament. In the Bush administration, the disarmament specialists had to work for Assistant Secretary of State for Arms Control and Disarmament John Bolton, an antidisarmament ideologue who had devoted the past several decades to stopping arms control measures.[4]

Clinton supported the Anti-Ballistic Missile Treaty and believed that building a national missile defense would harm the strategic position of the United States and compromise counterproliferation strategy. In one of his last acts as president, he deferred the construction of a radar site in Alaska that would have breached the ABM Treaty and started the NMD program. His decision to defer NMD was greeted in the international community (or what National Security Advisor Condoleezza Rice referred to as the "illusory international community") as a "wise" and "immensely welcome" move, particularly in Russia, China, Japan, and the leading NATO member countries. But deferral was not cancellation, and, in actual fact, Clinton merely kicked the dossier on NMD into his successor's in basket. Indeed, many foreign editorials prophetically warned that Clinton's "postponement, not cancellation" granted no more than a "temporary reprieve" and that the "debate in the United States is not whether but when and in what form to deploy missile defense."

The Bush Team and the End of Arms Control

The real villain of the campaign to stop international arms control and disarmament is President George W. Bush. At the very outset of his administration, he signaled his opposition to disarmament by making key appointments of antidisarmament ideologues to major policy positions throughout the foreign policy bureaucracy. Such neoconservatives as

Undersecretary of Defense Paul Wolfowitz, Undersecretary of Defense for Policy Douglas Feith, Deputy National Security Advisor Robert Joseph, and Undersecretary of State Bolton were positioned to block any bureaucratic support for disarmament. These individuals had spent the last three decades fighting arms control and they believed that, with the end of the Cold War, disarmament was irrelevant to the United States and that the absence of international constraints would allow the Bush administration to develop both offensive and defensive strategic weapons. They strongly favored deployment of a national missile defense system and low-yield nuclear weapons as well as withdrawal from the Anti-Ballistic Missile Treaty; they also opposed any ban on chemical and biological weapons. They supported the Strategic Offensive Reductions Treaty (SORT) with Moscow in 2002 that called for no destruction of strategic missiles and postponed the removal of strategic offensive warheads until 2012.

With the dissolution of the ACDA and the loyalty of the key policy bureaucracies assured, the Pentagon was free to lobby on Capitol Hill for the rejection of the CTBT, withdrawal from the Anti-Ballistic Missile Treaty, the deployment of a national missile defense, the lifting of the congressional ban on research on low-yield nuclear weapons, the weakening of the Chemical Weapons Convention, and the rejection of the Biological Weapons Convention. Bush's secretary of state, Colin Powell, may be more moderate than his neoconservative counterparts at other policy departments, but he has done nothing to promote an arms control agenda or protect the State Department's arms control expertise. As a result, the center of gravity for disarmament policy has shifted to the Department of Defense, which has never favored arms control.

We know very little about strategic planning in Russia and China, but it would be reasonable to assume that these two nuclear states will react strongly to U.S. nuclear modernization. The Russian navy, for example, has already allowed its strategic submarines to patrol more extensively in international waters in 2002 and 2003. India and Pakistan were prepared to join the Nonproliferation Treaty regime in return for U.S. ratification of the CTBT, but the two South Asian nuclear powers dropped discussion of possible membership in the NPT when the United States failed to ratify the CTBT and moved to develop low-yield nuclear weapons.

The Demise of the ABM Treaty

A major victory against the disarmament consensus took place on December 13, 2001, when President Bush announced withdrawal from the ABM Treaty, which became effective in six months according to the terms of the treaty. Bush wanted the abrogation in order to remove the legal barrier to deployment of a national missile defense. Ironically, the only effective criticism of the U.S. withdrawal came from a bipartisan group of former secretaries of defense (including Robert McNamara, Harold Brown, James Schlesinger, and Melvin Laird) who called on the United States and Russia to "avoid actions that would undermine the ABM treaty," let alone destroy it. Former secretary of state George Shultz had threatened to resign when President Ronald Reagan's Star Wars initiative for deployment of a national missile defense put the ABM Treaty at risk. Secretary of State Powell supported the Bush administration's death knell to disarmament, however; the U.S. Senate, its disarmament expert Sam Nunn having retired, made no attempt to challenge the new administration, although thirty-two members of the House sued the president for violating the Constitution by not receiving congressional consent when he abrogated the ABM Treaty (see appendix).

The Anti-Ballistic Missile Treaty of 1972 had been the cornerstone of the arms control regime for thirty years, limiting ballistic missile defense to a strategically insignificant deployment. The treaty had prohibited development of a costly missile defense system and prevented another spiral in any arms race involving strategic offensive systems. It helped reduce tensions between the United States and the Soviet Union and provided a basis for political détente. As understood in both Washington and Moscow, nationwide defensive deployments would lead to ever larger and more sophisticated offensive systems in the United States and the Soviet Union as well as in the nuclear inventories of China, Britain, and France.

The Rise of NMD: Decreased Security and Increased Risk

The abrogation of the ABM Treaty opened the door to the deployment of a national missile defense (NMD), a return to heightened military spending on strategic defense, and the prospect of another arms race. The prospect of NMD also promises to destroy the institutional framework for preventing the proliferation of nuclear weapons and nuclear technology. Curiously, the opponents of NMD have failed to exploit effectively the heavily publicized test failures of the program, the enormous costs and opportunity costs associated with deployment, and the instability such a program introduces.

Unlike President Clinton's modest plan to develop land-based interceptors to knock down enemy warheads in midcourse when a warhead is in space, President Bush wants a far more complex program that includes land- and sea-based interceptors, airborne lasers, and space-based weapons. This multilayered defense encompasses all three phases of the flight of a warhead—the boost, midcourse, and terminal phases. The system was proposed by President Ronald Reagan's science adviser, George Keyworth, whom former secretary of state Shultz called a "lunatic."

The midcourse defense, which is the largest part of the Bush system, is useless against missiles accompanied by decoys because interceptors cannot distinguish between warheads and decoys or chaff. A team of leading physicists and engineers, sponsored by the Massachusetts Institute of Technology and the Union of Concerned Scientists, determined that NMD can be rendered useless by simple decoys or other countermeasures easily within the grasp of any country capable of launching a nuclear warhead. Nations sophisticated enough to build a ballistic missile that could threaten the United States could develop the balloon decoys or aluminum shields that would deceive a defense interceptor. The panel concluded that shiny Mylar balloons, similar to the kind sold in grocery stores, could achieve the same results.

An extensive study by the American Physical Society, the largest U.S. association of physicists, concluded that the boost-phase system, designed to destroy missiles soon after launch, would be ineffective against the faster, solid-fuel missiles that Iran and North Korea may deploy within the next ten to fifteen years.[5] Even Pentagon officials have conceded that the midcourse system being deployed in Alaska and California has severe limits.[6] Nevertheless, the largest single weapons expense in the U.S. defense budget for 2004 was the allocation of $9.1 billion for NMD. The United States has placed both its strategic relations with

Russia and the international regime for nonproliferation at risk for a national defense system that may never work.

In May 2003 the United States, with little fanfare, began a $500 million construction project in Fort Greely, Alaska, using midcourse defenses. This project eventually will hold a vanguard force of rocket-propelled interceptors for defending the United States against ballistic missile attack, although it is clear that the system can be rendered virtually useless.[7] The Greely deployment represents the first strategic missile defense in the United States since 1975, when the Ford administration abandoned an antiballistic missile defense in North Dakota that had been in place for several months. The current timetable calls for placing six interceptors at Fort Greely and four additional interceptors at Vandenberg Air Force Base in California—a former strategic missile base—by 2004 and ten more missiles at Fort Greely in 2005.

Only a few flight tests have been held on the Alaska system, mostly unsuccessful. Expected test failures will presumably bring further delays, which calls into question why it was so necessary to withdraw from the ABM Treaty in 2002. The Pentagon, moreover, according to Sen. Carl Levin (D-MI), has begun to deny testing and evaluation data to the U.S. Senate, which is required by law. The tests are being dumbed down, with targets and interceptor missiles following a preprogrammed flight path to designated positions and decoys having a significantly different thermal signature and shape than the warhead to allow for easier identification. Even Defense Department officials have acknowledged that tests are "carefully scripted."

There are significant opportunity costs associated with the building of a national missile defense, which has already cost the U.S. treasury more than $120 billion since President Dwight D. Eisenhower first proposed a modest program. The billions of dollars for NMD will limit defense spending in such critical areas as counterterrorism and counterproliferation of WMD. Since the use of intercontinental ballistic missiles against the United States by rogue states or nonstate terrorist organizations is the most unlikely threat this country will face over the near and long term, those opportunity costs compromise the United States' ability to deal with more likely threats.

U.S. deployment of NMD has already prompted Iran and North Korea to advance their own efforts to procure nuclear missiles; this weakens the national security interests of the United States and will further complicate the international security agenda if Japan decides to enter the nuclear club. North Korea has withdrawn from the NPT, thus negating the success of the Clinton administration in negotiating Pyongyang's membership, and Iran has become less cooperative with NPT officials.

Walking Away from the Ban on Chemical and Biological Weapons

In addition to the abrogation of the ABM Treaty and the deployment of NMD, the Bush administration has walked away from the Chemical Weapons Convention and the Biological Weapons Convention. Both conventions had support from Democratic and Republican administrations for three decades, including the administration of George H. W. Bush. Republican president Richard M. Nixon began the negotiations for a ban on chemical weapons, and the convention was negotiated in the Republican administration of George H. W. Bush. The coauthors of the Cooperative Threat Reduction Act of 1992, Sen. Sam Nunn (D-GA) and Richard Lugar (R-IN), with the assistance of Sen. John Kerry (D-MA), were responsible for moving the convention through Congress for ratification.

The major opponent of the process was, predictably, then chairman of the Senate Foreign Relations Committee Jesse Helms, who opposed all arms control and disarmament legislation over a twenty-year period. Helms particularly opposed the intrusive inspection measures that would "compromise trade secrets," although the United States Chemical Manufacturers Association, which represented more than 90 percent of America's chemical manufacturing capacity and the majority of facilities that would be involved in treaty-monitoring activities, helped various administrations draft the treaty's implementing legislation and allowed trial inspections at their facilities to evaluate the verification process.[8]

The Bush administration also blocked effective compliance-monitoring and enforcement measures to constrain biological weapons, which were first limited in the 1925 Geneva Protocol in the aftermath of the large-scale use of chemical weapons in World War I. The protocol banned the use of chemical and bacteriological weapons but did not limit their development, production, testing, or stockpiling. The 1972 Biological Weapons Convention banned the development, production, stockpiling, and transfer of toxic agents for offensive military purposes. While the lack of formal verification measures made the convention "toothless and unable to address a series of alleged violations," the Bush administration has demonstrated no interest in adding politically binding transparency measures to the convention. Instead of strengthening the convention, the administration has abandoned it.

Halt to Disarmament with Russia

The most cynical disarmament step of the Bush administration has been the negotiation of the Treaty of Moscow, or the Strategic Offensive Reductions Treaty, in May 2002. Signed a month before the abrogation of the ABM Treaty, the Moscow treaty ostensibly reduced nuclear arsenals to between seventeen hundred and twenty-two hundred warheads within ten years. But there was no schedule for dismantlement or disarmament and no inspection or verification procedures. Not a single reduction of missiles or warheads has to take place before 2012. Bush negotiated a pretense of a treaty without any serious effort at disarmament. Putin had wanted a verifiable and comprehensive agreement with significant reductions to begin as soon as possible; he was totally unsuccessful. Moscow remains highly skeptical of the disarmament approach of the Bush administration, which it terms "mainly theoretical, its design uncertain, and its purpose highly secret."[9] Bush successfully silenced political demands for arms control and gave Putin no choice but to go along with this feckless exercise. In failing to destroy any nuclear warheads, both Putin and Bush were in violation of Article 6 of the NPT, which required the five declared nuclear powers (United States, Russia, Britain, France, and China) to take steps to eliminate their nuclear weapons.

More Nuclear Weapons

To make matters worse, the Bush administration is supporting new funding for the development and deployment of low-yield nuclear weapons and has revived the concept of using a nuclear deterrent to a nonnuclear threat or attack. The neoconservatives adroitly used the abrogation of the ABM Treaty and the deployment of NMD to reopen the debate on the utility of low-yield weapons. High-ranking uniformed members of the Joint Chiefs of Staff oppose these weapons because they

provide serious command and control problems and contaminate the battlefield where they are used, but the civilian leadership of the Defense
Department is charging ahead.

The decision of Congress in May 2003 to lift a ten-year-old ban on
the research and development of low-yield nuclear weapons marked a
major shift in American nuclear policy. It compromises diplomatic efforts
to stop such nuclear states as India and Pakistan and such developing
states as Iran and North Korea from pursuing longer-range systems. Secretary of Defense Rumsfeld wants to develop nuclear bunker busters in
the war against terrorism, which Senate Armed Forces Committee
chairman John Warner (R-VA) considers a "prudent step to safeguard
America from emerging threats and enemies."[10] Conversely, Sen. Jack
Reed (D-RI) refers to low-yield nuclear weapons as consistent with a
"small apocalypse."

FALLACY OF THE BUSH ADMINISTRATION'S STRATEGIC THINKING

The major strategic moves of the Bush administration demonstrate disdain for the profound opposition of other states or international organizations. The withdrawal from the ABM Treaty and the failure to submit the
Comprehensive Test Ban Treaty for ratification were universally condemned. The deployment of a national missile defense was opposed by
every major nation in the global community, with the exception of India.
The end to the ban on research on low-yield nuclear weapons was casti-
gated at home and abroad.

The abrogation of the ABM Treaty was unnerving to the international
community, particularly the smaller nations, because they believed and
hoped that international law and international treaties would provide
some protection from larger, more powerful nations. Moreover, the international community saw the ABM Treaty as the cornerstone of deterrence
and strategic stability and understood that it had helped keep the Cold
War cold. It particularly resented President Bush's reference to the treaty
as a document that "enshrined the past" and to NMD as part of the moral
imperative to protect the U.S. population. According to the president, the
United States needed "new concepts of deterrence that rely on both offen-

sive and defensive forces." The fact that a national missile defense could very well isolate the United States and make it and the rest of the world more insecure and vulnerable was lost on the Bush administration. Russia and China were particularly opposed to the development and deployment of low-yield weapons and such space-based missile defense components as sensors and "kill-vehicles," which are seen as dangerous steps toward the weaponization of space and the beginning of an arms race in space. The central and psychological importance of the ABM Treaty to Russia and China cannot be overestimated.

WHAT NEEDS TO BE DONE?

President Eisenhower's warnings about the military-industrial complex in 1961 and the importance of the nonproliferation regime established in 1968 have never been more pertinent. The NPT regime essentially created two categories of states: the nuclear weapons "haves" and "have-nots."[11] The "have-nots," or the nonnuclear states, argue that under the conditions now created by the United States, their countries are submitting to a "new colonialism" in remaining part of the NPT regime. Therefore, the "have-nots" insist that the United States abandon its hostility toward arms control, its nuclear threats, and its notions of preemptive attack in order to restore the NPT regime. The policies of the Bush administration have done nothing to accommodate the legitimate national security concerns of the nonnuclear states.

Nonproliferation must be put at the top of the strategic agenda if the international arms control and disarmament community is to gain some momentum in the battle for nuclear disarmament. The potential spread of weapons of mass destruction to terrorist organizations or to states that are willing to resort to terrorism is a frightening specter. We have learned that the use of military force, such as the U.S. invasion of Iraq, has not brought a solution to the problem of WMD but, instead, has increased the chances for proliferation of the weapons and associated technology. Ultimately, international negotiations, inspections, and sanctions provide the surest way to resolving this grotesque security problem; conversely, the unilateral use of military force provides the best path for breaking down the international and national constraints that are in place.

A major success for counterproliferation was registered in December 2003 when Libyan leader Col. Muammar Qadhafi renounced development and production of all weapons of mass destruction and agreed to inspections from the International Atomic Energy Agency to monitor the dismantling of all facilities. President Bush credited this decision to the military success of Operation Iraqi Freedom, but it is more likely that diplomacy played the key role. The Clinton administration and then the Bush administration responded positively to Qadhafi's initiative in the late 1990s to normalize relations with the United States, and both administrations used Saudi ambassador Prince Bandar bin Sultan to achieve a breakthrough. President Bush and Prime Minister Blair have claimed that the Libyan concession was a direct result of the use of force against Iraq, but critics of the war emphasize the role of diplomacy in gaining Qadhafi's renunciation of all weapons of mass destruction.[12]

Instead of searching for new uses for nuclear weapons and new deployments for a national missile defense, the Bush administration or its successor must find ways to revive old arms control regimes or introduce new ones. The Bush administration trumpeted a long-range missile threat from such "rogue nations" as North Korea, Iran, and Iraq—the "axis of evil." These states, however, do not possess delivery vehicles with ranges capable of striking the United States. According to State Department officials, "Only North Korea could threaten the United States homeland with ballistic missiles in this decade, and only if it abandons its current moratorium on long-range missile tests."[13] The intelligence community argues that the major threat to the United States emanates from terrorist organizations using short-range conventional weapons, but NMD supposedly counters a strategic attack from *long-range* nuclear weapons. A national missile defense could also be used to counter accidental or unauthorized launch, part of the Pentagon's worst-case planning, but early-warning data exchanges and enhanced transparency of nuclear activities and infrastructures would be a far better investment in global security.

Strategic stability would be served best by undertaking a renewed effort with Russia to reduce both nuclear inventories and the alert status of deployed weapons, to safeguard nuclear weapons and materials, and to establish confidence-building measures. We are currently investing insufficient funds to dismantle Russian nuclear systems and to prevent the proliferation of weapons and fissile materials from the former Soviet Union.

The Bush administration's efforts to gain a military foothold in the former Soviet republics in the Caucasus and central Asia have led to placing talks on strategic stability on the back burner. Action also could be taken to reduce nuclear arsenals, and the hair-trigger operational nuclear posture of the Cold War could be ended to reduce the danger of an unauthorized or accidental nuclear strike.

The five declared nuclear powers of the nonproliferation regime (the United States, Russia, Britain, France, and China) must cooperate to revive the NPT. Former secretary of defense Robert McNamara argues that all nuclear weapons states should report their holdings to the UN Security Council along with a plan to reduce their inventories and that the declared nuclear powers must be willing to provide security guarantees to those smaller nuclear powers (e.g., Israel, North Korea, India, and Pakistan) that agree to relinquish their nuclear weapons.[14] The most controversial aspect of McNamara's plan calls for compulsory international inspections of those nuclear states that fail to adhere to Security Council regulations, with violations leading to Security Council authorization of conventional military force to compel compliance. The authorization of force will not be accepted, but the McNamara plan could lead to a constructive discussion of ways to return to an effective nonproliferation regime.

The United States must develop a strategic policy designed to stop the proliferation of nuclear weapons based on the McNamara plan or another diplomatic initiative that relies on the collective security interests of the global community. At the same time, the United States needs to address more challenging situations in Iran, North Korea, and Pakistan that require diplomatic and collective efforts to stop their programs and prevent any transfer of materials and expertise to other nations or nonstate actors seeking a strategic capability. Strategic arsenals are used by these nations (and others) as a symbol of a modern and legitimate state, and for countering perceived nuclear threats, so there must be incentives for forgoing a nuclear capability. Thus the United States cannot continue a foreign policy based on threats without prompting countries to acquire nuclear weapons as a means of deterrence.

The safety and security of Russian nuclear facilities and military forces is the next most significant national security issue that confronts the United States. Moscow devotes scarce resources to maintaining its nuclear forces, but the obsolescence of Russian strategic systems and President Putin's military reform plans will probably result in Russia having fewer than two thousand strategic warheads by 2015. Nevertheless, a key arms control and proliferation issue revolves around Russian facilities that house weapons-usable nuclear material, which receive "low funding, lack trained security personnel, and do not have sufficient equipment for securely storing such material."[15] Weapons-grade and weapons-usable nuclear materials have been stolen from some Russian institutes as well as from institutes in former Soviet republics, including Belarus, Georgia, and Ukraine.

Finally, the United States must reexamine its withdrawal from the ABM Treaty, which served for nearly thirty years as an obstacle to a greater strategic arms race. The ABM Treaty ended strategic defense, offered the opportunity to all nuclear states to put fewer resources into its strategic arsenal, and persuaded China to maintain its strategic deterrent at fewer than twenty strategic nuclear warheads. The European allies looked at the ABM Treaty as an international guaranty of political and strategic stability, and the smaller nations of the third world saw the treaty as evidence of the role of international diplomacy to limit the strategic arsenals of the world's superpowers. The Bush administration fails to understand that U.S. pursuit of invulnerability in the security arena leads to greater vulnerability in the international arena, particularly in our relations with countries such as India, Iran, and North Korea, which have their own regional security problems and cannot ignore the global reach of the United States. As a result, U.S. security is undermined.

Until the inauguration of the Bush administration in 2001, Democratic and Republican administrations viewed the ABM Treaty as a necessary constraint on research and development and on military and industrial demands for greater defense spending. These administrations supported the treaty and believed that nonproliferation could be sold to the international community. The U.S. construction of a national missile defense and withdrawal from the ABM Treaty negate these reassurances, prompt proliferation, and threaten another strategic arms race. The Bush administration argued that the ABM Treaty "enshrined the past," but, in reality, the U.S. withdrawal from the treaty moved the international community to an uneasy future. Again, U.S. security is undermined.

The "revolution in military affairs" in the United States, which has seen the increased lethality of military weaponry and the increased influence of the Pentagon in national security policy, has marginalized the arms control and disarmament community. Within the policy community in Washington, only the Department of Defense engages in genuine long-term planning for both the development of weapons and the scenarios for using such weapons. The arms control community is virtually moribund, and the Policy Planning Department of the State Department is no more than a speech-writing office for the secretary of state. The intelligence community that once offered reassurance of the verification of disarmament treaties has become a handmaiden to the war fighter in its apparent inability to ensure verification. There is nothing comparable in the policy or intelligence communities to the Pentagon's Office of Net Assessment, which directs long-term research and prepares strategic studies to justify force modernization.

In terms of political power and influence, there is no government agency or department able to take on the Department of Defense. This is a dangerous situation for the United States; in its efforts to promote American invulnerability, the Bush administration actually is undermining the stability of the world—and the United States. Arms control and disarmament must be put into the hands of agencies that advocate rather than undermine these objectives. Only then will this country and the world see arms control and disarmament agreements that will help secure global security.

NOTES

1. Raymond Garthoff, *The Grand Transition: American-Soviet Relations and the End of the Cold War* (Washington, DC: Brookings Institution, 1994), pp. 319–20.

2. Michael Roston and David Smigielski, "Accomplishments of Selected Threat Reduction and Nonproliferation Programs in Russia," Russian American Nuclear Security Advisory Council, June 10, 2003.

3. Jacques Chirac, Tony Blair, and Gerhard Schröder, "A Treaty Is All We Need," *New York Times*, October 8, 1999, p. A31.

4. In his foreign policy memoir of the Clinton years, former deputy secretary of state Strobe Talbott does not even mention the defeat of the CTBT or the

dissolution of ACDA. Strobe Talbott, *The Russia Hand: A Memoir of Presidential Diplomacy* (New York: Random House, 2002).

5. The boost-phase system refers to a capability against the initial launch of a missile, when the missile's burners remain lit, thus offering targeting advantages and easier detection.

6. Bradley Graham, "Scientists Raise Doubts about Missile Defense," *Washington Post*, July 16, 2003, p. 2.

7. Bradley Graham, "New Breed of Missile Silos Put in Alaska," *Washington Post*, May 27, 2003, p. 3.

8. Amy E. Smithson, "Playing Politics with the Chemical Weapons Convention," *Current History* (April 1997): 163.

9. Jack Mendelsohn, "America, Russia, and the Future of Arms Control," *Current History* (October 2001): 323–29.

10. Associated Press, "GOP Blocks Democrats Efforts to Halt Nuclear Arms Studies," *Washington Post*, May 10, 2003, p. A2.

11. Jose Goldemberg, "Encouraging Proliferation," *Washington Post*, June 2, 2003, p. 29.

12. David Sanger and Judith Miller, "Libya to Give Up Arms Programs," *New York Times*, December 20, 2003, p. 1.

13. Statement by Acting Assistant Secretary for Intelligence and Research Thomas Fingar before the Senate Select Committee on Intelligence, February 7, 2001, as cited in Mendelsohn, "America, Russia, and the Future of Arms Control," p. 324.

14. Robert S. McNamara, "The Problem of Proliferation of Nuclear Weapons," June 11, 2003, unpublished memorandum.

15. National Intelligence Council, Central Intelligence Agency, "Annual Report to Congress on the Safety and Security of Russian Nuclear Facilities and Military Forces," Washington, DC, February 2002.

CHAPTER EIGHT
GOING IT ALONE

BUSH CHARTS HIS OWN COURSE

The neoconservatives of the Bush administration have spent the past two decades developing an ideology of unilateralism. As key members of the Bush team, they are positioned to incorporate unilateral acts into U.S. foreign policy. It is important to trace the thinking behind their policy and to understand the militant version of the policy that has been put into effect.

WHO NEEDS THE REST OF THE WORLD?

The unilateralists break with the idea of collective security, arguing that the United States must use its power to further its own national interests. Consultation and negotiation with other states are designed to gain support for our policies—not to identify common ground and build common positions. The latter requires compromise, and the neoconservatives have no patience for compromise. In an updated version of Secretary of Defense Charles Wilson's statement "What's good for General Motors is good for America," the neoconservatives argue, "What's good for America is good for the world." Bush's national security advisor Condoleezza Rice states, "To be sure, there is nothing wrong with doing something that benefits all humanity, but that is, in a sense, a second-order effect. America's pursuit of the national interest will create conditions that promote freedom, markets, and peace."[1]

After developing their doctrine for almost two decades, the unilateralists now control U.S. foreign policy. They believe that it is the mission of the United States, the world's only superpower, to create its own world order. This requires the use of force when its will is thwarted. William Kristol and Robert Kagan, ideologues who support the Bush team, maintain that "the United States can and should lead the world to a better future, one built around American principles of freedom and justice—but only if it has the power and the will to use that power. . . . American dominance can be sustained for many decades to come, not by arms control agreements, but by augmenting America's power and, therefore, its ability to lead."[2]

In proclaiming unilateralism, the Bush team picks up a strain in U.S. history that goes back to colonial times. John Winthrop, the leader of the Massachusetts Bay Colony, proclaimed in the early seventeeth century that his Puritans were establishing a new society in a virgin land as an example of purity before the eyes of God. Their colony would be a "city upon a hill," "an example to the nations," and free of all the "evils of the Old World." One can hear the echo of this phrase in Secretary of Defense Rumsfeld's references to "old Europe," which deliberately worsened relations with our most important allies on the continent, France and Germany. The Puritans thought of themselves as alone in the wilderness, creating the model society. Their society, they believed, must be invulnerable to attack and uncompromising in its dealings with other societies or countries. It should not be one among the nations of the earth, but in a class by itself, a beacon for all the world's less enlightened states. Those who opposed it would then rightly be called devils in a degenerate world.

George Washington, in his farewell address, called upon his countrymen to steer clear of permanent alliances and so continued the thinking of our Puritan ancestors. Except for the War of 1812, the United States steered clear of engagements in European wars until World War I. Our dealings with foreign powers had to do with securing land, like the

Louisiana Purchase from France or the Southwest from Mexico in the Mexican-American War, not in taking part as one among the powerful nations of the world. This gave the new nation time to grow and become strong as Washington had intended. At the same time, however, it nourished a culture of insularity that still runs deeply through the American political character. That insularity is complemented by a U.S. vision of itself as the best of all nations.

In one area of the world, however, the United States did assert its power—Latin America. With the 1823 Monroe Doctrine, the United States made clear that other European nations were not to interfere in our sphere of influence, although at that point we lacked the means to enforce the doctrine. In 1904 Theodore Roosevelt, in what came to be known as the Roosevelt Corollary to the Monroe Doctrine, went even further, claiming that the United States had the right to intervene in Latin American countries if conditions in those countries invited intervention by outside powers. This doctrine provided the United States the pretext to intervene in Latin America whenever we wished. In a sense the Bush policy today can be viewed as an extension of the Roosevelt Corollary to the global arena.

America's detachment from world politics changed briefly in World War I, when the Germans interfered with our shipping in the North Atlantic. At the end of the war, President Wilson, ahead of his time and ahead of U.S. political thinking, urged U.S. participation in the League of Nations and developed the Fourteen Points. These urged "open covenants of peace, openly arrived at," removal "so far as possible" of trade barriers, and reduction of armaments "to the lowest point consistent with domestic safety." Wilson's aim was to establish a world community, with strong U.S. participation, that would collectively guarantee the peace. Senate Republicans killed U.S. membership in the League, fearing that it might send Americans into battle without congressional consent. Sen. Henry Cabot Lodge (R-MA) and others insisted that U.S. interest alone should determine our foreign policy, not the negotiated common interests of the member states. Without U.S. membership, the League became an ineffective forum.[3]

With the League defeated at home, the United States returned to a period of isolation in the 1920s and early 1930s. It refused to join the Permanent Court of International Justice and to work with other nations in countering the world depression.[4] As the geopolitical crisis deepened in Europe, this country passed rigid neutrality laws that made it impossible to provide support to the victims of aggression. During a decade that saw the rise of fascism in Europe, the United States was unable to exert any constructive influence and passively watched the world drift toward war.

COLLECTIVE SECURITY

President Franklin Roosevelt recognized that stopping Hitler, Mussolini, and the Japanese would require a common effort that included the United States. He led this country into a series of arrangements, first with Great Britain and the Commonwealth, and then with countries all over the world. His strategy was based not on unilateralism but on collective security, and he had to battle unilateralists, led by Republican senators, to implement it.

In the last two years of World War II, Presidents Franklin D. Roosevelt and Harry S. Truman returned to Wilson's vision of world government and supported the creation of the United Nations to deal with future international rivalries. Roosevelt and Truman were careful architects of a Security Council that would protect U.S. interests and thus deflect the political resistance that Wilson had encountered in 1918 and 1919. Roosevelt and Truman urged our participation not only in the United Nations but in the World Bank, the International Monetary Fund, and other multilateral arrangements to secure stability and security in Europe. These agreements, in Arthur Schlesinger Jr.'s words, "bound the United States to the outside world in a way that isolationists, in their most pessimistic moments, could hardly have envisaged."[5]

President Truman even gave the welcome speech to the grand conference of the first meeting of the United Nations that took place in San Francisco on April 25, 1945, before the war ended. This makes a poignant contrast to the current president, George W. Bush, who addresses the United Nations reluctantly and at the behest of the only internationalist in his administration, Secretary of State Colin Powell.

In the postwar period, statesmen like Dean Acheson, George Marshall, and George Kennan guided this nation into a series of multilateral arrangements, including the Marshall Plan and NATO. When the United Kingdom could no longer guarantee security to the pro-Western governments of Greece and Turkey, the Truman Doctrine was advanced to supply military and economic aid to the governments in Athens and Ankara, which eventually became Western allies. Greece was already surrounded by communist neighbors—Albania, Bulgaria, and Yugoslavia— and probably would not have remained democratic without U.S. assistance. Turkey had a long and tense border with a Soviet Union that was applying pressure on its southern neighbors, including not only Turkey but also Iran and Afghanistan. Through the Marshall Plan and NATO, the United States firmly conveyed its commitment to contain the Soviet Union, and containment worked beyond any reasonable expectation.

DRIFTING INTO UNILATERALISM

In a radical departure from the bipartisan support for multilateralism that prevailed for over fifty years, the neoconservatives have thrown the country back to its unilateral beginnings. Whereas the United States in its infancy was relatively weak and self-contained, it is now a global power whose economy is inextricably linked with those of the world community. We no longer have the option of opting out. The neoconservative spin therefore is not that we withdraw but that we dominate.

The neoconservative attack on multilateralism began in 1994 when the Republicans gained control of Congress. President Clinton had briefly introduced the concept of "aggressive multilateralism" to justify extended U.S. efforts to cooperate with UN peacekeeping. Speaker of the House Newt Gingrich promptly accused President Clinton of having a "multilateral fantasy" and a desire "to subordinate the United States to the United Nations." Gingrich and the unilateralists won a major victory when Congress blocked payment of U.S. dues to the United Nations and its assessment for UN peacekeeping. Gingrich has reemerged as a spokesperson for the radical right with a vicious attack on the State Department, which he accused of engaging in a "deliberate and systematic effort" to undermine Bush's foreign policy and of favoring "process, politeness, and accommodation" over "facts, values, and consequences."[6]

In the period leading up to the election of 2000, the unilateralists in

Congress rejected the Comprehensive Test Ban Treaty and U.S. participation in the International Criminal Court (ICC). In opposing the ICC, the
United States opposed every member of the European Union, including
our NATO allies. Other examples of unilateralist moves at this time
included opposition to the global effort to ban land mines and to ban soldiers under the age of eighteen from combat (see chapter 7).

POLICY DRIVEN BY IDEOLOGY

Unilateralism is now the guiding principle of our foreign policy.[7] The ideological assertion of unilateralism and military power originated in 1992
when a draft version of the *Defense Policy Guidance* was leaked to the
Los Angeles Times. Written after the Gulf War of 1991, the *Guidance*
called for U.S. dominance by preventing the rise of any potentially hostile power. This document was written by a trio of neoconservatives now
managing U.S. foreign policy—Paul Wolfowitz; Lewis "Scooter" Libby;
and their boss, Richard Cheney, then secretary of defense. It defended the
preemptive use of force against states suspected of developing weapons
of mass destruction. The United Nations and various international
treaties, such as the Nonproliferation Treaty, were not even mentioned.
When he read it, Sen. Joseph Biden (D-DE) was appalled; he immediately
denounced the document as a prescription for "a Pax Americana."

The administration's assertion of unilateral U.S. military power is not
what might have been expected in view of candidate George W. Bush's
endorsement of a "humble" foreign policy. Discretion, not aggression,
seemed indicated, particularly in view of Bush's narrow and disputed
election. After all, George H. W. Bush and National Security Advisor
General Brent Scowcroft had pursued multilateral cooperation through
the United Nations and a cautious realism in their assertion of U.S. power.
Close observers of George W. Bush recorded his disparagement of
nation-building and multilateral peacekeeping but believed his appointment of Colin Powell as secretary of state and Condoleezza Rice as
national security advisor pointed to moderation.

Moderation and multilateralism were not the goals of the Bush
administration, however. In addition to appointing a significant number of
neoconservatives to important positions in the State Department, Defense

Department, and National Security Council, the president has relied on the work of right-wing think tanks and conservative groups. These groups include the Heritage Foundation, the American Enterprise Institute, the Project for the New American Century, and the Center for Security Policy, which provided the personnel and ideology for the turnaround in American foreign policy.

Neoconservatives first gained power during the Reagan administration but the "rules of the game" of the Cold War restrained both the United States and the Soviet Union from aggressive moves that risked confrontation. Despite the constraints, Reagan's administration saw the largest increase in the defense budget during peacetime, the attempted creation of a national missile defense, and an anticommunist crusade throughout Latin America. Many of the leading members of the Bush administration also served in the Reagan administration.

After the fall of the Soviet Union, the neoconservatives lost momentum as the United States under George H. W. Bush pursued a moderate foreign policy. While Bush was frustrating to this group, Bill Clinton was intolerable. Clinton's support of international cooperation on climate change and the control of AIDS, humanitarian intervention and peacekeeping, nation-building, and the creation of the International Criminal Court were anathema to them. This "globaloney," as the neoconservatives called it, failed in their view to deal with the new realities of power as the United States moved into the post–Cold War world.

An influential group of neoconservatives and members of the defense industry formed the Project for the New American Century in 1997.[8] The neoconservative pundits Kristol and Kagan brought this group together.[9] The project's first official policy declaration stated that conservatives had failed to "confidently advance a strategic vision for America's role in the world. . . . We aim to change this. We aim to make the case and rally support for American global leadership." The group declared, "A Reaganite policy of military strength and moral clarity may not be fashionable today. But it is necessary if the U.S. is to build on the success of this past century and ensure our security and greatness in the next."

The group wrote a letter to President Clinton in January 1998, declaring, "We may soon face a threat in the Middle East more serious than any we have known since the end of the Cold War. . . . We urge you to . . . enunciate a new strategy that would secure the interests of the U.S.

and our allies around the world. That strategy should aim, above all, at the removal of Saddam Hussein's regime from power." The issue was Hussein's weapons of mass destruction. "If Saddam does acquire the capability to deliver weapons of mass destruction, as he is almost certain to do if we continue along the present course, the safety of American troops in the region, of our friends and allies like Israel and the moderate Arab states, and a significant portion of the world's supply of oil will all be put at hazard." The letter was signed by a group including Elliott Abrams, John Bolton, Richard Perle, Rumsfeld, and Wolfowitz. Five years later the views in this letter became the justification for the war in Iraq.

The right-wing Center for Security Policy is directed by Frank Gaffney, who signed the project's statement in 1997 and has been a strong proponent of a national missile defense. Richard Cheney served as a member of the board of the Center for Security Policy, and Donald Rumsfeld received its Keeper of the Flame award. The center brings together politicians and defense corporations in a way that would have appalled President Eisenhower, who, at the end of his presidency, warned the American people against the "military-industrial complex."

The neoconservatives have aligned themselves with U.S. religious fundamentalists, including the Christian Right and Jewish and Catholic conservatives. They invoke absolutist values, including the moral and cultural superiority of the United States in a throwback to the Puritan views of John Winthrop. America's mission, according to the neoconservatives, is to maintain its military supremacy and spread our values around the world—not to cooperate with other countries or join multilateral organizations.

The collection of right-wing groups has been buttressed by think tanks heavily supported by corporations that benefit from neoconservative policies.[10] Spokespersons for groups such as the American Enterprise Institute and the Heritage Foundation can be read in op-eds and magazine articles around the country as they aggressively promote their positions and ideology. They can be most easily found in the pages of the *Weekly Standard*, published by Kristol, the *Wall Street Journal*, *National Review*, *Commentary* magazine, and the *Washington Times*. They push their agenda on radio and TV talk shows. Their style is coercive, dismissive, and arrogant. In the Bush administration, it is evident in the dismissive language used by Rumsfeld and Cheney against those who differ with them. The world they evoke is one in which U.S. force prevails, and the purpose of diplomacy is to achieve only U.S. ends. Their position dismisses multilateralism and international law and asserts aggressive unilateralism and U.S. economic dominance.

THE NEOCONS

The neoconservatives, who spent years on the sidelines, are running the game. The principal players share a number of common features, including:

- A long history of advocating militant unilateralism. In the words of Kristol,[11] they want an "unapologetic, idealistic, assertive" America that will promote prodemocratic revolutions around the world, if necessary at the point of an American gun.
- Association in right-wing ideological groups, lobbying organizations, the media, corporations, and the government, creating an interlocking and powerful network.
- The belief that foreign affairs are the prerogative of the executive branch and that Congress and the public should be only minimally involved and selectively informed. An atmosphere of secrecy pervades the group, which frequently withholds information and hides behind classification. From the Iraq war, to missile defense, to energy policy, information released is far below previously accepted levels, a move which tends to shift power away from Congress to the executive foreign policy team. The Office of Special Plans at the Pentagon, which misused intelligence to make the case for war in Iraq and failed to prepare for the transition, was made up of leading neoconservatives such as William Luti and Abram Shulsky, associates of Richard Cheney.
- A history of government service that has often been used to promote personal interests. The possibility of conflict of interest is often so strong that it cannot be discounted as a significant motive in the making of foreign policy. Several members of the group, such as John Poindexter and Elliott Abrams, also have a history of lying to Congress.

As we review the players, we see these common features. With the exception of Secretary of State Colin Powell and his deputy, Richard Armitage, the Bush foreign policy team is more militant, more secretive, and more ideologically unified than any in recent memory.[12]

Vice President Richard Cheney

Background

Cheney came to Washington in 1968 as a congressional fellow and became a protégé of Rep. Donald Rumsfeld (R-IL). When President Ford tapped Rumsfeld to be his chief of staff in 1974, Rumsfeld made Cheney his deputy. Cheney then served as chief of staff, a member of Congress, House Republican whip, and secretary of defense under George H. W. Bush. Today, as vice president, he chairs Bush's Budget Review Board and the administration's energy task force, is Bush's chief emissary to Capitol Hill, and is a major spokesman on foreign affairs.

Policies

With Paul Wolfowitz and Lewis Libby, Cheney developed the Pentagon's *Defense Policy Guidance*, ostensibly to be applied in the years 1994–1999 but shelved by the election of President Clinton. The *Guidance* stated as its first objective the establishment of a "new order" and the prevention of any new rival to the United States. It proclaimed the use of preemptive military force, including the ability to strike first against any threat from nuclear, chemical, or biological weapons. It argued that the United States should expect that future alliances would be "ad hoc assemblies, often not lasting beyond the crisis being confronted," and that the U.S. should be ready to act alone when "collective action cannot be orchestrated." This work has become American policy. As Rep. John B. Larson (D-CT) noted of Cheney, "One has to admire, in a way, the Babe Ruth–like sureness of his political work. He pointed to center field ten years ago, and now the ball is sailing over the fence."

Cheney has championed the war in Iraq, a national missile defense system, the weaponization of outer space, the rejection of the International Criminal Court, and the ending of the U.S. moratorium on nuclear testing. The administration's endorsement of "forward deterrence," preemptive use of nuclear weapons against nonnuclear states, and retreat from arms control show a strong Cheney influence. He is the last remaining member of the Bush administration who believes that the United States will find large stockpiles of WMD in Iraq.

Conflicts of Interest and Credibility

Cheney's career has been marked by conflict of interest and disingenuous statements. At the end of the Iraqi war, Kellogg, Brown and Root Services, which is owned by Halliburton Company, received without competition Pentagon contracts worth $5 billion, with a potential value of $15 billion. The company has come under investigation for overcharging for petroleum by $67 million.[13] Cheney was CEO of Halliburton for years before becoming vice president. In that post Cheney collected more than $10 million in salary and stock payments and held stock worth another $35 million. In 1998 and 1999 Halliburton racked up $23.8 million in sales to Iraq through two European subsidiaries after Cheney repeatedly stated that his company would not do business with Iraq.[14] Halliburton also came under investigation by the Securities and Exchange Commission for accounting irregularities similar to those practiced by Enron, which had occurred while Cheney was chairman. He claims to have broken his ties to Halliburton when he became a candidate for vice president in August 2000, but still holds 443,000 stock options and receives $150,000 a year from the company.

Lewis "Scooter" Libby

Background

The vice president's chief of staff and national security adviser is, in the words of Evan Thomas of *Newsweek*, "the most powerful Washington figure most people never heard of." Libby entered government in 1981 as a member of the Policy Planning Staff of the secretary of state; he then became director of special projects in the Bureau of East Asian and Pacific Affairs. He also has served as legal adviser to the U.S. House of Representatives Select Committee on U.S. National Security and Military/Commercial Concerns with the Peoples' Republic of China. During the administration of President George H.W. Bush, he was deputy undersecretary of defense for policy.

Policies

With Cheney and Wolfowitz, Libby drafted the *Defense Policy Guidance* document of 1992. Like Wolfowitz, he is known for aggressively pushing intelligence analysts to secure the information that fits his particular policy views. Before the war he strongly pushed the line that Saddam Hussein possessed WMD and was linked to terrorists working to attack the United States.

Secretary of Defense Donald H. Rumsfeld

Background

Rumsfeld's career includes four terms as a U.S. congressman, various economic posts in the Nixon administration, ambassador to NATO, and secretary of defense under President Ford. He is both the youngest and oldest defense secretary in U.S. history. Rumsfeld was an active member of both the Project for the New American Century and the right-wing Center for Security Policy.

Policies

Rumsfeld argues that the United States should assert its dominance through its military presence, and, if necessary, through the active use of force. He urges forward deployment of force to intimidate the potential enemy or actively engage it on its home ground, including the preemptive use of force against possible military competitors to the United States and countries seeking WMD.

Before September 11 he called for a massive change in the U.S. defense posture and declared before the Senate Armed Services Committee, "The old deterrence of the Cold War is imperfect for dissuading the threats of the new century and for maintaining stability in our new national security environment." His proposed reorganization would eventually lead to an increase of almost $100 billion in the defense budget.

As secretary of defense, Rumsfeld has moved strongly into areas of policy normally reserved for the secretary of state and into areas of intelligence formally under the authority of the director of central intelligence. He has arrogated to himself military decisions normally made by the professional military. His caustic remarks, such as those labeling the European governments that opposed the U.S. invasion of Iraq as "old Europe," have made the work of Secretary of State Powell more difficult. In every sphere, he has supported policies or acted in ways to enhance his power and increase the military presence of the United States.

Conflict of Interest and Credibility

As secretary of defense under President Ford, Rumsfeld awarded the M-1 tank deal to the Chrysler Corporation, a key political contributor in Michigan to his boss, without competitive bidding, which had every appearance of bias and politics.[15] In 1998, as chairman of the Commission on the Ballistic Missile Threat to the United States, Rumsfeld flagrantly distorted available intelligence to present a threatening picture justifying a missile defense system.[16]

Deputy Secretary of Defense Paul Wolfowitz

Background

Trudy Rubin, the intrepid columnist for the *Philadelphia Inquirer*, has called Deputy Secretary of Defense Paul Wolfowitz "the administration's preeminent intellectual" and a mentor to a number of Bush team members who have worked with him in the past.[17] From 1989 to 1993 he was undersecretary of defense for policy under Secretary of Defense Cheney. Under President Reagan he was assistant secretary of state for East Asian and Pacific Affairs and then U.S. ambassador to Indonesia. He had also served in the Pentagon as deputy assistant secretary of defense and has worked for the Arms Control and Disarmament Agency. Prior to coming into the present administration, he was dean and professor at the School of Advanced International Studies (SAIS) of Johns Hopkins University.

Policies

With Cheney and Libby, Wolfowitz developed the draft for the Pentagon's Defense Policy Guidance. Wolfowitz has been a particularly strong and consistent proponent of regime change in Iraq. In calling for the demise of Saddam Hussein, Wolfowitz asserted that it would be a defeat for terrorists globally. He declared that "[Saddam's] demise will open opportunities for governments and institutions to emerge in the Muslim world that are respectful of fundamental human dignity and freedom."

Credibility

Wolfowitz, as part of the Reagan team, supported a number of Asian dictators, such as President Suharto of Indonesia, Chun Doo-hwan in South Korea, and Ferdinand Marcos in the Philippines, although in subsequent speeches and writings, he dismissed the dictatorial nature of these regimes or denied his role in supporting them.

Undersecretary of Defense Douglas J. Feith

Background

Feith served in the Reagan administration as deputy assistant secretary of defense for negotiations policy and as special counsel to Assistant Secretary of Defense Richard Perle.

Policies

Feith has a long history of opposing arms control agreements, leading efforts to block ratification of the Chemical Weapons Convention negotiated by George H. W. Bush and calling the Biological Weapons Convention "worthless." He criticized the Intermediate Nuclear Forces Treaty and declared that the ABM Treaty was obsolete and invalid, arguing that Russia was not the legal heir of the Soviet Union; prevalence of such a view would invalidate treaties signed before 1989.

On Middle East policy, Feith has been a consistent hawk. In 1996 he cowrote the report recommending a "clear break" with the Oslo peace process. When Prime Minister Netanyahu did not make the break, Feith called upon Israel to reoccupy the territories controlled by the Palestinian Authority. He wrote in the *Washington Times* in August 1997, "Supporters [of the Oslo peace process]—like so many distraught battered wives—simply cannot be persuaded there is no romance, there is no peace process."

Conflicts of Interest and Credibility

As an attorney in his nongovernment years, most of Feith's casework involved Israel or other foreign interests, including a leading Israeli armaments manufacturer interested in establishing joint ventures with U.S. aerospace manufacturers. He was a registered foreign agent for Turkey, seeking to promote defense cooperation between the United States and his client, a company called IAI, which also retained Richard Perle. Feith also represented the Loral Corporation, which the Pentagon has accused of selling sensitive technology to China. His former law firm, Feith and Zell, has established a task force to assist companies engaged in "infrastructure and other reconstruction projects in Iraq." At the time of Feith's confirmation as undersecretary of defense for policy, James J. Zogby wrote in the *Baltimore Sun*, "His pattern of behavior and obvious conflicts of interest should have disqualified him from such a sensitive post; the issues raised at his confirmation hearing demonstrated that."[18]

Undersecretary of State for Arms Control and Disarmament John R. Bolton

Background

Bolton's confirmation carried the Senate with a 57–43 vote, with only seven Democrats joining the unanimous Republicans. Sen. Jesse Helms said on his behalf in January 2001, "John Bolton is the kind of man with whom I would want to stand at Armageddon, if it should be my lot to be on hand for what is forecast to be the final battle between good and evil in this world." At Bolton's nomination, Senator Biden (D-DE), the ranking Democrat on the Senate Foreign Relations Committee, said, "I do not believe Mr. Bolton has the vision or the experience necessary for this position."

Bolton was assistant secretary for International Organization Affairs at the Department of State from 1989 to 1993 and held important positions in the Agency for International Development during the Reagan administration. Prior to his appointment, Bolton was senior vice president of the American Enterprise Institute, a member of the Project for the New American Century, and an adviser for the Jewish Institute for National Security Affairs, as were Cheney and Feith. He also was a regular contributor to Kristol's *Weekly Standard.*

Policies

Bolton's nomination, which Colin Powell opposed, was controversial because of Bolton's outspoken disdain for arms control and various international treaties, his call for diplomatic recognition of Taiwan in opposition to the official "one-China" policy, and his opposition to payment of U.S. dues to the United Nations. On North Korea, Bolton declared that "we are indifferent to whether we ever have 'normal' relations with it, and that achieving that goal is entirely in their interest, not ours."[19]

In 1997 Bolton maintained that disenchantment with the United Nations had occurred because of its attacks on Zionism, its suggestion that first world countries have an obligation to help the third world, and the failure of peacekeeping and nation-building. Accordingly, he stated that "the United Nations has a limited role to play in international affairs for the foreseeable future."[20] At his confirmation hearing Sen. Barbara Boxer (D-CA) reminded the nominee that he had said, "If the UN Secretariat building in New York lost ten stories, it wouldn't make a bit of difference." As early as 1999, he targeted Secretary General Kofi Annan for special attack.

As for arms control, Bolton had characterized its supporters as "misguided individuals following a timid and neopacifist line of thought." He opposed the Comprehensive Test Ban and the ABM treaties. At a speech at the Heritage Foundation on May 6, 2002, Bolton falsely claimed that Cuba was developing biological weapons and sharing its expertise with U.S. enemies.

Conflict of Interest and Credibility

John Isaacs, the respected head of the Council for a Livable World, stated, "There is good reason to question not only Mr. Bolton's experience and policy positions, but his ethics as well." In 1986 Bolton helped Senator Helms's National Congressional Club flout federal laws, resulting in a $10,000 fine from the Federal Election Commission in 1986. In the 1990s Bolton was charged with funneling political contributions through foreign businessmen and the Taiwanese government, which paid him $30,000 over three years for research papers on UN membership issues. When Bolton advocated full membership for Taiwan in the United Nations before subcommittees of the House Foreign Affairs Committee, he was asked if his testimony was related to such payment. Bolton replied that he had "never been paid by anybody for any testimony" and that his appearance and payment for the paper were "completely separate transactions."[21] Paper writing and testimony on behalf of Taiwan continued. Bolton was also president of the tax-exempt National Policy Forum, a GOP subsidiary, but left the post shortly before a 1997 congressional probe into whether the group illegally took foreign donations during the 1996 elections. No charges were filed.[22]

National Security Advisor Condoleezza Rice

Background

The *New York Times* describes Condoleezza Rice as President Bush's "longtime foreign policy tutor."[23] A political science professor and former provost at Stanford University, Rice was a member of a group of foreign policy advisers to Bush nicknamed "The Vulcans," which also included Cheney, Wolfowitz, and former secretary of state George Shultz. Her past experience includes a stint as a Soviet expert with Brent Scowcroft, George H. W. Bush's national security advisor.

Policies

Rice's major positions were spelled out before her appointment in an article in *Foreign Affairs* titled "Promoting the National Interest," which demonstrated her enthusiasm for tough power politics and her disdain for internationalism.[24] "Many in the United States are (and have always been) uncomfortable with the notions of power politics, and great powers, and power balances. In an extreme form, this discomfort leads to a reflexive appeal instead to notions of international law and norms, and the belief that the support of many states—or even better, of institutions like the United Nations—is essential to the legitimate exercise of power. The 'national interest' is replaced with 'humanitarian interests' or the interests of 'the international community.'" Rice dismissed any possibility that the need to seek UN approval should bar the United States from pursuing its national interest. She charged that "multilateral agreements and institutions should not be ends in themselves" and dismissed the Kyoto Treaty on climate control and the Comprehensive Test Ban. She disparaged humanitarian intervention and nation-building as too problematic and stated clearly that in the next administration, "Military readiness will have to take center stage."

Conflicts of Interest and Credibility

Like other members of the foreign policy team, Rice came to the administration with a history of corporate connections. She was a major stockowner and director of Chevron from 1991 to 2001, an oil corporation which has strong connections to Cheney's Halliburton Corporation.[25]

National Security Council Senior Director for Near East and North Africa Affairs Elliott Abrams

Background

Abrams came to his post with a controversial past. In the 1980s Abrams served as Reagan's assistant secretary of state for human rights and then as assistant secretary for Inter-American affairs. During the Contra War in Nicaragua, the Reagan administration trained Nicaraguans to fight a brutal war largely against the civilian population of Nicaragua in an attempt to oust the Sandinista government. In the interim years Abrams headed the Ethics and Public Policy Center and was in close association with Richard Perle and former UN ambassador Jeanne Kirkpatrick at the

American Enterprise Institute. James Zogby, the director of the Arab-American Institute, wrote that his appointment sent "a very dangerous message to the Arab world" and added to the "lock that the neocon set now has on all the major instruments of decision making except for the State Department."[26]

Policies

Prior to taking his present post, Abrams had called for "regime change" in Iraq and for cracking down on the Palestinian Authority. He is not an Arab-Israeli specialist but has long supported the Israeli Likud Party's emphasis on overwhelming military force. He also supports a military alliance between Israel and Turkey to oppose any grouping of Arab states jeopardizing Israel's position.

Conflict of Interest and Credibility

Abrams was indicted by the Iran-contra special prosecutor for giving false testimony about his role in illegally raising money for the contras but pleaded guilty to two lesser offenses of withholding information to Congress in order to avoid a trial and possible jail term. He received a sentence of two years probation and one hundred hours of community service. President George H. W. Bush pardoned him in 1991 along with several other contra defendants. When asked what he learned from this experience, Abrams replied that he "learned to destroy all messages before he left the office for home." David Corn of the *Nation* reports: "In 1993 after a UN truth commission, which examined 22,000 atrocities that occurred during the twelve-year civil war in El Salvador, attributed 85 percent of the abuses to the Reagan-assisted right-wing military and its death-squad allies, Abrams declared, 'The Administration's record on El Salvador is one of fabulous achievement.' "[27]

At the time of Abrams's appointment as senior director for democracy, human rights, and international operations at the National Security Council, White House spokesman Ari Fleischer declared, "The President thinks that's a matter of the past that was dealt with at the time, and that Mr. Abrams is held in high regard by Democrats and Republicans alike, and that he'll do an outstanding job in this position." Other officials who were involved in deceiving Congress during the contra period have also surfaced in the Bush administration.[28] These include John Negroponte, ambassador to Honduras from 1981 to 1985, who covered up the gross human rights abuses of the Honduran government and U.S. operations during the Contra War and is now U.S. ambassador to the United Nations, and Otto Reich, head of the public diplomacy office in the Reagan White House and a former assistant secretary of state for the Western Hemisphere, who received a recess appointment from the White House when it was clear he could not be confirmed.

Key Adviser Richard Perle

Background

Richard Perle served as an assistant secretary of defense during the Reagan administration and is a resident fellow at the American Enterprise Institute. Perle was active in the Project for a New American Century and other right-wing organizations with defense industry ties, such as the Center for Security Policy. With Abrams and Wolfowitz, he was a contributor to the Project for a New American Century book, edited by Kagan and Kristol and entitled *Present Dangers: Crisis and Opportunities in American Foreign and Defense Policy,*[29] which came out during the 2000 election. He was also an adviser to the pro-Likud Jewish Institute for National Security Affairs, along with Cheney, Feith, Abrams, and Bolton.

Policies

Perle strongly backed the administration's position on Hussein's possession of WMD. At a Senate Foreign Relations subcommittee hearing in March 2001, he declared, "Does Saddam now have weapons of mass destruction? Sure he does. We know he has chemical weapons. We know he has biological weapons. . . . How far he's gone on the nuclear weapons side I don't think we really know. My guess is it's further than we think. It's always further than we think, because we limit ourselves, as we think about this, to what we're able to prove and demonstrate. . . . And, unless you believe that we have uncovered everything, you have to assume there is more than we're able to report."

For years Perle was known for his strong opposition to nuclear arms control agreements. As an adviser to candidate Bush in 2000, Perle strongly advocated a missile defense system and abrogation of the ABM Treaty. He resigned from the Reagan administration because of the negotiation of the INF Treaty of 1987, which eliminated an entire class of intermediate-range missiles.

Conflicts of Interest and Credibility

In 1996 Perle and Feith wrote a paper for Israeli prime minister Netanyahu that endorsed Israel's biblical land claims and called on Israel to make "a clean break" with the policies of negotiating with the Palestinians and trading land for peace. The paper repudiated the Oslo peace process and reasserted Israel's claim to Gaza and the West Bank. The report also said, "Israel can shape its strategic environment by weakening, containing, and even rolling back Syria. This effort can focus on removing Saddam Hussein from power in Iraq." This policy, originally designed for Israel, has become basic U.S. policy.

Perle resigned as chairman of the Defense Policy Board on March 27, 2003. The board, while ostensibly private, provided counsel and advice to Rumsfeld and the Department of Defense. Perle had been employed as a consultant by bankrupt telecommunications firm Global Crossing, which was trying to get Pentagon clearance to be sold to Asian investors. Perle would have received $725,000 for his work, including $600,000 if the government approved the deal.[30] Reports indicated he had been soliciting investment money, reputedly $100 million, from a Saudi who was seeking to influence U.S. policy on Iraq. Despite apparent conflicts of interest, he was allowed to keep his membership on the Defense Policy Board. As columnist William D. Hartung remarked on March 28, 2003, "The fact that Rumsfeld accepted the resignation on Perle's terms—stepping down as chair of the policy board, but remaining a member—underscores how tone deaf our defense secretary is when it comes to perceptions of conflict of interest."[31] Retired rear admiral Thomas Brooks, who served on the board during the Clinton administration, said, "It sounds like he's squeezing every nickel out of the Defense Policy Board."

Secretary of State Colin L. Powell

Background

Secretary of State Colin L. Powell is the one key figure in the Bush administration who has never been a part of the neoconservative movement and, as a result, has drawn fire from them for his positions on a variety of issues. Powell arrived at the State Department with thirty-five years' service as a professional soldier, becoming a four-star general and chairman of the Joint Chiefs of Staff. In 1987 he had served as assistant to the president for national security affairs. After retirement from the military, Powell chaired America's Promise, a civic organization dedicated to helping youth through education and through mentoring and after-school programs.

Policies

Powell represents the one clear exception to the militant unilateralism of the Bush foreign policy group. Indeed, one of the neoconservatives' greatest successes has been to limit his influence as secretary of state. As the article by Gingrich indicates, Powell continues to be the object of virulent criticism by the radical right wing of the Republican Party.

While charming and cajoling diplomats and audiences around the world, Powell has been unable to dispel an image of American arrogance. Despite his support of multilateralism, he has been unable to realize this vision in policy. Nevertheless, he remains more committed to diplomacy than most members of the Bush team and favors a role for the UN and Europe in the Iraqi transition process.

Since September 11, Powell had taken a backseat to Rumsfeld, Cheney, and Rice, until the problems of the Iraqi occupation allowed the secretary of state to lobby the president that the United States needed the support of the United Nations in Iraq. Once a moderate on Iraq, he became a hawk when the president decided on war.[32] On February 5, 2003, Powell presented to the UN Security Council the Bush administration's specious case that Iraq had weapons of mass destruction and was closely connected to al Qaeda. While Powell has disagreed with a number of Bush policies, he has loyally backed decisions once they were made. On the Israel-Palestinian issue, he has been a moderating influence on the neoconservatives; his influence can be seen in the "road map" agreement between Israel and the Palestinians.

Powell has conceded to being frustrated with his role in the Bush administration but has indicated he would not resign before the 2004 election. In an interview with the *New York Times*, he noted that one thing he admired most about his predecessor George C. Marshall was that the retired general did not resign even after his advice not to recognize Israel in 1948 was rejected.[33]

Credibility

When Powell was Defense Secretary Caspar Weinberger's senior military assistant, he was involved in the cover-up of the secret effort to provide funds to the Nicaraguan contra rebels from profits gained by selling arms to Iran. Iran-contra was conducted despite congressional legislation prohibiting such aid.

*   *   *

The neoconservatives in the Bush administration have taken positions on policy and the political process that are far to the right of the American mainstream and the moderate wing of the Republican Party. The country still believes in the balance of power between the executive and legislative branches, but the neoconservatives do not. The Republican Party endorses the limited use of force for defense, but this group believes in an aggressive assertion of power. Their party and the country still value international agreements, particularly arms control, international law, and the United Nations, but this group disdains them or sees them at best as limited expedients. Their party and the country believe that civil service means an abnegation of private interest and a full concentration on the interests of the country, but members of this group frequently cannot separate their private interests from their public involvements.

NOTES

1. Condolezza Rice, "Promoting the National Interest," *Foreign Affairs* 79, no. 1 (January/February, 2000): 45.

2. Robert Kagan and William Kristol, "Reject the Buddy System," *New York Times*, October 25, 1999, p. A31.

3. President Wilson's inept handling of the question, however, may have done as much damage as the substantive issue in preventing U.S. membership.

4. With the Hawley-Smoot Tariff of 1930, the United States passed the highest tariff in its history, which was instrumental in cutting down world trade and in maintaining the world depression.

5. Arthur Schlesinger Jr., "Unilateralism in Historical Perspective," in *Understanding Unilateralism in American Foreign Relations*, ed. Gwyn Prins (London: Royal Institute of International Affairs, 2000).

6. Newt Gingrich, "Rogue State Department," *Foreign Policy* (July/August 2003): 42.

7. For a superb analysis of the takeover of American policy by the neoconservatives, see Tom Barry and Jim Lobe, "The Men Who Stole the Show," Special Report, *Foreign Policy in Focus* (October 2002).

8. In many ways, the Project for a New American Century was the natural heir of the Coalition for a Democratic Majority and Committee on the Present Danger, which had flourished during the Carter years by attacking Carter's policies of detente and support of arms control.

9. See their essay "Toward a Neo-Reaganite Foreign Policy," *Foreign Affairs* (July/August 1996). For a recent study of the contrast between U.S. unilateral power politics and Europe's enchantment with international law, multilateralism, and diplomacy, see Robert Kagan's *Of Paradise and Power: America and Europe in the New World Order* (New York: Alfred A. Knopf, 2003). Kagan's position is that Europe endorses these relics of foreign policy because it lacks the military means to assert power.

10. In her *Way Out There in the Blue: Reagan, Star Wars, and the End of the Cold War* (New York: Simon & Schuster, 2000), Frances Fitzgerald provides a detailed analysis of the connection between think tanks, weapons labs, politicians, and the arms industry in missile defense.

11. William Kristol is the son of Irving Kristol, a former editor of *Commentary* magazine. Another editor was Norman Podhoretz, who is the father-in-law of Elliott Abrams. The magazine exercised a strong early influence on the development of the neoconservative movement.

12. Several attempts have been made to connect the Bush foreign policy

team to the philosophy of University of Chicago professor Leo Strauss (1899–1973), particularly as Paul Wolfowitz, Richard Perle, Irving Kristol (William's father), and Stephen Cambone, the undersecretary of defense for intelligence, consider themselves Straussians. The problem is the immense gap between Strauss's teachings and Bush's administration and policies. As James Atlas asks in his "A Classicist's Legacy: New Empire Builders" (*New York Times*, May 4, 2003), "Just what would Leo Strauss think of the policies being carried out in his name?" Our sense is that he would be appalled. Also see Jeet Heer, "The Philosopher," *Boston Globe*, May 11, 2003, and Seymour M. Hersh, "Selective Intelligence," *New Yorker,* May 12, 2003, p. 44.

13. Douglas Jehl, "U.S. Sees Evidence of Overcharging in Iraq Contract,*" New York Times*, December 12, 2003, p. A1.

14. Sandra Sobieraj, "Bush, Cheney Have Millions in Assets," Associated Press, June 1, 2001.

15. Craig Eisendrath, Melvin A. Goodman, and Gerald E. Marsh, *The Phantom Defense: America's Pursuit of the Star Wars Illusion* (Westport, CT: Praeger, 2001), p. 37.

16. Ibid., pp. 35, 65–66.

17. Trudy Rubin, "Paul Wolfowitz: Not Just Any Optimist," *Philadelphia Inquirer*, November 17, 2002, p. C5.

18. James J. Zogby, "Resolving Door Poses Danger to Defense," *Baltimore Sun*, August 7, 2001.

19. John Bolton, "Perspective on Foreign Policy: U.S. Must Stand Up to North Korea," *Los Angeles Times*, September 22, 1999, p. 7.

20. John Bolton, "America's Skepticism about the United Nations," *USIA Electronic Journal* 2, no. 2 (May 1997).

21. Walter Pincus, "Bolton's Objectivity on China Is Questioned," *Washington Post*, April 9, 2001, p. A17.

22. Bill Nichols, "Dems to Challenge Conservative Nominees," *USA Today*, March 29, 2001, p. A1.

23. Richard Oppel Jr. and Frank Bruni, "Bush Adviser Gets National Security Post," *New York Times*, December 18, 2000.

24. Rice, "Promoting the National Interest."

25. Martha Smilgis wrote in the *San Francisco Examiner*, on June 7, 2001, "With Condoleezza in charge, the interests of the oil companies will dominate foreign policy decisions." Rice had an oil tanker named after her, but it was quietly renamed. See Marinucci, "Chevron Redubs Ship Named for Bush Aide Condoleezza Rice Drew Too Much Attention," *San Francisco Examiner*, May 5, 2001, p. A1.

26. "Neoconservatives Consolidate Control over U.S. Mideast Policy," http://www.fpif.org/commentary/2002/0212abrams.html.

27. David Corn, "Elliot Abrams: It's Back!" *Nation*, June 14, 2001, p. 5.

28. For the connection between the Reagan administration and drug traffickers in the Iran-contra scandal, see Alfred W. McCoy, "Mission Myopia: Narcotics as Fallout from the CIA's Covert Wars," in *National Insecurity: U.S. Intelligence after the Cold War*, ed. Craig Eisendrath (Philadelphia: Temple University Press, 2000).

29. Robert Kagan and William Kristol, *Present Dangers: Crisis and Opportunity in American Foreign Policy and Defense Policy* (San Francisco: Encounter Books, 2000).

30. James McIntyre, "Top Pentagon Adviser Resigns under Fire," CNN, March 28, 2003, http://www.cnn.com/2003/US/03/27/perle.resigns/.

31. World Policy Institute, Research Project, March 28, 2003, http://www.worldpolicy.org/projects/arms/updates/032803.html.

32. Glenn Kessler, "Moderate Powell Turns Hawkish on War with Iraq," *Washington Post*, January 24, 2003, p. A1. Powell did everything possible to persuade France, Russia, and other critics of the Iraq war to back the use of force to disarm Hussein. When the Europeans turned him down, Powell became a hawk.

33. "Powell Defends Diplomacy, Saying He Wants Record Straight," *New York Times*, December 23, 2003, p. 1.

CHAPTER NINE
THE WAR AT HOME

Restriction of free thought and free speech is the most dangerous of all subversions. It is the one un-American act that could most easily defeat us.

— Supreme Court Justice William O. Douglas

I think secrecy is the friend of democracy.

— U.S. Attorney General John Ashcroft

Since its inception, American leaders have portrayed the United States as morally superior to other nations. We have confidently projected this image to a world that for many years has viewed the United States as the promised land. U.S. rhetoric has reflected pride in our open institutions. Democracy and a free-market economy are cited as the vehicles bringing equal opportunity and fair treatment to all.

Even as it continues to proclaim U.S. moral superiority, the Bush administration is undermining the policies and institutions that have protected individual rights, provided fair treatment under the law, and offered equal opportunity to its citizens. Six weeks after 9/11, Congress passed the USA PATRIOT (Uniting and Strengthening America by Providing Appropriate Tools Required to Interrupt and Obstruct Terrorism) Act, which gave the government unprecedented power to intrude into private lives, to use military tribunals rather than civilian courts to try suspected terrorists, and to deprive defendants of basic rights. Invoked as an emergency measure to stop terrorism, the PATRIOT Act erodes constitutional provisions, authorizing "sneak and peek" searches, which allow the government to search people's homes without immediate notification. Provisions of the act allow the government to gain access to sensitive data, including medical and library records, and even records concerning the purchase or rental of books, music, and videos.

Attorney General John Ashcroft, one week after 9/11, issued an order authorizing the detention of foreign citizens for an unspecified amount of time; he has refused to apply the Geneva Convention or prisoner of war status to al Qaeda suspects and Taliban members, who have been incarcerated at Guantanamo Bay since 2001. Several teenagers have been held at Guantanamo since October 2001 with no charges against them. Ashcroft's techniques are reminiscent of the McCarthy era when the fears of the American people were exploited at the expense of civil rights.

At the same time, the Bush administration is breaking the social contract that Democrats and Republicans established in the wake of the depression seventy years ago. The wealthy classes are gaining from key tax provisions while the social safety net is being methodically weakened. Legislation is being introduced to reduce government services and protections—in education, welfare, health, and social insurance. While the military budget soars to $450 billion, if expenses in Iraq and Afghanistan are included, the domestic budget is being cut for lack of funds. Reductions of government programs, which hurt the working and middle classes, have created a widening gap in income and standards of living between the rich and the rest of the society.

MILITARY TRIBUNALS

Despite President Bush's declarations that the war on terrorism is a war to protect human rights, his administration plans to try aliens accused of terrorism in military tribunals, an approach that denies defendants the rights guaranteed to all by our legal system. Military tribunals lack credibility at home and abroad. Verdicts of such tribunals are seen not as acts of justice, but as arbitrary and high-handed.[1] Defendants are likely to be considered martyrs and heroes, particularly in the Islamic world, rather than justly condemned criminals.

The military tribunals lack credibility because they deprive defendants of a trial by an independent court, deny their right of appeal, lower due process standards for noncitizens, and restrict the rights of the accused to prepare an effective defense. These restrictions inhibit defense lawyers' ability to access classified materials and to interview potential witnesses. At the same time, evidence obtained under duress, including torture, can be admitted. The government can also monitor conversations between defense attorneys and their clients. Finally, the military tribunals are more likely to favor the government's case than would an independent civilian court.

The government has also threatened the use of military tribunals to restrict rights provided in civilian courts. In the case of Zacarias Moussaoui, the so-called twentieth highjacker, the government denied Moussaoui's lawyers access to evidence and a witness critical in his defense. When a judge ordered the government to make the witness available, it refused, claiming that questioning the witness would pose a threat to national security. The government indicated that if it did not like the way the judge was handling the case, it would transfer Moussaoui to a military tribunal, thus evading the Sixth Amendment of the Constitution that guarantees rights to a fair trial. Without such guarantees, military tribunals can render verdicts, including possible death sentences, that are dictated by policy, not justice.[2]

The United States has detained about 680 males from forty-three countries at Camp X-Ray, the specially constructed prison at Guantanamo, on the southeastern tip of Cuba. Most of these individuals, some of them teenagers, were swept up in Afghanistan during the rout of the Taliban. Prime Minister Tony Blair, disturbed by the lack of rights granted to defendants by the Bush administration, intervened in July 2003 to have two British teenagers held at Guantanamo returned to Britain. The two had been held despite repeated requests by Foreign Secretary Jack Straw over a two-year period that they be returned. A federal appeals court in San Francisco declared in December 2003 that the U.S. policy of holding detainees at Guantanamo without legal protection was unconstitutional and a violation of international law.

DETAINEES

In the months following 9/11, about twelve hundred Muslim men were picked up in the United States and often held in secret. In the name of national security, they were detained without charges, denied attorneys and contact with their families and the outside world, and often treated brutally.[3] Most of these men had entered the United States without proper immigration papers; many were held on criminal charges unrelated to September 11. Hundreds were deported. In addition, nearly seventy-seven thousand immigrants from Arab and Muslim countries were questioned, fingerprinted, and photographed as part of the government's special registration program.

The roundup was similar to a sweep of suspected subversive immigrants that occurred in 1919, conducted under the authority of Attorney General A. Mitchell Palmer. Known as the "Palmer Raids," they were led by J. Edgar Hoover, then head of the Alien Radical Division of the Justice Department. Those who were detained were often interrogated without access to legal counsel, often held in secret, and sometimes tortured.[4] In the end, over five hundred were deported, usually for their political associations, not for acts of terrorism or subversion.

Secretary of Defense Rumsfeld suggested in March 2002 that the detainees who had not been tried or acquitted might be kept for the duration of the conflict with terrorism. When asked "When would that be?" he responded, "When we feel that there are not effective global terrorist networks functioning in the world that these people would be likely to go back to and begin again their terrorist activities."[5] In a war without end, this could be forever. Not only were the detainees being held indefinitely, but they were denied any right of appeal through the courts. In April 2003 Attorney General John Ashcroft reaffirmed the government policy of holding groups of asylum seekers and other noncitizen groups who enter the United States without proper documents in detention indefinitely, even if they individually posed no danger to the United States.

This suppression of rights was criticized by the Department of Justice's own Office of the Inspector General in an exhaustive report issued in June 2003 and again in a follow-up report in July. The reports charged that the detainees were denied basic legal rights, including prompt notification of charges and access to bail, and subjected to "a pattern of physical and verbal abuse." Some of the most serious cases were under continuous investigation without decisive action being taken. The Justice Department's spokesperson, Barbara Comstock, defended indefinite detention against even such internal criticism. She said, "We detained illegal aliens encountered during the September 11 terrorist investigation until it was determined they were not involved in terrorist activity, did not have relevant knowledge of terrorist activity, or it was determined that their removal was appropriate. . . . We make no apologies for finding every legal way possible to protect the American public from further terrorist attacks."[6]

Following September 11, aggressive measures were considered necessary to protect the country from terrorism. But this did not require fundamental violations of human rights, nor is there convincing evidence that we have enhanced our security or acquired significant intelligence through these measures.[7] In January 2004 the Supreme Court rejected an appeal seeking the identity of hundreds of these men who had not been charged with a crime.

Another class of detainees, suspected al Qaeda operatives and Taliban commanders, are being held in detention centers under shocking conditions. The *Washington Post* recorded, "Those who refused to cooperate inside this secret CIA interrogation center are sometimes kept standing or kneeling for hours, in black hoods or spray-painted goggles. At times, they are held in awkward, painful positions and deprived of sleep with a twenty-four-hour bombardment of lights—subject to what are known as 'stress and duress' techniques. . . . Some who do not cooperate are turned over—'rendered,' in official parlance—to foreign intelligence services [in such countries as Morocco, Egypt, and Jordon] whose practice of torture has been documented by the U.S. government and human rights organizations. . . . Each of the current national security officials interviewed for this article defended the use of violence against captives as just and necessary. . . . 'If you don't violate someone's human rights some of the time, you probably aren't doing your job,' said one official."[8]

In June 2003 President Bush lashed out against torture practiced by other countries, stating, "The United States is committed to the world-wide elimination of torture and we are leading this fight by example."

After 9/11 nearly three thousand suspected al Qaeda members and their supporters were detained in Afghanistan, Guantanamo, the island of Diego Garcia, and Charleston, South Carolina, without prisoner-of-war (POW) status.[9] While U.S. officials have denied torture, three inmates have died in U.S. custody in Afghanistan, and eighteen prisoners at Guantanamo reportedly have attempted suicide. Interviews with a number of officials confirm regular beatings and use of violence, thus setting a precedent for the treatment of U.S. prisoners of war by other nations. As Thomas Paine said, "He that would make his own liberty secure must guard even his enemy from oppression; for if he violates this duty he establishes a precedent that will reach himself."

Basic rights, such as a fair trial, adequate defense, and freedom of communication, have been denied to aliens and even American citizens. José Padilla, an American citizen, was arrested at a Chicago airport in May 2002 and held as a material witness by the Justice Department during a grand jury probe into an alleged conspiracy to detonate a radioactive dirty bomb in a U.S. city. In June 2002 the government transferred him to military custody and cut off all contact with his attorney. The transfer was made on the basis of an order by President Bush designating Padilla to be an "enemy combatant" closely associated with al Qaeda. Padilla has been held in solitary confinement since that date at the U.S. naval base in Goose Creek, South Carolina. In this case, the rights of an American citizen are violated by his designation as an "enemy combatant," a designation that is entirely a matter of executive discretion, not subject to judicial review. This precedent would allow any American citizen to be so designated and thus denied basic civil rights. A federal appeals court in New York ruled in December 2003 that Congress, not the president, has the authority to detain an American citizen as an "enemy combatant" and that Padilla should be released from military cusody. In addition, the Supreme Court agreed to hear appeals on behalf of sixteen foreigners held at Guantanamo.[10]

The other U.S. citizen being detained indefinitely as an "enemy combatant" is Yaser Esam Hamdi, arrested during the war in Afghanistan and held at Guantanamo and a naval base in Norfolk, Virginia, since April

2002. He has not been transferred to civilian custody, allowed to meet with a lawyer, or charged with any crime, and in July 2003 a federal appeals court ruled that he could be jailed indefinitely without seeing an attorney. The Supreme Court has recently agreed to hear this case as well.

Such incarceration, as indicated by the federal appeals court, violates the basic rights of citizens. Concentrating such power in the hands of the executive also seriously alters the balance of power under the Constitution. The president has the power to command U.S. armies in a war but not to set the legal framework for conducting the war, such as determining who is the enemy, whether to use military tribunals, or whether to suspend basic civil rights.

The actions and plans of the administration are reminiscent of the Star Chambers, which issued summary executions after sham trials, that the English abolished in 1641. These were a symbol of the kind of autocracy that the United States as a new nation wished to avoid. Alexander Hamilton wrote in *The Federalist Papers* that a policy that allows "confinement of the person, by secretly hurrying him to jail, where his sufferings are unknown or forgotten," is a "dangerous engine of arbitrary government."

In its treatment of all three classes of detainees—immigrants and other suspicious noncitizens detained in the United States, combatants apprehended in Afghanistan or other countries, and American citizens considered as "enemy combatants"—the administration has acted not as the executive branch of a constitutional government but as a unilateral power without legal or constitutional restraints. This precedent could seriously undermine our system of government.

USA PATRIOT ACT

Congress passed the USA PATRIOT Act on October 26, 2001, with overwhelming votes—357 to 66 in the House and 98 to 1 in the Senate. Passed as a measure to combat terrorism, the USA PATRIOT Act has given the executive branch license to seriously infringe on civil rights. The act allows law enforcement agencies to conduct secret searches, tap phones and e-mails, and access medical, financial, mental health, and student records with minimal judicial oversight. Such actions need not be based on "probable cause" but on a simple declaration that records are "sought for" in an ongoing investigation. For the first time, the CIA has been granted access to grand jury information. The PATRIOT Act also allows FBI investigations of U.S. citizens without probable cause of crimes under the rubric of "intelligence purposes." Finally, it permits noncitizens to be jailed on mere suspicion and held indefinitely without conviction; it also loosens requirements for deportation.

Sections of the PATRIOT Act are clearly subject to abuse. Once an organization is classified as being a domestic terrorist organization—a designation at the discretion of the executive branch—it loses many traditional rights under our legal system. Section 806, for example, allows assets of the organization to be seized without a prior hearing and without the organization being convicted of a crime; there need only be an assertion of probable cause to believe that the assets were involved in domestic terrorism. Since it may be months between seizure and forfeiture, the government can bankrupt the organization without due process. Individuals can be tracked and monitored by the government and subjected to harassment, intimidation, and imprisonment not only for terrorism but for conduct, such as "democratic opposition," perceived as intolerable by the government.[11]

Attorney General Ashcroft has jumped on the act with alacrity. In December 2001 he stated, "Within hours of passage of the USA PATRIOT Act, we made use of its provisions to begin enhanced information sharing between the law enforcement and intelligence communities. We have used the provisions allowing nationwide search warrants for e-mail and subpoenas for payment information. And we have used the act to place those who access the Internet through cable companies on the same footing as everyone else. . . . We have waged a deliberate campaign of arrest and detention to remove suspected terrorists who violate the law from our streets." Disdaining criticism of the act, he said, "Charges of 'kangaroo courts' and 'shredding the Constitution' give new meaning to the term, 'the fog of war.' "[12] By June 2003 Ashcroft declared, "Hundreds of suspected terrorists have been identified and tracked throughout the U.S., with more than eighteen thousand subpoenas and search warrants issued."[13] In January 2004 he denied that the PATRIOT Act had resulted in any violations of civil rights.

In many ways, the 342–page law has resurrected the COINTELPRO programs of the 1950s, 1960s, and 1970s, during which the FBI and the

CIA engaged in surveillance of domestic groups in a program to counter communism. Investigations in the U.S. Congress, presided over by Sen. Frank Church (D-ID) and Rep. Otis J. Pike (R-NY), led to legislation outlawing such surveillance and establishing special oversight committees over the intelligence community to prevent further abuses of power. In bringing back the domestic surveillance and police techniques of an earlier era, the PATRIOT Act has extended the war against terrorism abroad to a war against democracy at home. Rather than striking a balance between needed police techniques to counteract terrorism and the protection of civil rights, it tips the scale precariously in the former direction.

Unfortunately, U.S. history demonstrates that in times of tension, civil rights and the First Amendment often have been casualties. One thinks of the Alien and Sedition Acts passed as tension mounted with England in the first years of the Republic; Lincoln's suppression of habeas corpus and his monitoring of the press during the Civil War; the Espionage Act of 1917 and the Sedition Act of 1918 making criticism of the war effort illegal; the internment of 110,000 Japanese Americans during World War II; and the post–World War II McCarthy era, which capitalized on the fear of communism.

In this dubious tradition, we find the PATRIOT Act. It contains such a broad definition of "terrorism" that the legislation can be used against any domestic political protester, such as environmentalists and antiabortion activists. A bipartisan effort led by Sen. Ron Wyden (D-OR) and Rep. Lisa Murkowski (R-AL) would force the government to be more specific about the targets of wiretaps under the PATRIOT Act and would restrict the kind of information collected on Internet and e-mail use.

Along with PATRIOT Act provisions, public surveillance has increased in other areas. Studies have indicated that these systems are not effective in stopping either terrorism or petty crime, and that they can be abused to spot people engaged not in terrorism but in peaceful protest.

A provision of the November 2002 Homeland Security Act prohibits the recruitment of mail carriers and utility technicians, who are "well positioned to recognize unusual events," to be spies for the government. Called TIPS (Total Information and Prevention System), the program had conjured up images of the Soviet Union and Big Brother. Although TIPS was stopped by Congress, a similar practice is suggested in guidelines issued in May 2002 by Ashcroft to allow the FBI to infiltrate "any event that is open to the public," including public meetings, church services, and political conventions. These guidelines are still in effect.

The Pentagon designed a program called Total Information Awareness to give officials access to all possible government and commercial databases in order to provide advance warning of terrorist attacks. Congress denied funding in July 2003, and the program subsequently was renamed the Terrorism Information Program. Its director, John Poindexter, was the former Reagan-era national security advisor who received a suspended jail sentence for withholding information on Iran-contra from Congress. Concerned that the records of millions of American citizens would be subjected to government scrutiny, Congress enacted an amendment, offered by Sen. Ron Wyden (D-OR), which banned the use of funds to implement the surveillance program domestically against U.S. citizens without further consent from Congress. When the amendment expires, however, the program could be reinstated.

Poindexter was forced to resign from the government in August 2003 after his proposal for a terrorist futures-trading market, an online betting parlor, became public. The program rewarded investors who forecast terrorist attacks, assassinations, and coups. Even such neoconservatives in the administration as Paul Wolfowitz said they were mortified that the program's developers could be so politically tone deaf.[14]

A program for airline security, the Computer Assisted Passenger Pre-screening System II (CAPPS II), would assemble every passenger's travel history and living arrangement, plus other personal and demographic information. Data would be pulled together from a variety of sources, including criminal and commercial records. The system, attacked by the European Union, civil libertarians, and the Bush administration's own budget office, had still not been installed in January 2004.[15] Nevertheless, the program is busily creating a color code security system for all airline passengers.

Such programs depart in principle from Anglo-American law, which holds that police may conduct surveillance *only* when there is evidence of involvement in wrongdoing. Ashcroft's strategy—the accumulation of massive amounts of information on the entire population—is capable of infinite abuse.

These methods, moreover, are not effective. The government has already shown its inability to connect the information it has on terrorism.

Computers in the Immigration and Naturalization Service, the FBI, and the State Department are notoriously primitive. In this situation, as the American Civil Liberties Union pointed out, "You don't find a needle in a haystack by bringing in more hay."

Another program under discussion by the executive branch has been the establishment of a national ID card for all citizens. The ID card would combine a number of new technologies, such as biometrics and signaling chips with powerful databases, which would provide an instant record of people's lives and whereabouts. While initially designed as a counterterrorism tool, it is easily expandable to allow citizen surveillance for purposes that have nothing to do with terrorism. These programs use "Big Brother" techniques whose possible marginal value in the fight against terrorism may be far less important than their effect on our free society.[16]

Finally, the PATRIOT Act gave the CIA unprecedented access to grand jury information, which would appear to be a violation of the 1947 National Security Act, the CIA's charter, prohibiting any role for the agency in the field of law enforcement, including subpoena power. Actually, the White House and Senate Republicans wanted to authorize the CIA and the military to issue "national security letters," an administrative subpoena to compel Internet providers, libraries, and others to produce information about their users.[17] Senate Democrats and a small number of Republicans defeated the proposal only after Republican members of the Senate Select Intelligence Committee argued for the right of subpoena in secret session. Bush revived the concept of administrative subpoenas in a speech in September 2003.

Thus far, only one portion of the PATRIOT Act has been declared unconstitutional. In January 2004 a federal judge in California ruled that the ban on providing "expert advice or assistance" was too vague and in violation of the First and Fifth Amendments."[18]

PATRIOT ACT II

Even as the administration was preparing a preemptive strike on Iraq in early 2003, the Justice Department was drafting a new PATRIOT Act; there is considerable opposition to the act, led by Sens. Carl Levin (D-MI) and Patrick J. Leahy (D-VT). A copy, leaked in February 2003, proposed giving additional powers to the federal government and threatened more attrition of civil rights. The new act would:

- make it easier to initiate surveillance and wiretapping of U.S. citizens;
- shelter federal agents engaged in surveillance without court orders;
- loosen constraints on electronic eavesdropping;
- give the government access to credit reports without consent and without judicial process;
- allow the sampling and cataloging of genetic information without court order and without consent;
- terminate limits on police spying;
- authorize secret arrests in immigrant and other cases;
- limit the right of defense attorneys of American citizens to challenge the use of secret evidence in criminal cases; and
- strip even native-born American citizens of the rights of citizenship if they provide support to organizations designated as terrorist by the government, allowing them to be indefinitely imprisoned as undocumented aliens.

The new act, if adopted, would seriously undercut personal privacy, reduce government accountability, and erode the rights of all persons, citizens and noncitizens, to due process. It also would subject American citizens to having their citizenship arbitrarily removed.[19]

Fortunately, both congressional Democrats and Republicans are resisting passage of a second PATRIOT Act, and there have been a series of legal challenges of the more threatening provisions of the first PATRIOT Act. The American Civil Liberties Union sued in July 2003 over a provision that allows the government to secretly seize business records in terror investigations. The Center for Constitutional Rights, based in New York, filed papers in federal court in the same month to challenge the PATRIOT Act's infringement of free speech protections by outlawing "expert advice and assistance" to groups that the United States has labeled terrorist organizations.[20] One of the plaintiffs' attorneys stated, "In its rush to pass the PATRIOT Act just six weeks after the September 11 attacks, Congress overlooked one of our most fundamental rights: the right to express our political beliefs, even if they are controversial."

In the summer of 2003 Attorney General Ashcroft launched a charm offensive around the country to rally support for the PATRIOT Act, involving U.S. attorneys in a way that violates laws prohibiting members of the executive branch from engaging in grassroots lobbying. Fortunately, one member of Congress, Rep. John Conyers Jr. (D-MI), is looking into this matter and may put an end to such offensive barnstorming tours. In January 2004 Ashcroft renewed his efforts to have the PATRIOT Act continued.

DOMESTIC MILITARY COMMAND

With the establishment of the U.S. Northern Command (Northcom), the Pentagon has created a military command for the domestic United States to use armed forces to defend the country against a terrorist attack. The command was first proposed in a study called "Defending the U.S. Homeland," published by the Center for Strategic and International Studies in 1999, suggesting that the Department of Defense be responsible for domestic antiterrorism as well as "monitoring crossings of the U.S. border" and "protecting the perimeter of key cities." A key figure in the writing of this study was Lewis Libby, Vice President Cheney's chief of staff (see chapter 8).

Northcom maintains permanent liaison with the FBI, the CIA, the National Security Agency, and the Geospatial-Intelligence Agency. Members of Northcom gather domestic intelligence and exchange information with local and state police as well as U.S. intelligence agencies. Northcom also works closely with the Department of Homeland Security (see below).

Maj. Ted Wadsworth, a spokesman for the Pentagon, says, "The consistent DoD [Department of Defense] view has been that the president has sufficient legal authority to use the military in the United States when he determines that doing so is appropriate." Troops were used after 9/11 at airports and downtown intersections and flew combat air missions over major U.S. cities. They were used at the insistence of the George H. W. Bush White House during the Los Angeles riots in 1992 and extensively, in 2002, at the Winter Olympics, at the insistence of George W. Bush. We need a clear understanding of how and when such forces may be used, since their continued use could represent a dangerous extension of federal power.[21]

HOMELAND SECURITY DEPARTMENT

President Bush signed the Homeland Security bill into law on November 25, 2002, marking the largest reorganization of the federal government since the National Security Act in 1947. The new Department of Homeland Security (DHS), funded by the Senate on July 24, 2003, at $28.5 billion, combines the personnel of twenty-two federal agencies and innumerable state and local agencies and organizations. Headed by Tom Ridge, former governor of Pennsylvania, the DHS is designed to make "a concerted national effort to prevent terrorist attacks within the United States, reduce America's vulnerability to terrorism, and minimize the damage and recover from attacks that do occur." The DHS handles such issues as border, coastline, and air patrolling; shipping and airline screening; visas and immigration; protection of vulnerable facilities; financial disruption of terrorist groups; disaster programs; cyber or computer security; and public information. Its predecessor, the Office of Homeland Security, gained immediate recognition in March 2002 by its color coding of the danger of terrorist attack, a system which eventually seemed to do little but create alarm while providing no security.

The department is off to an extremely slow start, and experts do not believe that the DHS can ensure that the United States has strategic warning of another terrorist attack. The rest of the government perceives the department as a backwater; the FBI and the CIA have not been willing to send their best personnel to rotation assignments to the DHS, and the Pentagon has not been sending representatives to interagency meetings. President Bush was never enthusiastic about establishing the department and created his own Homeland Security Council that has been critical of Ridge's handing of the department. Paul C. Light, a scholar of government at New York University, has called the DHS a "very thin operation," with an unsophisticated hierarchy.[22]

The department has been plagued both by its inability to coordinate its many pieces and by its failure to create effective liaisons with state and local law enforcement organizations. Due to institutional resistance by the FBI and the CIA, it has failed to create a central repository of information for domestic security issues, which was one of the main purposes in establishing it. Lines of authority are unclear, and funding issues are unresolved. At this point, the DHS provides another layer of bureaucracy but does not address all the key aspects of domestic security.

Given the sheer numbers of immigrants and visitors, the extent of imported goods, and the miles of coastlines and borders, the job of the DHS is daunting, if not impossible. At present, the funding of the department seems inadequate. In June of 2003 a Council on Foreign Relations task force found that the United States is still underfunding homeland defense by $98.4 billion over five years, particularly for first-responders: police, fire, and ambulance personnel. The report, "Emergency Responders: Drastically Underfunded, Dangerously Unprepared," reads, "Although the American public is now better prepared in some respects to address aspects of the terrorist threat than it was two years ago, the United States remains dangerously ill-prepared to handle a catastrophic attack on American soil." The report identifies biological, chemical, and nuclear weapons as the gravest terrorist threats and indicates that unless drastic measures are taken, the next terrorist attack could be even more devastating than that of September 11.[23] The Immigration and Naturalization Service (INS) is particularly underfunded, given its huge responsibility.

The DHS was immediately politicized in the summer of 2003 when it was involved with the FBI in trying to find Texas Democratic representatives who had gone to Oklahoma to prevent an illegal legislative redistricting effort (they returned in September 2003). The effort itself was managed by House majority leader Tom DeLay (R-TX), who pressed the Justice Department and the DHS to intervene in the state matter. Fortunately, the inspector general of the Justice Department intervened and called attention to the questionable role played by DeLay's congressional office. There is no record that the DHS investigated the matter or took corrective action, and Secretary Ridge has refused to comment.

National security, in any event, can never be complete. As federal dollars are limited, we must determine how best to spend them. Are tens of billions better spent on outmoded Cold War weapons systems, on a missile defense system that does not work, on adventurous extensions of U.S. military might in the Middle East, or in securing our homeland? To this question, the present administration has provided no satisfactory response.[24] Unfortunately, we may never get serious answers from the DHS, which is protected from inquiries under the Freedom of Information Act, from compulsory Inspector General audits, and from protected whistle-blowers. As in the deployment of a national missile defense system, a vital aspect of U.S. policy has been protected from meaningful criticism.

In its handling of domestic security, the Bush administration appears to be mimicking the actions of the British in the 1970s when the British government was faced with terrible acts of violence in Northern Ireland, the so-called Troubles. Its response was draconian, involving "widespread detention; extended powers of arrest, search, and seizure; increased surveillance capabilities; and the creation of a special court to try terrorist suspects."[25] These measures proved counterproductive in Northern Ireland, and there is no guarantee that such measures will be effective in this country's fight against terrorism.

ROLLING BACK THE TWENTIETH CENTURY

The Bush administration has increased military and intelligence spending significantly and has cut or eliminated key aspects of domestic legislation, including federal health, housing, social security, and assistance to the poor. Moreover, it is turning many of these programs over to state governments that have become increasingly strapped for funds due to the tax measures and security policies of the administration.[26] The *Washington Post's* Jonathan Weisman noted, "Tax changes in Bush's 2004 budget would cost the Treasury $1.46 trillion over ten years, a number that dwarfs all the changes he is seeking in social spending."[27]

The message is clear. Responsibility for the relief of poverty, cure of diseases, provision of security in old age, and protection of our nation's children no longer belongs to the government; nor do the wealthy bear social responsibility in relation to their wealth as tax cuts are going almost entirely to benefit upper income groups. Households earning more than $1 million receive an average income increase of $93,500 from tax cuts; more than half of all U.S. households receive a tax cut of $100 or less in 2003; and 36 percent receive no tax relief whatsoever. In the minds of neoconservatives running the government, this policy rightly rewards those who have succeeded and disdains those who have not.

The use by the administration of the average tax cut across the whole population totally misrepresents the benefits. The Treasury Department reported that "91 million taxpayers will receive, on average, a tax cut of

$1,126." Actually, the average tax cut in 2003 for households in the middle of the income spectrum was only $256, according to the Urban Institute–Brookings Institution Tax Policy Center. Thus, the Treasury Department has been transformed into a public relations agency providing the best possible face for administration policies.[28] Princeton economist Paul Krugman noted, "From the beginning, the key to Mr. Bush's domestic vision has been massive tax cuts, which Republican ideologues see both as a reward to the well-heeled, and a key to starving the government of money that might be spent on programs like health care or housing. Conservatives once viewed deficits as the height of bad fiscal policy. Now, they embrace them. There is no danger that a government swimming in red ink will come up with new programs to protect the environment, to extend health care for the poor or provide affordable housing to the homeless."[29]

With majorities in both houses, the Republicans are confident of success and have in the president a true believer. A key figure in pushing this plan is Grover Norquist, president of Americans for Tax Reform, who remarked, "My goal is to cut government in half in twenty-five years, to get it down to the size where we can drown it in the bathtub." Each move by the government represents a clear advantage to a high-income special interest group, such as the pharmaceutical industry that will gain by federal subsidies for prescription drugs for the elderly but without limits on the prices. The government bails out airlines, insurance companies, and banks while introducing vouchers that will have the public paying for private schools.

Under President Bush the departments and agencies of the government are made to serve the administration and not the American people. Treasury Department reports are skewed to put the best possible face on administrative policies. In the wake of 9/11, the Bush administration had the Environmental Protection Agency cover up the fact that the air in New York City had reached unhealthy proportions, thus endangering the lives of American citizens who returned to their homes without adequate safety measures. The Bush administration also tried to use the Federal Communications Commission to consolidate the communications industry, but in this case Congress resisted.

"IT'S THE ECONOMY, STUPID"

Over 2.5 million jobs were lost in the first three years of the Bush administration, more than in any administration since Herbert Hoover's. Economic growth had been lowered to 2.4 percent in 2002 and less in 2003, and the deficit in 2003 is $375 billion and is projected for $477 billion in 2004, after years of surplus during the Clinton era. At 4.2 percent of the gross domestic product (GDP), the deficit is significantly higher than the deficits during the Great Depression, which averaged 3.5 percent. The national debt stands at $6.7 trillion, with an additional $5.2 trillion projected for the next ten years.

The president has blamed the wars in Afghanistan and Iraq and the recession for the deficit, ignoring the far greater impact of the tax cuts. Bush stated in April 2003 that "this nation has got a deficit because we have been through a war. . . . And we had an emergency and a recession, which affected the revenue growth of the U.S. Treasury." Congressional Budget Office data show, however, that tax cuts from 2001–2004 will cost nearly three times as much as the combined costs of the battles and occupation in Afghanistan and Iraq, homeland security, and other costs of the war against terrorism.[30]

While the administration has defended the deficits as "manageable," an aging population will increasingly require more services, particularly Social Security and Medicare. Instead of getting the nation's accounts in order, we are putting our future at risk as the country sinks into red ink. Senior analysts at Goldman Sachs, a major U.S. investment house, call the nation's long-term outlook "terrible, far worse than the official projections suggest."[31]

Most economists predict further loss of jobs and do not expect tax cuts for the wealthy to stimulate the economy. Hundreds of economists, including ten winners of the Nobel Prize, issued a statement opposing the Bush tax cuts as ineffective and not credible as stimulus measures. They stated, "Regardless of how one views the specifics of the Bush plan, there is wide agreement that its purpose is a permanent change in the tax structure and not the creation of jobs and growth in the near-term. . . . Passing these tax cuts will worsen the long-term budget outlook, adding to the nation's projected chronic deficits. This fiscal deterioration will reduce the capacity of the government to finance Social Security and Medicare benefits as well as investments in schools, health, infrastructure, and basic research. Moreover, the proposed tax cuts will generate further inequalities in after-tax income."[32] As the *New York Times* commented, "The Bush budget, with tax cuts, is hard to justify using any model of growth."[33]

Why is the president doing all this? "The president learned that the only way to really, really help the people at the bottom is to have a few years of really great growth," said Kevin A. Haassett, an economist at the American Enterprise Institute. However, with no such growth predicted and cuts to social programs, there is little likelihood that any but the wealthiest could benefit, and even their position will worsen if the economy founders. Most Americans believe in paying for homeland security and social security and for schools, health care, and basic infrastructure, not in creating greater income gaps in our society.

NOTES

1. President Bush's Military Order of November 13, 2001, authorized the use of military tribunals to try non-U.S. citizens who are or were members of al Qaeda who engaged in acts of international terrorism or who knowingly harbored such persons. The military order violates the 1949 Geneva Conventions relating to prisoners of war, which require they be tried in "the same courts according to the same procedure as in the case of members of the armed forces of the Detaining Power," and "shall have, in the same manner as the members of the armed forces of the Detaining Power, the right of appeal or petition from any sentence pronounced upon him." International agreements that the United States has signed also restrict military tribunals to immediate battlefield conditions, not, for example, to prosecute those financing terrorism or harboring terrorists.

2. See editorial, "The Trial of Zacarias Moussaoui," *New York Times*, July 28, 2003.

3. Amnesty International, "Report on U.S. Antiterrorism Law Alleges Violations of Civil Rights," *New York Times*, July 21, 2003. See also "USA: Watchdog Agency Finds Post 9/11 Detaineees Were Deprived of Rights," June 4, 2003.

4. New Jersey superior court judge Arthur D'Italia quoted the U.S. District Court for the District of Columbia in a ruling, "The requirement that arrest books be open to the public is to prevent any 'secret arrests,' a concept odious to a democratic society." *M o rrow* v. *District of Columbia*, 417 F.2d 728, 741–42 (DC Cir. 1969).

5. Anthony Dworkin, "U.S. Administration Defends Its Rules for Treatment of Afghan Captives," March 29, 2002, http://www.crimesofwar.org/news-captive.html.

6. Barbara Comstock, press release, Department of Justice, June 2, 2003. See also Office of the Inspector General, "The September 11 Detainees: A Review of the Treatment of Aliens Held on Immigration Charges in Connection with the Investigation of the September 11 Attacks," June 2003; Office of the Inspector General, "Report to Congress on Implementation of Section 1001 of the USA PATRIOT Act," July 17, 2003; and Stuart Gorin, "Justice Department Reviews Treatment of Alien Detainees," U.S. Department of State, International Information Programs, June 2, 2003.

7. While the government appears to have had no evidence linking the overwhelming majority of the detainees with terrorism, it charged two individuals, Zacarias Moussaoui (who was already in custody on September 11—see above) and Richard Reid, with terrrorist crimes out of the over twelve hundred arrested.

8. Dana Priest and Barton Gellman, "U.S. Decries Abuse but Defends Interrogations," *Washington Post*, December 26, 2002, p. A1. For a report on improvement at Guantanamo, see Pamela Falk, Gitmo Journal, CBSNews.com, July 17, 2003. See also John Mintz, "6 Could Be Facing Military Tribunals," *Washington Post*, July 4, 2003, p. A1.

9. Mark Bowden, "The Dark Art of Interrogation," *Atlantic Monthly* (October 2003): 56.

10. Neil A. Lewis and William Glaberson, "U.S. Courts Reject Detention Policy in 2 Terror Cases: Appellate Judges Rebuff Bush on Citizen and Afghan Captives," *New York Times*, December 18, 2003, p. A1.

11. See American Civil Liberties Union, "Interested Persons Memo on the Indefinite Detention without Charge of American Citizens as 'Enemy Combatants,'" September 13, 2002. For the use of the PATRIOT Act beyond crimes involving terrorism, see Eric Lichtbau, "U.S. Uses Terror Law to Pursue Crimes from Drugs to Swindling," *New York Times*, September 28, 2003, p. A1.

12. "The Attorney General's Statement," Online NewsHour: Attorney General Ashcroft on civil liberties, December 6, 2001.

13. Testimony of Attorney General John Ashcroft before the House Committee on the Judiciary, June 5, 2003.

14. Eric Schmitt, "Poindexter Will Be Quitting over Terrorism Betting Plan," *New York Times*, August 1, 2003, p. A11.

15. Ariana Eunjung Cha, "Pentagon Details New Surveillance System," *Washington Post*, May 21, 2003, p. A6.

16. See Jay Stanley and Barry Steinhardt, "Bigger Monster, Weaker Chains:

The Growth of an American Surveillance Society," American Civil Liberties Union, January 2003.

17. Eric Lichtbau and James Risen, "Broad Domestic Role Asked for CIA and the Pentagon," *New York Times*, May 2, 2003, p. A21.

18. "Federal Judge Rules Part of PATRIOT Act Unconstitutional," Associated Press, January 26, 2004.

19. A detailed section-by-section analysis is provided in a study by the American Civil Liberties Union memo of February 14, 2003.

20. Dan Eggan, "PATRIOT Act Faces New Challenge in Court," *Washington Post*, July 29, 2003.

21. A domestic role for federal troops in law enforcement, however, has been prohibited by the 1878 Posse Comitatus Act. See Robert Dreyfuss, "Bringing the War Home," *Nation*, May 26, 2003.

22. John Mintz, "Government's Hobbled Giant," *Washington Post*, September 7, 2003, p. 19.

23. John Mintz, "Study: First Responders Underfunded," *Washington Post*, June 29, 2003, p. A21. See also, "Council for a Livable World, "Homeland Defense Underfunded by $98.4 Billion," July 1, 2003.

24. In July 2003 Democratic candidate Sen. John Kerry stated, "Just as we did not have a viable plan for Iraq after the capture of Baghdad, today we still do not have a real plan and enough resources for preparedness against a terrorist attack." *New York Times*, July 17, 2003.

25. Laura K. Donohue, "The British Trade Rights for Security, Too," *Washington Post*, Outlook Sec., August 3, 2003, p. 1.

26. See William Greider, "Rolling Back the 20th Century," *Nation*, April 24, 2003.

27. Amy Goldstein and Jonathan Weissman, "Bush Seeks to Recast Federal Ties to the Poor," *Washington Post*, February 9, 2003, p. A1.

28. See Paul Krugman, "Everything Is Political," *New York Times*, August 5, 2003.

29. Paul Krugman, "The War at Home," *New York Times*, April 20, 2003.

30. The Center on Budget and Policy Priorities projects a deficit of $4.1 trillion over the coming decade if tax cuts are extended and other likely costs are incurred. With higher deficits will come higher interest payments, projected during the coming decade at $3.5 trillion. Richard Kogan, "The Causes and Significance of the New Deficit Figures," Center on Budget and Policy Priorities, July 15, 2003.

31. Goldman Sachs, "Budget Blues: Play It Again, Uncle Sam," press release, March 14, 2003.

32. See http://www.epinet.org/stml/woo3/statement_signed.pdf.

33. David E. Rosenbaum, "Bush's Next Test," *New York Times*, April 17, 2003, p. A22. See also the report of the Committee for Economic Development, "Exploding Deficits, Declining Growth: The Federal Budget and the Aging of America," March 2003.

PART THREE
FROM THE
WRONG TO
THE RIGHT PATH

CHAPTER TEN
WHERE IN THE WORLD IS WORLD IS BUSH TAKING US?

The terrorist attacks of September 11 and the U.S. invasion of Iraq in March 2003 have unleashed a cycle of international violence that seems to have no end. In many ways the apocalyptic vision of Osama bin Laden is being realized. Nearly 150,000 American forces are occupying an Islamic country and attracting Islamic fighters from far and wide to counter Western infidels. Islamic-inspired terrorist attacks have taken place in North Africa, the Middle East, the Persian Gulf, and South Asia, creating their own brand of chaos and raising additional questions about the role of bin Laden and the al Qaeda organization. Nearly all American forces were pulled out of Saudi Arabia in 2003, one of bin Laden's original goals when he began his reign of terror in the early 1990s.

The initial U.S. response to the September 2001 attacks was the October invasion of Afghanistan to overthrow the Taliban regime and rout the al Qaeda forces; this action was designed to protect the vital interests of the United States and, in the words of Secretary of State Colin Powell, the "civilized world." Instead, in three years, the Bush administration has undermined the foundations of American foreign policy, compromised the credibility of the White House, weakened the national security position of the United States, eroded civil liberties, and created greater chaos in the international arena.

There probably has never been an American president so willing to use military force as President Bush or a secretary of defense so influential and so enamored with the use of force as Secretary Rumsfeld. The president uses language that is redolent of a celluloid Clint Eastwood; "make my day" has become "bring 'em on." The White House manipulated the return of troops to the United States from the Persian Gulf in order to allow the president, who dodged service in the Vietnam War, to make a carrier landing in full combat gear.

Secretary Rumsfeld, for his part, is the first secretary of defense to dominate the national security process, the intelligence community, and even the administration itself with a mix of self-confidence, self-aggrandizement, and hubris. The diplomatic tradition of the United States and the American style in international negotiation have been largely European in origin, but Bush, Rumsfeld, and Cheney have gone out of their way to antagonize our most important European allies and to create significant political tension with the continent.[1] This book has demonstrated how the administration, ostensibly seeking to enhance U.S. security, has in fact recklessly increased our insecurity. Now we will examine the possibility that threats to American security interests will get far worse before they get better. It is often foolhardy to create worst-case scenarios in the international environment, but, in the wake of the Iraq War, some of these worst cases are becoming more probable.

PARADIGM LOST

Unlike his Democratic and Republican predecessors, including his father, President George H.W. Bush, the current President Bush approaches the global community with a posture of unilateralism and triumphalism. The Bush administration abruptly walked away from the Kyoto Protocol, the Anti-Ballistic Missile Treaty, and the Comprehensive Test Ban. Washington, declaring a worldwide and continuous war on terrorism, now has deployed more than 368,000 soldiers overseas in 120 countries, with more than half of the army's combat-ready forces tied down in Iraq for the foreseeable future. These are the characteristics of a military empire.

American forces are making decisions on the ground in some of the most unstable areas of the world. They are engaged against the Abu Sayyaf guerrillas in the Philippines, where the United States has been holding joint counterterrorism exercises annually since 1999. Colombia is now the third largest recipient of U.S. military aid, and, as part of Plan Colombia, the United States is equipping and training counterdrug forces there and is in effect intervening in a civil war on behalf of the government although much of the drug traffic is conducted by paramilitary units with strong government ties. Small contingents of U.S. forces are also deployed to such unstable and unpredictable places as Tajikistan, Georgia, and Macedonia; U.S. combat troops have never left Bosnia and Herzegovina following the breakup of Yugoslavia. And Secretary of Defense Rumsfeld is talking about more U.S. forces, greater mobilization of the National Guard and army reserves, and more forward support bases and facilities, with the defense budget projected to be more than $500 billion by 2008. More defense spending is becoming classified, with the so-called black budget reaching nearly $25 billion for 2004, the highest secret budget since the defense buildup of the Reagan administration in the 1980s.[2] Traditionally, increases in the "black budget" have meant increases in CIA covert action

WORST-CASE SCENARIOS

The United States and U.S. interests have become increasingly vulnerable in the wake of the invasion of Iraq, but there has been no debate of the public policy process for national security. In 2001 Congress convened the bipartisan *United States Commission on National Security Strategy/21st Century* that concluded that the national security structure in the United States was "dysfunctional" and badly in need of overhaul. When the United States faced a similar crisis after World War II, President Truman authorized the National Security Act that addressed problems confronting the nation. The Bush administration, facing a similar crisis, has worsened the dangerous scenarios that it confronts. Although the following scenarios are labeled as "worst case," the rapid deterioration of the international scene suggests that each worst case is rapidly becoming more likely.

The Iraqi and Afghan Quagmires

Iraq is not yet President Bush's Vietnam, but evidence is accumulating that the military "victories" in Afghanistan and Iraq are becoming political "failures," increasingly costly in terms of lives and treasure. Foreign terrorists could not operate freely in Iraq before the U.S. and British invasion, but they are free to do so now, and foreign elements are entering the country from Syria, Yemen, Sudan, Afghanistan, and Pakistan. America may eventually be "sucked into a quagmire" similar to that in Vietnam forty years ago. American forces will be unable to leave either Afghanistan or Iraq in the near term; over-reliance on the use of force will further weaken America's national security position.

The United States placed Hamid Karzai in power in Kabul, but he has no influence outside of Afghanistan's capital, and warlords and thugs control much of the country. Elements of the Taliban are returning to old haunts, and there was never any reason to believe that al Qaeda members, perhaps even Osama bin Laden himself, ever left the country. In view of the porous nature of the Durand Line separating Afghanistan and Pakistan (there is no official border), it is difficult to prevent Taliban and al Qaeda elements from going back and forth between the two countries. The CIA and U.S. Army special forces continue to bribe warlord leaders to foster stability, but these gang leaders continue to commit crimes in wholesale fashion; the enhanced power of the warlords has weakened the central government.

American forces are being killed and wounded almost daily as a guerrilla presence has formed in Iraq, and the large American presence provides a target-rich environment for former Ba'athist Party elements and assorted Sunni supporters of Saddam Hussein. During a three-week period in the summer of 2003, anti-U.S. forces bombed the Jordanian Embassy and UN headquarters in Baghdad, the most important Shiite religious site in Najaf, and oil and water pipelines. These forces have the ability to strike anywhere in the country. As a result, the Bush administration, which had declared in the spring of 2003 that the Pentagon would soon be discussing withdrawal and rotation plans, instead had to bolster U.S. forces and activate National Guard and reserve units to expand the U.S. presence.[3]

Before the war, the State Department, the Central Intelligence Agency, and the Agency for International Development had warned the Pentagon that it needed to seek guidance from other departments of the U.S. government as well as international expertise on rebuilding the Iraqi infrastucture. After almost a year, with little such assistance, the reconstruction remains controversial and largely unsuccessful.

The reliance of Vice President Cheney and Secretary of Defense Rumsfeld on Iraqi National Congress leader Ahmed Chalabi, whom the Pentagon secretly airlifted into southern Iraq several weeks after the war began, clearly backfired, just as the State Department and the intelligence community had warned. Wolfowitz antagonized U.S. specialists on Iraq even before the war ended when he snubbed the experts in the State Department's Bureau of Near Eastern Affairs and appointed an inexperienced political appointee and daughter of the vice president, Elizabeth Cheney, to advise the U.S. transition team in Baghdad. Ms. Cheney turned around and appointed a political colleague from the International Republican Institute to be her deputy. Again, instead of fleshing out the staff with genuine experts, Cheney turned to the Pentagon's Office of Special Plans, a political creation of the secretary of defense, and to the Pentagon's Middle East and South Asia policy office.

With U.S. forces unable to enforce security and economic reconstruction unacceptably slow, the administration began making overtures to the formerly spurned international community, particularly the United Nations, to play a larger role and pay part of the price tag. The international community had opposed providing forces and assistance for these postwar tasks until the United States agreed to share power. Such power sharing would require joint decision making on the use of police forces, economic development and contracting, as well as recognition that the United Nations was acting in its own name and not as an agent of the United States. With security uncertain, the United Nations has been wary of returning to Iraq, let alone of assuming responsibility for Iraqi sovereignty.

Violence and Civil War in Iraq

Even if the United States and Britain have success in stabilizing the Iraqi situation, such stability might not survive the eventual withdrawal of coalition forces. Eventually Iraq might return to the Iraqis and the likelihood of ethnic and religious violence is not a worst-case scenario but a likely one.

The guerrilla efforts of former Ba'athist leaders, including forces loyal to Saddam Hussein, are exacerbating the internecine struggles in Iraq between Sunnis and Shiites in central Iraq and between Kurds and Turkmen in the north. An added element of tension will develop if such outside powers as Turkey or Iran decide to exploit Iraqi vulnerability. The introduction of additional foreign forces and terrorist elements presents a recipe for disaster. The United States is likely to fare no better in Iraq than did the British after World War I when foreign occupation failed to make reforms that were durable, and continued violence was the general result. The CIA station in Baghdad reported in January 2004 that Iraq may be on a path to civil war, which contradicts the upbeat assessments of the Bush administration.

Dangers of Regime Change

> The Bush administration has apparently learned nothing from this nation's egregious experiences with "regime change" that had disastrous consequences for U.S. national interests and international politics during the worst days of the Cold War.

The U.S.-UK collaboration in Iran in 1953 overthrew the popularly elected regime of Muhammad Mossadegh and replaced him with a dictator, the shah of Iran, who paved the way for Ayatollah Khomeini's fundamentalist revolution in 1979. The United States assisted the bloody coup d'état against South Vietnamese leader Ngo Dinh Diem, setting in motion a series of events that led to more than fifty thousand U.S. deaths in Vietnam and an embarrassing withdrawal in 1975. The White House and the CIA conspired against the regime of the popularly elected Chilean president, Salvador Allende, which led to the death of Allende and the ugly and brutal rule of dictator Augusto Pinochet. With the exception of a totally vanquished Germany and Japan after World War II, the United States has never successfully conducted an exercise in regime change. Nevertheless, members of the Bush administration are discussing the need for U.S.-imposed regime changes in Iran, North Korea, and Syria, despite this long history of failure.

Before the situation in Iraq worsened, the administration was considering regime change in Iran. Pentagon neoconservatives who report directly to Undersecretary of Defense Feith held secret meetings with Manucher Ghorbanifar, the Iranian middleman in Iran-contra.[4] The White House contends that the meetings were not authorized, but the fact that Feith reports directly to Secretary of Defense Rumsfeld points to at least preliminary high-level discussions of regime change in Iran. The individuals who met with Ghorbanifar are also involved in regular discussions with Ahmed Chalabi. One of these individuals was Harold Rhode, a protégé of Michael Ledeen, the neoconservative who introduced Ghorbanifar to National Security Council aide Oliver North at the start of the Iran-contra affair. Ledeen once described Ghorbanifar as "one of the most honest, educated, honorable men I have ever known."[5] But the CIA revealed that Ghorbanifar had failed several polygraph tests during Iran-contra and that it had warned CIA officers not to deal with him, asserting that he "should be regarded as an intelligence fabricator and nuisance."

The Problem of Proliferation

U.S. discussion of "regime change" in Iran and North Korea has led directly to a quicker pace for the nuclear programs in both countries, where leaders in Tehran and Pyongyang believe there is need for a deterrent against another U.S. preemptive action. International inspectors in Iran have found traces of highly enriched uranium at the Natanz uranium enrichment plant, which points to progress in developing a nuclear warhead for the Shahab-3 missile that can carry a 2,200-pound payload as far as 1,500 kilometers.[6] North Korean diplomats told their U.S. counterparts at six-party talks in Beijing in August 2003 that Pyongyang was about to test a nuclear weapon.[7]

The environmental sample at Natanz points to a serious violation of the Nonproliferation Treaty that includes Iran as a member. Iran has admitted that it received substantial foreign assistance in building Natanz, and the international community strongly believes that Pakistan once again is the culprit.[8] In addition to the enriched uranium facility, Iran has been developing a separate reactor that can be used in the production of plutonium.

The strategic situation is complicated by the fact that both Iran and

North Korea receive secret assistance from Pakistan on *nuclear technology*, and Pakistan receives *missile technology* from North Korea that it probably shares with Iran. The Bush administration has proclaimed that it would not "tolerate" nuclear weapons in Iran, as in North Korea, and Undersecretary Bolton told the BBC in the summer of 2003 that "all options are on the table."[9] National Security Advisor Rice, who is a major supporter of the Bush administration's doctrine of preemption, has used threatening language regarding both Iran and North Korea. Unlike North Korea, there has been no discussion of using economic strangulation against Iran, which would be counterproductive in view of Iran's energy independence and its growing economic ties to many European states and Russia.

In contrast to North Korea, Iran has been conducting its policies methodically and incrementally and does not appear to be bluffing. Eventually, the Bush administration will have to devise a coherent policy for Iran. Once again, however, the mindset of the neoconservatives is on the application of coercive pressure and perhaps even force rather than diplomacy and multilateral pressure that require patience and have been effective in the past.

As for North Korea, Kim Jong-Il presumably believes that his country's possession of a nuclear weapon will eventually convince the United States to pursue direct talks and a diplomatic solution. Kim Jong-Il and his generation remember that North Korea fought the United States to a standstill in the Korean War in the early 1950s. Indeed, some believe that Pyongyang won the war, and even many South Koreans respect North Korean tenacity in facing up to the United States. In any event, North Korean leaders do not appear to fear U.S. pressure tactics as the rest of world warily watches the continuation of this dangerous minuet. Officials in China, Japan, Russia, and South Korea share a worry over North Korea's incremental moves toward the production of fissile materials for nuclear weapons, and they are trying to move both Pyongyang and Washington to the negotiating table. It is not yet clear which capital will prove more intransigent. Thus far the United States has refused to make any concessions unless North Korea first destroys its nuclear facilities and allows full inspection.

Now that Pyongyang has announced that it has produced enough plutonium to make six to eight nuclear bombs and plans to test its first nuclear weapon, the international community hopes that the Bush administration will accept a diplomatic approach to the North Korean problem.[10] The United States could pursue negotiations with North Korea to freeze plutonium production and introduce confidence-building measures, or it could continue to posture and fulminate. In that case, we would soon learn that North Korea had tested a nuclear weapon and had even begun deployment of missiles with nuclear warheads that could reach Japan or South Korea, as well as parts of Alaska and Hawaii.

If North Korea genuinely believes that the Bush administration is prepared to use preemptive force against Pyongyang, there will be no reason for it to stop development of nuclear weapons, the only possible deterrent to a U.S. attack. Thus the U.S. strategy of confrontation and unilateral pressure may be encouraging the proliferation of nuclear weapons on the Korean Peninsula.

The Threat of War with North Korea and Iran

The neoconservatives seem to welcome the idea of using military force against North Korea; as former secretary of defense William Perry warns, however, "Military action . . . could result in a conflict comparable to the first Korean War, with casualties that would shock the world." South Korea would take the worst losses with the possible devastation of the capital of Seoul from conventional artillery. There could be more than one million casualties and fatalities in such a confrontation.

Any introduction of nuclear weapons on the Korean peninsula would worsen the geopolitical situation, creating a worst-case situation. The acquisition of nuclear weapons in North Korea would institute debates in Japan and Taiwan that could lead to nuclear programs there; a Chinese decision to bolster its offensive and defense forces; and a South Korean decision to rely less on an American deterrent and to seek its own nuclear capability. The United States has threatened to interdict North Korean ships to search for WMD, and North Korea has stated that such tactics would be considered acts of war.

Many neoconservatives consider Iran the major source of chaos in the Middle East and the Persian Gulf and believe that "regime change" in Tehran is an essential prerequisite to successfully completing the peace process in the Middle East. These officials seem to believe that the prewar

Iraqi situation serves as a template for justifying war against Iran; they are again charging that Iran has both weapons of mass destruction and close links with terrorist organizations, including al Qaeda. The Iranian situation is further complicated by the lack of diplomatic relations between the United States and Iran, the mutual suspicions between the two sides, and U.S. determination to correct the strategic setback that occurred when the shah was overthrown by the ayatollahs.

Again, the worst-case scenario is not improbable, and unsatisfied U.S. demands to Tehran to turn over al Qaeda officials finding sanctuary in Iran could be used by the Bush administration as a pretext for war.

War with Syria and the Road Map

Although the Bush administration has a full docket of troubles in the post-Iraq period, there are forces within the administration that favor a fight with Syria as well. The repercussions of such a policy would seriously complicate U.S. diplomatic efforts toward Israel and the Palestinian Authority.

In July 2003, at the very time that American soldiers were being killed in Iraq and evidence was mounting of energized nuclear production programs in North Korea and Iran, Undersecretary of State Bolton scheduled a hard-line briefing for the House International Affairs Committee intending to throw down a gauntlet to Syria. The United States had become increasingly frustrated with reports of Iraqis fleeing U.S. forces to enter Syria, foreign fighters entering Iraq from Syria to oppose U.S. forces, and the reported transiting of military equipment across the Syrian-Iranian border in both directions.[11] U.S. officials were even charging that the United States could not find WMD in Iraq because Saddam Hussein had moved these weapons and materials to Syria; this was most likely disinformation that had originated in Israel, however. The neoconservative view was that Syrian actions were complicating the U.S. mission in Iraq. Bolton planned to tell the congressional committee that Syrian chemical and biological weapons programs were threatening the stability of the entire region, thus endangering the chances for the success of the so-called road map between Israel and the Palestinian Authority.

As a result of Washington's pressure tactics, Syria, which had cooperated with the United States against al Qaeda following 9/11 and had even cosponsored a resolution in the UN Security Council to ban WMD in the Middle East, suddenly took a strong stand against allowing UN inspectors in Syria to search for WMD. Thus, there is unfinished diplomatic business between the United States and Syria, but Bolton's charges were counterproductive, putting Syria in a defensive and less cooperative position. The United States also has unfairly labeled Syria a sponsor of terrorism; in the past, Washington could cite the infamous Bekaa Valley in Lebanon as a Syrian-operated terrorist area prior to the Israeli withdrawal from southern Lebanon, but this is no longer true.

Only several days before Bolton's testimony, which would have turned up the heat in the already torrid Middle East, the CIA and other intelligence agencies blocked the testimony, and the hearing was postponed. This dispute between the intelligence agencies and the Bush administration was not unlike the dispute regarding Iraqi weapons of mass destruction. The embarrassment of fabricated intelligence from Niger presumably emboldened the intelligence community to challenge Bolton's testimony with a thirty-five-page memorandum detailing the errors in Bolton's statement.[12] The weakened credibility of the entire Bush administration for its handling of the case for war against Iraq meant that the president could not afford another contretemps before Congress.

Bolton, Abrams, and Feith, who are leading the pressure campaign against Damascus, may simply not understand that complicating relations with Syria would compromise the road map toward Israel and the Palestinian Authority. It is more likely, however, that they have adopted this policy in an effort to derail the "road map" that points to the creation of an independent Palestinian state, which many analysts view as the most important contribution to a policy of ending terrorism in the Middle East.

The provocative nature of the hard-line rhetoric against Syria in the wake of the war with Iraq led Secretary Powell to state that the United States had no "war plans" for regime change in Syria.[13] Conversely, whenever Powell or others within the administration have recommended or taken a diplomatic tack for dealing with the Arab-Israeli imbroglio, the neoconservatives close to Cheney and Rumsfeld have moved to undercut the policy. On several occasions neoconservatives blocked Secretary Powell's plans to travel to Syria to hold talks with President Assad.

Once again, the strength of the neoconservatives in the Bush administration presents the possibility of a worst-case scenario, one that involves war between the United States and Syria. The most vituperative of the neoconservatives roundly regret that Syria was not placed in the "axis of evil" and have long considered the regime in Damascus as ripe for "regime change." As long as U.S. forces remain in Iraq in such large numbers, there will always be the risk of a confrontation between these forces and Syria. Any deterioration of relations between the two countries would complicate the geopolitical situation in the region, including the national security position of Israel; would make the United States even more unwelcome in the Arab world than it already is; and would create yet another motivation for Islamic terrorists.

If the United States were to use military force against Syria, the Israelis would opportunistically move against Yasir Arafat in Ramallah, expelling him from the West Bank once and for all and annihilating both political and spiritual members of Hamas, which would lead to more civilian casualties. A Likud government headed by Sharon or Netanyahu might take these brutal steps in any event. The U.S. use of force in the Middle East provides Israel with the pretext to take additional military action.

Other Trouble Spots

In addition to the most prominent worst-case scenarios in Iran, North Korea, Pakistan, and Syria, there is the risk of greater chaos involving the internal situations in Colombia and Indonesia, the instability in the Caucasus and Central Asia, the lethal tensions between India and Pakistan, and the possibility of Islamic fundamentalist challenges to U.S. clients such as Egypt, Jordan, or Saudi Arabia.

Colombia's new president, Alvaro Uribe, is confronting a protracted internal war and moving to assert national political authority.[14] But no government in Colombia has been able to govern and control national territory for the past decade, and an increase in violence greeted the Uribe government, which declared a limited state of emergency and increased taxes to pay for larger allocations for defense. Any worsening of the internal conflict that involves illegal armies, paramilitary forces, and narcotics traffickers will have dangerous consequences for the United States throughout South America, especially in the Andean region where criminal and terrorist networks have deep roots.

In Indonesia human rights activists are terrorized on a regular basis, and peace negotiators are often arrested and sent to jail. It is conceivable that in several years U.S. troops also will be sent to Indonesia, where a separatist struggle has been waged for decades. A parallel case is in the Philippines where U.S. troops are working with the Filipino army in pursuit of terrorists.

In the Caucasus and Central Asia oil and natural gas have attracted a great deal of U.S. attention, and the need for a U.S. presence in the region has increased. The United States is already overcommitted in these fractious regions, but the Bush administration once again has used the war on terrorism to establish a military presence and create military facilities. The leaders of the mostly Muslim states in the Caucasus and Central Asia are antidemocratic strongmen, probably the same individuals who would have held power even if the Soviet Union had not disintegrated. At the very least, the increased U.S. presence in these regions will create unneeded problems with Russia, China, and Iran, which have their own interests there and are concerned about the emergence of the United States as the preeminent power in the region.

A Nuclear Exchange between India and Pakistan

Finally, the greatest risk of a nuclear exchange is in South Asia, where India and Pakistan, nonmembers of the Nonproliferation Treaty, have nuclear weapons and lack any strategic dialogue.

As long as Kashmir remains unsolved, there is always the possibility of a flash point developing between India and Pakistan. The United States has not had a strategic policy toward India for decades and has ignored Pakistan's instability and covert nuclear activities. It may seem paradoxical to offer the Middle East as a model for negotiation in South Asia, but the step-by-step process and Camp David summitry that the United States began in the 1970s could provide an example for innovative and tenacious U.S. brokering between the two long-term antagonists.

The End to Counterproliferation

> The hard-line unilateral tactics that the Bush administration is pursuing in Iraq, its use of preemptive force, and its failure to rule out the use of nuclear weapons against nonnuclear states have complicated the bipartisan counterproliferation strategy of the past three decades. These tactics have almost certainly created an international environment that encourages proliferation of weapons of mass destruction. For the first time in decades, the number of nuclear weapons is likely to increase, which marks a defeat for long-standing U.S. goals. The Bush administration's hostility to arms control and disarmament measures has reversed the previous Democratic and Republican commitment to build on the success of the NPT. By its rhetoric and its policies, the administration is contributing to instability in the world and to greater threats to U.S. security.

The Bush administration has encouraged greater nuclear proliferation in third world countries because of its own provocative policies, particularly the decision to pursue new nuclear weapons. Secretary of Energy Spencer Abraham has called for a major investment in "low-yield weapons" and new "weapons concepts" that will ultimately produce new mushroom clouds and compromise the counterproliferation strategy of the international community.[15]

Abraham has been leading the way toward relaxing or ending the ban on the research and development of low-yield nuclear weapons or so-called mini-nukes and powerful bunker busters that could lead to a resumption of underground nuclear testing. The use of bunker busters is particularly threatening because they could cause the venting of chemical and biological agents into the atmosphere; this would replicate the venting that occurred in Iraq in Desert Storm in 1991 when the U.S. Air Force bombed a strategic weapons depot in Khamasiyah. The use of bunker busters against such sites, with the venting of lethal agents, would prevent nuclear inspectors from examining controversial facilities.

In addition to returning to measures that were adopted or considered during the worst days of the Cold War, Abraham has made other decisions that have worsened the counterproliferation picture. In terminating the Nuclear Cities Initiative with Russia, he ended a program that had been designed to shrink nuclear weapons facilities in the so-called secret cities of the former Soviet Union where weapons of mass destruction were tested and produced and to find jobs for Russian nuclear scientists outside the weapons industry. This has renewed fears of a "brain drain" of these scientists, attracted to high-paying jobs in third world states pursuing nuclear weapons programs. Abraham also ended an important agreement to eliminate thirty-four metric tons of weapons-grade Russian plutonium. If the Russians and Chinese decide to match U.S. efforts in the field of low-yield nuclear weapons, there could be another nuclear arms race only a decade after the collapse of the Soviet Union held so much hope for constraints and limits on nuclear weapons.

AN APOCALYPTIC VISION

In Joseph Conrad's novel *The Secret Agent*, there is a minor character, an anarchist called the professor, whom no one dares to touch because he has wired himself to a powerful bomb. The novel ends with a view of the mad professor walking like a "pest in the street full of men." This grotesque vision, familiar to many in Colombia, Iraq, Israel, and Lebanon, is now a clear and present danger to Americans. This vision brings home the vulnerability of American interests around the world and even at home. The United States is overextended in the Middle East and the Persian Gulf and has unwisely deployed forces in former Soviet republics in Central Asia and the Caucasus, where chaos and discontinuity dominate the landscape.

In the past several years, the position of the United States in the international community has plummeted to an unusual place. Foreign countries continue to emulate American goals regarding democratization and free markets but abhor American political and military practices around the world. Instead of trying to prevent conflict, the United States has made major efforts to increase its own military power in order to dominate the international community. The United States is now perceived as too willing to use overwhelming lethal force and far too unwilling to seek the advice and counsel of others. Foreign representatives at the United Nations question virtually every position taken by U.S. representatives on a wide variety of international issues; they are particularly vexed by U.S. unwillingness to contribute to environmental and security problems the world over. It would be possible for moderate political forces to reverse these aspects of U.S. policy and diplomacy in a relatively short period of time, perhaps avoiding some of these worst-case scenarios. It is difficult to imagine, however, that the heavy-handed neoconservative ideologues of the Bush administration will reverse course and seek to find common cause on controversial international issues.

Since January 2001 we have witnessed the Bush administration's disdain for multilateral diplomacy, a breakdown of the international arms control systems, a militarization of national security policy, and an increased reliance on secrecy. At the same time, there has not been a genuine debate of such controversial aspects of U.S. policy as the expansion of NATO, the withdrawal from the ABM Treaty, and the deployment of an unworkable national missile defense. The Bush administration has eroded the international sympathy that developed for the United States in the wake of the 9/11 attacks, compromised the international cooperation needed to fight terrorism, given terrorists new sanctuaries and recruitment tools, and threatened the dismantlement of the international system. Having diagnosed and described the disease, the next chapter will discuss what is to be done.

NOTES

1. See Robert H. Ferrell, *American Diplomacy: A History* (New York: W. W. Norton, 1969).

2. Dan Morgan, "Classified Spending on the Rise," *Washington Post*, August 26, 2003, p. 22.

3. Vernon Loeb, "Pentagon Unveils Plan to Bolster Forces in Iraq," *Washington Post*, July 24, 2003, p. A8.

4. Knut Royce and Timothy M. Phelps, "Secret Talks with Iranian Arms Dealer," *Long Island Newsday*, August 8, 2003, p. 1.

5. Ibid.

6. Felicity Barringer, "Traces of Enriched Uranium Are Reportedly Found in Iran," *New York Times*, August 27, 2003, p. 1.

7. Peter Slevin and John Pomfret, "N. Korea Threatens Nuclear Arms Test," *Washington Post*, August 29, 2003, p. 1.

8. Joby Warrick, "Iran Admits Foreign Help on Nuclear Facility, *Washington Post*, August 27, 2003, p. 17.

9. David E. Sanger, "Two Nuclear Weapons Challenges, Two Different Strategies," *New York Times*, June 21, 2003, p. 9

10. David E. Sanger, "North Korea Says It Has Made Fuel for Atom Bombs," *New York Times*, July 15, 2003, p. 1.

11. Martha Kessler, "Avoid the Road to Damascus," *Los Angeles Times*, April 18, 2003, p. 18.

12. Douglas Jehl, "New Warning Was Put Off on Weapons Syria Plans," *New York Times*, July 18, 2003, p. 11. In 2002 Bolton pulled a similar maneuver, falsely charging that Cuba had a biological weapons program.

13. Nicholas Blanford, "Syria Yields—a Bit—to Pressure," *Christian Science Monitor*, April 18, 2003, p. 5.

14. See John A. Cope, "Colombia's War: Toward a New Strategy," Institute for National Strategic Studies, National Defense University, October 2002.

15. Spencer Abraham, "Facing Nuclear Reality," *Washington Post*, July 21, 2003, p. 21.

CHAPTER ELEVEN
ROAD MAP
TO THE FUTURE

WHAT IS TO BE DONE?

At this precarious juncture in American history, America needs more humility than hubris in the applications of American military power, and the recognition that our interests are best served through alliances and consensus.

— Sen. Chuck Hagel (R-NE), January 24, 2003

The rising number of fatalities and casualities among American forces in Iraq as well as the deteriorating security position there led the Bush administration to take more pragmatic steps in the summer of 2003. Former ambassador to India Robert D. Blackwill, who served in the National Security Council for George H. W. Bush, was named a deputy assistant to George W. Bush and a coordinator for strategic planning of policy under National Security Advisor Condoleezza Rice. This unheralded step indicated that Rice had failed to provide either strategic direction or a framework to the Bush foreign policy and that some rethinking of policy was essential.[1] Rice issued a memorandum in November 2003 to place control for all postwar policy in Iraq in the hands of the National

Security Council and to limit the role of Secretary Rumsfeld and the Pentagon. The administration also indicated that Undersecretary of State Bolton, who had already traveled to Asia for talks with North Korea, would not take part in the Beijing talks that were about to begin. The promotion of Blackwill and the demotion of Bolton, the leading neoconservative in the State Department, reflect signs of self-criticism within the administration and beg questions about the proper direction for U.S. foreign policy and the specific steps that need to be taken.

Secretary of Defense Rumsfeld conceded that change was in order. In mid-August he quietly closed down the Office of Special Plans with no fanfare, in fact no announcement whatsoever. The office was the major villain in the campaign to go to war against Iraq, creating specious intelligence information out of whole cloth and dropping the ball on the need for transition arrangements in the postwar period. The personnel who staffed the office remained at the Pentagon, however, so there is no guarantee that attempts to politicize intelligence will not continue. But there is at least some recognition on the part of the secretary of defense that the small group was becoming an embarrassment to the Bush administration. Rumsfeld has become a less visible spokesperson for Iraqi policy and has turned over the job of interrogating Saddam Hussein to the CIA.

There are other indications that the bureaucracies within the foreign policy community are beginning to assert themselves and take positions at odds with the neoconservatives in control of the National Security Council and the Pentagon. Deputy Secretary of State Richard Armitage, for example, told a press conference in August 2003 that the United States would consider a new UN resolution to place U.S. forces in Iraq under UN authority. Armitage and Secretary of State Powell had to push aside Vice President Cheney and Secretary of Defense Rumsfeld, the toughest unilateralists in the Bush administration, in order to make a case for a major role for the United Nations in Iraq. However, even in early 2004, the administration was still hedging on offering a significant role to the United Nations. Following Armitage's remarks, Paul Bremer, who oversees the reconstruction of Iraq, told the editorial board of the *Washington Post* in early September that it will cost "several tens of billions" to rebuild Iraq. In a much-needed attempt to level with the American people, the president announced the following week on national television that he would be requesting nearly $90 billion for the military occupation and the reconstruction in Afghanistan and Iraq.

In addition to signaling support for six-power talks to end all nuclear programs in North Korea, the Bush administration has stepped back to allow the Europeans to take the lead in limiting the nuclear programs in Iran and has stopped referring to Iran as part of the "axis of evil." Washington also seems to realize that the major assistance for Iran's nuclear program does not come from Russia, but from North Korea and Pakistan, and that international cooperation is necessary to apply an effective counterproliferation strategy.

These events suggest that the neoconservatives are being confronted by the facts of their policy failures. It is not clear to what extent these events will weaken their strong grip on the foreign policy machinery of the Bush administration and whether there will be significant changes, if only to prepare the president for his reelection campaign. Nor is it clear that President Bush has the sophisticated understanding of international developments necessary to develop and guide a coherent strategic framework.

What is clear is that this country needs to move in a very different direction. This chapter marks an attempt to create a strategic road map for broader U.S. interests that would improve the U.S. standing in the international community and, more important, strengthen U.S. national security policy.

FOREIGN POLICY

As we have seen, U.S. foreign policy under the stewardship of Bush, Cheney, Powell, and Rumsfeld has been based on unilateralism and militarism. The United States has clearly overreached in invading and occupying Iraq, which explains the criticism of the decision to go to war from such leading retired generals as Brent Scowcroft, Norman Schwarzkopf, John Shalikashvili, and Anthony Zinni.

The United States, the world's only superpower, already has too many "boots on the ground." The condition of continuous, worldwide war has created an operational tempo that the United States cannot afford and the Pentagon cannot endure. The U.S. doctrine of preemptive war creates a dangerous precedent for other nations, perhaps justifying an Indian attack against Pakistan or an Israeli attack against Syria.

The major international problems that we face today, including terrorism and crime, AIDS, environmental pollution, and currency crises, cannot be addressed unilaterally nor can they be resolved by the use of force. These problems require multilateral involvements and solutions.

In Both Afghanistan and Iraq, the Efforts of Nation-Building and Peacekeeping Must Be Internationalized as Quickly as Possible

While some critics of the wars in Afghanistan and Iraq have called for immediate American withdrawal, we believe that would be a mistake. To leave now would invite chaos, including bloody confrontations between Sunni and Shiite forces in Iraq; such a power vacuum would create more breeding grounds for terrorism in both Iraq and Afghanistan.

But this is a job that the United States cannot do alone. We have tied up more than half of this country's ground forces in Afghanistan and Iraq, and we are spending at least $5 billion a month in the process. Neither the U.S. government nor the American public is prepared for the burdens of empire; U.S. military forces are overextended and in no position to deal with emergencies we may face in the future, such as the possibility of a genuine crisis on the Korean peninsula. If we are to have the military units and resources to respond to other crises, we must participate with other nations in peacekeeping, not attempt these tasks alone.

These efforts must be under civilian, not military control. The Pentagon is not equipped to run a transition process, particularly those that include nation-building on a grand scale.

Under military and still largely unilateral occupations, Afghanistan and Iraq are rapidly becoming the black holes of nation-building. The United States has made modest moves in each country, introducing a NATO element in Afghanistan and a Polish-led multilateral force in southern Iraq. But we need to involve the United Nations and nongovernmental organizations (NGOs) far more extensively in order to share the burden of government with other countries and elicit collective resources for the job of reconstruction. Many of the international community's most experienced countries in the field of peacekeeping are prepared to commit troops and treasure only if the United States is willing to yield its domination of the transition process. Only with collective responsibility can the United States avoid the heightened opposition, not to speak of the mounting expense of an extended occupation.

We must also stop the preferential contracts for American firms, particularly in the oil industry, and allow the Iraqi government to manage its energy resources. In order to attract international investment for economic reconstruction, we must stop the excessive profiteering by firms with close ties to the administration, such as Halliburton or Bechtel. The United States has been seriously understating the income these firms have earned in Iraq where they dominate the reconstruction field. Nor should we coerce the Iraqi government to deal with the United States in preference to such former Iraqi economic partners as France and Russia. Finally, we must open bidding for reconstruction to France, Germany, and Russia.

Intelligence and Law Enforcement Are the First Options against Terrorism; Military Force Should Be the Last

West Europeans had to deal with terrorist movements throughout the 1980s; they did so effectively with law enforcement and intelligence agencies. Now that the problem is international terrorism, close liaison relations with other intelligence services are essential along with the knowledge of languages and regional studies in key areas. Cooperation between law enforcement and intelligence agencies, not the application of unilateral military force, is the key to success. In the post-9/11 period, there have been no arrests or captures of key al Qaeda leaders that have not been based on liaison intelligence and support.

International Diplomacy, Not Military Action, Must Be the First Option in Crisis Management

The Bush administration has downplayed the role of international diplomacy in such crisis situations as the Israeli-Palestinian peace process and the North Korean and Iranian nuclear programs. In the Middle East our aim should be the creation of a viable Palestinian state and security for Israel. This is probably best pursued by insisting that Israel abandon the settlements and by fostering the creation of a Palestinian capital in East Jerusalem. The United States also should insist on the end of terrorism against Israel and the support for this policy by members of the Arab League, including their diplomatic recognition of Israel. In North Korea and Iran, we must establish or reestablish diplomatic relations, offer a combination of security guarantees and economic arrangements, and create regional alignments to end the isolation of Pyongyang, particularly, and Tehran. Finally, we cannot expect to create a stable Iraq without fostering cooperation between Iraq, Iran, and Syria.

We Must Work to Strengthen the United Nations with a Rapid Deployment Force, and We Should Support Creation of a NATO Peacekeeping Force

The Bush administration refuses to recognize the key lesson of Afghanistan and Iraq, which is the need for multilateral organizations to create world order. Most members of the United Nations and NATO favor the creation of effective rapid deployment forces to meet crises as they occur around the world. Units forming the force can come primarily from countries that have disciplined services capable of effective military action. U.S. participation is needed for financial, logistical, and intelligence support. Such units could relieve the United States of the burden of unilateral intervention as the only viable option.

NATO has put too much energy into the expansion of its membership, which has weakened the alliance, and not enough energy into dealing with regional crises. With the collapse of the Soviet Union, NATO still has an important role to play in international affairs, but its expanded membership has made decision making more cumbersome.

The United States Must Participate with Both the United Nations and NATO as a Member of a Group, Not a Hegemonic Power

Through cooperation we can achieve objectives that are not possible alone, as exemplified in the multilateral success of East Timor. An example of failure to act with other nations is Rwanda in 1994, when the Clinton administration failed to provide modest logistical assistance to prevent a genocide that led to the slaughter of more than eight hundred thousand people. The same logic of cooperation applies to Liberia and the Congo, where the United States has dragged its feet and failed to support the work of Kofi Annan, an outstanding secretary general.

The United States must join the International Criminal Court, which is providing the beginnings of a juridical basis for world order. Such a court makes more legal and moral sense than the military tribunals we are establishing for terrorists. There are ample provisions for the United States to try its citizens in its own courts. Our boycott of conventions to end the use of teenage soldiers in combat or the deployment of land mines is reprehensible and should be reversed.

We Must Support Arms Control and Disarmament and Stop the Proliferation of WMD

The United States must preserve and enhance an effective arms control regime, not dismantle it. This means adhering to outstanding agreements, not abrogating treaties we have signed. It means desisting from actions that compromise agreements or open new areas for competition.

The United States must return to the ABM Treaty, end the deployment of a national missile defense, and adhere to the Comprehensive Test Ban Treaty to end underground testing. A moratorium on such testing has been in effect for over a decade. U.S. support of arms control could end nuclear testing worldwide and even attract India and Pakistan to the Nuclear Nonproliferation Treaty. We must press for adherence to the NPT by North Korea and Iran and for inclusion in the treaty of India, Pakistan, and Israel.

For its part, the United States must return to the agendas of George H. W. Bush and Bill Clinton to significantly reduce nuclear weapons and adhere to international conventions on chemical and biological weapons. We must not allow private interests, such as the U.S. pharmaceutical industry, to prevent intrusive verification measures. Such verification is also needed to enhance the effectiveness of the NPT. International inspection teams, using the expertise of the International Atomic Energy Agency, will enhance the credibility and effectiveness of these inspections.

The United States must end its development of low-yield nuclear weapons, such as bunker busters, and deployment of a national missile defense. In order to return to the high moral ground in the search for disarmament, the United States must prevent the weaponizing of outer space. The United States has isolated itself from the international community in pursuing these policies.

The United States Must Decrease the Record-Level Budgets for the Department of Defense and the Intelligence Community and Provide Necessary Resources to the Department of State and the Department of Homeland Security

We must return to the sound tradition whereby the secretary of state, not the secretary of defense, has the leading role in our foreign policy. The State Department's budget must include sufficient funds for the management and extension of economic assistance to address international needs and enhance the effectiveness of U.S. diplomacy. The Defense Department must be limited to the management of military policy. The director of central intelligence must coordinate and arbitrate intelligence disputes and not be involved in diplomatic negotiation or political support for administration positions. The position of director of national intelligence must be created to ensure against the politicization of intelligence, and the entire intelligence community must support a blue-ribbon independent investigation of the intelligence system.

The Department of Defense Must Be More Accountable to Congress

Research and development and military procurement are insufficiently debated in Congress. Congress should insist on tight financial controls, including greater budgetary accountability and restrictions on the influence of defense contractors to secure contracts through financial contributions. It should also insist on verifiable weapons testing before deployment and limit the Pentagon's use of secrecy, particularly secret budgets.

The United States Must Reform Trade and International Financial Policies to Complement Increased Economic Aid

The United States must increase its economic aid to help produce conditions that create rising expectations in the third world and decrease the root causes of terrorism. At the same time, unfulfilled promises of development assistance merely reinforce support for terrorist and extremist organizations in the developing world.

We must also alter our trade policies that undercut the effects of economic aid. We need to reduce high tariffs on the goods produced by developing countries, and we need to eliminate subsidies for our agricultural producers that enable them to unfairly compete with producers from the third world. The Bush administration must also end its support of the "Washington consensus," whereby it uses its influence in the International Monetary Fund and the World Bank to impose conditions supporting the financial community and depressing living standards. The United States must allow fiscal regulations that restrict the import of capital, government programs that provide social and economic benefits, and even protective tariffs to support new industries.

DOMESTIC POLICY

There are indications that the American political system is under duress as the Bush administration has exploited acts of terror to erode our democratic and social compact. American cynicism toward politics and politicians is increasing; the United States ranks next to last in electoral turnout among the world's so-called mature democracies. At the same time, the policy process has failed to address many homeland security problems created by 9/11.

We Must Modify the Complex Structure of the Department of Homeland Security and the Excesses of the PATRIOT Act to Protect Our Security and Democratic Rights

The PATRIOT Act has taken an overly restrictive approach toward civil liberties and civil rights. Congress and the public must recognize the dangers inherent in actions that erode our democracy.

Policies must be altered so that detainees and prisoners are given fair trials and handled humanely. We cannot rely on military tribunals to do this, and we need to create stringent regulations that restrict the use of torture, and, to the extent possible, allow for open trials and adequate defense. Arbitrary designation of American citizens as "enemy combatants" and the denial of their constitutional rights are intolerable.

Congress and the People Must Act to Maintain the Balance of Power between the Executive Branch and Congress

This balance has been shattered by the use of secrecy to insulate the administration from legitimate congressional control; the refusal to conduct the normal testing of weapons, such as the missile defense system, to give Congress periodic opportunities for review; and the abrogation of such treaties as the ABM Treaty without congressional review.

The Department of Homeland Security Must Be Strengthened to Become an Effective Combatant against Terrorism

The DHS has not adequately strengthened border and infrastructure security, intelligence collection and analysis, and interagency cooperation, that allowed 9/11 to occur.

We Must Use Federal Troops at Home in Genuine Crises, Not to Perform Tasks That Might Be Done by the National Guard or Local Police.

The Northern Command should be held in reserve, not used if local police or even national guards can do the job. Civilian public services must be adequately funded, particularly fire, police, and rescue departments that have important public safety functions.

The Government Should Once Again Assume Responsibility for Maintaining Needed Social Services and Assistance in Areas like Education, Housing, Welfare, and Social Security

The administration is turning back the clock to the period of President McKinley and is ignoring the history and sense of civic responsibility agreed upon by both political parties in the last century. We need to restore social services, stop the trend of cutting benefits that enhance our nation's health and education, and provide sustenance for our aged and poor. The federal government must work with state and local agencies, not undercut their programs and undermine their fiscal positions.

Tax Cuts That Benefit a Small Percentage of the Population Should Be Ended and a Graduated Income Tax and Corporate and Estate Taxes Restored That More Fairly Distribute the Burden on Those Better Able to Pay.

The tax cuts of the Bush administration have crippled the economy and widened the gap between the wealthy and the rest of the country. We have lost nearly three million jobs in the first three years of the Bush administration; the economy is running record deficits of $375 billion in 2003 and a projected $477 billion in 2004. An additional deficit of $5.2 trillion is projected in the next ten years. Our tax policies must be reversed, the graduated income tax revived, and the burden of governance borne in proportion to income.

We Need Strict Campaign Finance Laws to Restrict Use of Private Funds to Influence Elected Officials

Despite a Supreme Court decision in December 2003 upholding campaign finance restrictions, the United States does not restrict the power of money to control elections. We are still allowing special interests to have a totally disproportionate influence on our foreign and domestic policy. Our democracy is severely compromised by such influence.

WHAT IS TO BE DONE?

We need an agenda that reverses the domestic and international actions of the Bush administration and supports the following objectives:

- Internationalization of nation-building in Afghanistan and Iraq and the provision of adequate support;
- Use of diplomacy as the first option in dealing with international crises in North Korea, Iran, and Syria;
- Active participation in the creation of a viable Palestinian state and a secure Israel;
- Greater use of law enforcement and intelligence, rather than military force, in the fight against terrorism;

- Multilateral peacekeeping, including the strengthening of NATO and the United Nations with rapid deployment forces;
- Multilateralism in such areas as the control of disease and drugs, environmental security, and the regulation of trade and intellectual property;
- Membership in the International Criminal Court, ratification of the Comprehensive Test Ban Treaty, participation in conventions on chemical and biological weapons, and reaffirmation of the ABM Treaty;
- Adequate funding for the Department of State, and a more limited role for the Department of Defense with rigorous oversight of budgets and restrictions against the undue influence of arms manufacturers; and
- Greater economic aid, reduction or elimination of tariffs and subsidies that penalize third world countries, and International Monetary Fund and World Bank policies that raise incomes in the third world.

At home, these policies find their natural counterpart in the following policies:

- Revision of the PATRIOT Act so that civil rights are not sacrificed in the fight against terrorism;
- Equitable handling of detainees and prisoners, and the use of federal troops only for grave crises;
- Strengthening of the Homeland Security Department;
- Restoration of the balance of power between the executive branch and Congress;
- Reassertion of the government's responsibility in key areas, such as education, housing, welfare, and social security; and
- Fiscal responsibility, the restoration of a fair and graduated income tax, corporate and estate taxes, and effective campaign finance laws.

Four decades ago in Vietnam the United States fought the wrong war, at the wrong time, in the wrong place. The costs to this country in terms of loss of life and treasure as well as the social and political implications were incalculable. In doing so, Presidents Kennedy, Johnson, and Nixon weakened the international position of the United States. Once again, the United States has chosen without debate or discussion to put its forces in harm's way in a part of the world that has successfully resisted previous foreign invaders and their occupation. This time the policies of President Bush have recklessly endangered our international and national security. In the past this nation has found the energy and resolve to avoid dangers confronting us, secure a more peaceful world, and provide a more prosperous and democratic society at home. This is the challenge we face today.

NOTE

1 Associated Press, "New Job for Former Envoy," *New York Times,* August 16, 2003, p. 5.

APPENDIX
PURSUING THE PHANTOM OF A NATIONAL MISSILE DEFENSE

Nothing better illustrates President Bush's unilateral approach to security affairs than his decision to withdraw from the ABM Treaty and to develop an expensive national missile defense system. By withdrawing from the treaty, Bush asserted that the president alone, without the consent of Congress, could withdraw from treaties, a position that runs counter to the intent of the Constitution. Withdrawal from the ABM Treaty sent a signal to other nations that the entire fabric of arms control was at risk. The deployment of a missile defense system, which doesn't work, saps funds from vitally needed programs both in foreign and domestic policy. The persistence of the Bush administration in insisting on deployment demonstrates the corrupt collusion between the administration, defense industries, and conservative congressmen.

A SHORT HISTORY OF "STAR WARS"

Once the Soviets acquired nuclear weapons and Intercontinental Ballistic Missiles (ICBMs), the need for a defense against a doomsday strike

251

seemed imperative.[1] A nuclear exchange with our principal Cold War rival, with its prospect of one hundred million deaths or even total annihilation, was the nightmare scenario that haunted the first planners of an antiballistic missile defense as they began their work in earnest in the 1960s.

The more scientists and technicians worked on such a system, however, the less feasible it seemed. Prototype systems failed test after test or passed tests that greatly simplified their task, rendering the result useless. As the planners knew, it would always be possible for the Soviets in a *real* situation to overwhelm the system by launching many incoming missiles, and it would always be possible to prevent incoming missiles from being hit by confusing the defending missiles with chaff and decoys.

The truth was inescapable. In 1972 President Richard Nixon and Soviet leader Leonid Brezhnev agreed to the ABM Treaty, which eventually limited deployment of missile defenses to one site each and prevented testing to create a national missile defense system. The United States installed its system in Grand Forks, North Dakota, at a cost of $6 billion, only to dismantle it immediately when it became clear it would be ineffective. The Soviets deployed a limited missile defense system around Moscow, called *Galosh*, which U.S. military planners discounted as ineffective.

Despite passage of the ABM Treaty, the Reagan administration took up the cause again in the 1980s, driven by overoptimistic claims by scientist Edward Teller and the Livermore Laboratory. "Star Wars" was pushed hard by lobbying groups made up of representatives of the Pentagon, the arms industry, and conservative think tanks. This formidable lobbying machinery, put together in the 1960s, is still in operation and has succeeded again in pushing the country toward missile defense. The system still has little prospect of working.

Ultimately, the Reagan administration spent tens of billions of dollars on the development of a missile defense system that the vast majority of scientists knew couldn't work and that was banned by the ABM Treaty. While President Reagan promised a "nuclear shield" that would achieve "ultimate security" for the American people and render missiles "impotent and obsolete," such a system was never feasible. The claims of Teller and the Livermore Lab were quietly dropped in 1984 when it became clear their ideas were not viable, although the public was not told. Other options were explored with equally dismal results. No system has been found to be technically feasible.

Evaluation of a national missile defense is made problematic by the fact that the Bush administration has tested it in situations considerably simpler than battlefield conditions. Decoys pose the most persistent problem. Technically easy to build and orders of magnitude cheaper than the warhead, they can be used by any country attacking the United States. In a number of cases, defense contractors with the most to gain have conducted flawed evaluations. In one instance, Dr. Nira Schwartz, a computer software expert at TRW, a major missile defense contractor, maintained that the company had forced her to misrepresent her findings. Dr. Theodore A. Postol of MIT made similar allegations of misrepresentation.

On September 1, 2000, President Clinton announced that he would defer the decision to deploy a national missile defense system to the next administration, citing the system's unproven technology, as dramatically brought home by a series of failed tests; the likelihood that countermeasures, such as decoys, could foil it; and the objections of Russia, China, and our NATO allies that deployment would jeopardize the 1972 ABM Treaty. Analysts also pointed out that deployment could erode the entire fabric of arms control and lead to a new arms race. If China, for example, in response to a U.S. missile defense system, greatly strengthened its force of ICBMs, India and possibly Japan would respond.

President George W. Bush ignored these problems and called for early deployment of a national missile defense system. Many of the same people and institutions that had lobbied successfully for a missile defense system in the earlier Reagan and Bush periods were back in the game. These included Donald Rumsfeld, Richard Perle, Paul Wolfowitz, and Frank Gaffney, who heads the Center for Security Policy; the right-wing Heritage Foundation; and corporations such as Boeing, TRW, Raytheon, and Lockheed-Martin that donated millions of dollars to members of Congress to push through the national missile defense.

THE THREAT

In 1998 Donald Rumsfeld chaired the Commission to Assess the Ballistic Missile Threat; the commission's report provided much of the justification for Bush's proposed national missile defense system.[2] The report claimed that within a few years North Korea, Iran, and Iraq could deploy operational intercontinental ballistic missile systems with "little or no warning." Close analysis of the report revealed, however, that Rumsfeld had essentially changed the verbs of earlier, less threatening CIA estimates from "mights" and "coulds" to "wills." It reflected a shift to a series of worst-case assumptions, despite the lack of evidence of significant changes in real missile capability. The report was driven not by facts but by ideology. A year later the CIA issued a national intelligence estimate that copied some of the techniques and conclusions of the Rumsfeld report, thus supporting the case for deployment of a national missile defense. A more balanced net assessment of global ballistic missile arsenals, undertaken by Joseph Cirincione of the Carnegie Endowment for International Peace, revealed that the ballistic-missile threat was confined, limited, and changing relatively slowly.[3]

President Bush has claimed that a national missile defense will protect the country against terrorism. Given the enormous expenses and technical difficulties involved in their development, however, intercontinental ballistic weapons are highly unlikely weapons for terrorists to acquire; nor do terrorists have the capability to launch them. The CIA has stated that weapons delivered by ships or planes, or hand-carried, or even cruise or short-range missiles are much more likely weapons for terrorists,[4] as the attacks of September 11 brought home. These delivery systems could not be countered by NMD.

THE SYSTEM DOESN'T WORK!

The most obvious problem facing the Bush administration in its rush to deployment is that it still does not have a system that works.[5] The difficulties with current models are no different than the problems that plagued earlier systems, including the inability to distinguish decoys from warheads and the problem of lasers rapidly losing energy when attempting to destroy missiles as they are getting off the ground. The United States is not conducting realistic tests that could provide military and political leaders with the confidence needed to deploy these weapons.

Testing of antimissile defenses, including prototypes of the system to be installed in Alaska and California, has continued to reveal the vulnerability of missile defense to decoys. On those few occasions in which decoys have been employed, they have been distinguished by different shapes and temperatures than the warhead, have been limited to one or two, and have had their flight characteristics programmed into the defense system—hardly wartime conditions. The 2002 report of the director of operational tests and evaluations of the Department of Defense put it bluntly: the elements of a possible deployable system, such as guided energy and laser systems, have "yet to demonstrate significant operational capability."

To compensate for these problems, the administration has given its missile defense system a unique immunity. For all other systems, the director of the Defense Department's operational test and evaluation office has to certify that the systems work before they are put in the field. There is a good reason for this. When testing goals have been reduced, the results have often been negative. For example, the marines' V-22 Osprey was tested 33 times instead of the scheduled 103. It has since been plagued with problems, crashing twice and killing twenty-three marines in 2000. The missile defense program relies on far more exotic technology than the Osprey, and accordingly requires more testing. As Sen. Diane Feinstein (D-CA) wrote in a letter to Rumsfeld in February 2003, "I believe that any deployed missile defense system must meet the same requirements and standards that we set for all other fully operational weapons systems. Indeed, given the potential cost of a failure of missile defense, I believe that, if anything, it should be required to meet more stringent test standards than normally required."

To block criticism and meet its deployment deadline in 2004, the Bush administration has moved to exempt all missile defense programs from the normal oversight of the Joint Requirements Oversight Council; this council has the responsibility of ensuring that weapons programs perform well enough to be useful on the battlefield. Sen. Carl Levin (D-MI), former chief of the Senate Armed Services Committee, revealed on February 13, 2002, that the Defense Department had formally asked Congress for permission to bypass operational testing requirements altogether.

Heightened classification of information also has blocked review of the programs by Congress. In 2002 defense officials stopped providing

Congress with detailed cost estimates and timetables for antimissile systems and restricted information about targets and decoys used in flight tests. "These are disturbing trends," said Sen. Jack Reed (D-RI), then chairman of the Armed Services subcommittee on strategic weapons. "You get the suspicion this is as much to avoid scrutiny of the program as to shield it from adversaries." As John Isaacs of the Council for a Livable World pointed out, "The illogic of the administration's request is a sure sign that it is driven by politics. Speedy deployment is favored by defense contractors like Lockheed Martin, for which missile defense is a potential financial bonanza. . . . Without testing, the Pentagon—and the U.S. taxpayers—has no way of knowing whether the defense system is just a high-tech Maginot line, providing the illusion without the substance of national security."[6]

Despite the president's rush to deployment, the Pentagon has raised serious doubts about the system. Thomas P. Christie, director of operational testing and evaluations, declared on February 20, 2003, "One of my chief concerns is the potential for systems to circumvent the rigorous acquisition process and enter into full-rate production or into the hands of our warfighters without learning the operational capabilities and limitations demonstrated by adequate operational testing and evaluation."[7] He questioned the readiness and adequacy of every major component of the missile system. Most damning of all is Christie's statement, "Early entry of any weapon into production [is] questionable."

Thus President Bush is claiming a capacity his system does not have and may well not have for many years. He is clearly responding to decades of lobbying by the defense industry and years of ideologically driven pressure by the neoconservatives who now control U.S. defense and foreign policy. As for a system that is more modest than President Reagan's Star Wars program, Defense Secretary Rumsfeld smugly remarked, "To the extent we have a capability, it will have a deterrent effect. To the extent it has a limited capacity, it will have a deterrent effect only to that limit."[8] Senator Levin countered, "What the Pentagon has tried not to emphasize is that this 'initial capacity' is likely to be marginally effective, if it works at all. Declaring this untested, marginal system ready to deploy is like declaring a newly designed airplane ready to fly before the wings have been attached to the airframe and the electronics installed in the cockpit."[9]

As a result, the United States will have the most expensive military development program in history, going full-steam ahead with inadequate testing and virtually no congressional supervision. In fiscal 2004 the Bush administration will spend $9.1 billion, making missile defense the largest single development item in the military budget. This is only the beginning. A study prepared by the Center for Arms Control and Non-Proliferation in Washington, and Economists Allied for Arms Reduction in Pearl River, New York, states that the total cost of a national missile defense system could be between $800 billion and $1.2 trillion through 2035. If full deployment is reached by 2015, half the costs will be incurred in the next thirteen years, perhaps reaching to $50 billion a year by 2007 at a time when the country already is projecting over $450 billion in annual deficits.

What is driving the system is not its contribution to national defense but ideology and the intense lobbying of contractors such as Boeing, TRW, Raytheon, and Lockheed Martin—and those congresspeople whose districts house their facilities or whose campaigns are dependent on support from these corporations. Figures supplied by the Federal Election Commission indicate that supporters of the system have been the recipients of major contributions in the hundreds of thousand of dollars.[10] The present lobbying group, first formed in the late 1960s, has never slackened in its efforts of developing a national missile defense system.

SUING THE PRESIDENT

A strong attempt to stop the president from withdrawing from the ABM Treaty of 1972 and developing a national missile defense system was instituted on June 11, 2002, when thirty-two congresspeople, led by Rep. Dennis Kucinich (D-OH), sued the president for "illegal" abrogation of the treaty without congressional consent.[11]

The lawsuit named the president, Secretary of State Powell, and Secretary of Defense Rumsfeld as defendants. The lawsuit asked a decision from the federal courts on whether or not the Constitution permits the president to withdraw from the treaty without the consent of Congress. According to the suit, the Constitution says treaties, once approved by the Senate and White House, are federal law and that the president does not enjoy the power to repeal federal laws without congressional approval.

At stake was not just the ABM Treaty but all treaties to which the United States is presently signatory. If the president could withdraw from the ABM Treaty, he could, without congressional consent, withdraw from any treaty to which the United States is a signatory: the United Nations, the Limited Test Ban of 1963, or the Nonproliferation Pact of 1968. As Kucinich stated, "The president's termination of the ABM Treaty represents an unconstitutional repeal of a law duly enacted by Congress. If the president is allowed to repeal laws at his own instance, it would be destructive of our Constitution."[12]

The president's announcement to withdraw from the ABM Treaty had been cleverly timed. A little over a year after the September 11 attacks, with a limitless war against terrorism and the possibility of conflict with Iraq, President Bush had acted within a well-developed convention that Congress does not oppose the president on strategic issues during wartime. Despite severe misgivings on the part of a number of U.S. senators on both sides of the aisle, no senator was willing to step up to the plate and join Representative Kucinich and his colleagues to become a coplaintiff in the suit. On December 30, 2002, Justice John Bates of the District Court of Columbia, a Bush appointee, dismissed the lawsuit. The lead attorney for the plaintiffs, Peter Weiss, concluded that the decision represented "a considerable advance toward the imperial presidency and a commensurate retreat from constitutional government."[13]

STRATEGIC DANGER OF THE NATIONAL MISSILE DEFENSE

The withdrawal from the ABM Treaty and the deployment of a national missile defense could very well lead to another arms race, particularly if Russia and China decide to increase their strategic offensive force.[14] For the past two decades, China has had approximately twenty ICBMs. If China decides to deploy one hundred missiles, as the CIA predicts, and the U.S. national missile defense system is only partially effective, the country will be less secure from Chinese attack than it was before. A Russian decision to place multiple warheads on its ICBMs would create even greater strategic problems.

If North Korea in the future were to have the capacity to hit American cities, a future American president could not rely on a partially effective defensive system. North Korea has been the country cited most frequently to justify the national missile defense system. Yet it is important to realize how small and economically weak North Korea is—a country continuously facing famine with a GNP only 4 percent of Taiwan's. It has only tested two medium-range missiles (it has not tested its missiles since 1998), its test facilities are quite primitive, and its missile system is not capable of sustaining multiple launches of missiles.

In fact, the threat of military retaliation has deterred North Korea from launching another attack on South Korea for fifty years and would prevent it from launching a missile attack against either the United States or South Korea. Ironically, President Bush focused on North Korea as the raison d'être for NMD at the very time that Pyongyang was moderating its policies, improving its relations with South Korea and Japan, and looking for ways to moderate its modest strategic programs. It would be far wiser to deal with the North Korean problem diplomatically than rely on a missile defense that doesn't even work.[15]

The other troubling case is Iran. In July 2000 Iran completed its first successful test of a medium-range missile capable of hitting targets in Saudi Arabia, Israel, and Turkey. The missile has not been tested to its claimed range of thirteen hundred kilometers and is highly inaccurate, with only about a 50 percent chance of landing within four kilometers of its target. In any case, Iran's priority would not be to threaten the U.S. homeland but to establish regional hegemony by challenging the supremacy of U.S. military forces in the Middle East. For this objective, ICBMs are unnecessary.

It was clear at the time of Bush's election that changes in the diplomatic environment could greatly reduce the Iranian threat. If U.S.-Iranian relations continued to warm and the domestic influence of Iranian conservatives waned, Iranian financial support for missile programs could be cut. Successful U.S. efforts to prevent North Korean, Chinese, and Russian missile exports, upon which the Iranian program depends, would strangle any Iranian program. Again, by invading Iraq and militarily threatening Iran, the president has provided the motive for Iran to develop a nuclear deterrent and a missile system capable of delivering it.

NOTES

1. See Frances Fitzgerald, *Way Out There in the Blue: Reagan, Star Wars, and the End of the Cold War* (New York: Simon & Schuster, 2000). See also William J. Broad, *Teller's War: The Top Secret Story behind the Star Wars Deception* (New York: Simon & Schuster, 1992); Janne E. Nolan, *Gardians of the Arsenal: The Politics of Nuclear Strategy* (New York: Basic Books, 1989); Associated Press, "New Job for Former Envoy," *New York Times*, August 16, 2003, p. 5; and Craig Eisendrath, Melvin Goodman, and Gerald E. Marsh, *The Phantom Defense* (Westport, CN: Praeger, 2001).

2. "Report of the Commission to Assess the Ballistic Missile Threat to the United States"; National Intelligence Council, "National Intelligence Estimate (NIE) Foreign Missile Development and the Ballistic Missile Threat to the United States through 2015," unclassified summary, September 1999.

3. See Joseph Cirincione, "Assessing the Assessment: The 1999 National Intelligence Estimate of the Ballistic Missile Threat," *Nonproliferation Review* (Spring 2000).

4. CIA, national intelligence estimates of 1999 and 2000.

5. See George N. Lewis, Theodore A. Postol, and John Pike, "Why National Missile Defense Won't Work," *Scientific American* (August 1999). For a more technical study, see George N. Lewis and Theodore A. Postol, "Future Challenges to Ballistic Missile Defense," *IEEE Spectrum* (September 1997).

6. David Ruppe, "Missile Defense: Critics Say Administration Misled Congress on Missile Deployment Order," Global Security Newswire, June 23, 2003.

7. Council for a Livable World, "Pentagon Report: Bush Missile Defense of Questionable Quality," February 25, 2003, http://www.clw.org/nmd/christiereport .html.

8. Rumsfeld press conference, Frontiers of Freedom Institute, December 7, 2002.

9. Carl Levin, "Untested Missile Defense Setup Poses Risks: Can Missile Shield Be Built," *Congressional Record Weekly Update* (February 10–14, 2003): S2183.

10. Journalist William D. Hartung contributed this insight.

11. See Craig Eisendrath, "Suing the President," *USA Today Magazine*, May 2003.

12. Dennis Kucinich, "Anti-Ballistic Missile Treaty: Statement from Dennis Kucinich," http://www.Kucinich.US/issues/antiballistic.php.

13. On February 13, 2003, six members of the House, joined by members

of the military and parents of service personnel, filed a lawsuit seeking to prevent President Bush from invading Iraq without an explicit declaration of war from Congress. Here, members of the House went to the courts, again unsuccessfully, to affirm congressional powers being challenged by the president.

14. The Council for a Livable World has maintained a running account of the strategic issues involved in missile defense at http://www.clw.org. See also George Lewis, Lisbeth Gronlund, and David Wright, "National Missile Defense: An Indefensible System," *Foreign Policy* (Winter 1999–2000), and Joseph Cirincione, "The Asian Nuclear Reaction Chain," *Foreign Policy* (Winter 1999–2000).

15. See David E. Sanger, "Bush Issues Directive Describing Policy on Antimissile Defenses," *New York Times*, May 21, 2003.

INDEX